Dreams
and
Nightmares

The New Theory
on the Origin and
Meaning of Dreams

Other Books by Ernest Hartmann

Adolescents in a Mental Hospital
with Betty A. Glasser, Milton Greenblatt, Maida H. Solomon,
and Daniel Levinson

The Biology of Dreaming

Boundaries in the Mind

The Functions of Sleep

The Nightmare

The Sleep Book

Sleep and Dreaming, Editor

The Sleeping Pill

Dreams
and
Nightmares

THE NEW THEORY
ON THE ORIGIN AND
MEANING OF DREAMS

ERNEST HARTMANN, M.D.

PERSEUS BOOKS
Cambridge, Massachusetts

Library of Congress Cataloging-in-Publication Data

Hartmann, Ernest, 1934–
    Dreams and nightmares : the new theory on the origin and meaning
of dreams / Ernest Hartmann.
        p.   cm.
    Includes bibliographical references and index.
    ISBN 0-306-45996-5
    1. Dreams.   2. Dream interpretation.   3. Nightmares.   I. Title.
BF1091.H365   1998
    154.6'3--dc21
                                                        98-28475
                                                          CIP

ISBN 0-306-45996-5

©1998 Ernest Hartmann

Perseus Books is a member of the Perseus Books Group.

3 4 5 6 7 8 9 10   03 02 01 00

Printed in the United States of America

I would like to dedicate this book to several people who have recently disappeared from my waking world, but who still visit me in my dreams: Al Moffitt, a tough, yet wonderfully tender dream researcher; Bob Watson, a sleep specialist and colleague, and perhaps the sweetest and most decent person I've ever met; Viola Bernard, a wise psychiatrist and social activist who has helped the world greatly; my wonderful, incisive friend, Andrea Wilson, with whom I've had the most delightful breakfast conversations of my life; my dearest old friend and colleague, Myron Sharaf, who had perfect pitch for the emotional moment; and my mother Dora Hartmann, who died some years ago, but is still here in every cell of my body and every page of this book.

Contents

ACKNOWLEDGMENTS

I had a dream just a few nights ago in which I was pulling a complicated baggage cart across a park. The details were not quite clear. As is typical in my dreams, the place seemed to be both Central Park in New York and a park in Boston and my destination was both downtown New York and a university in Boston. I was pushing and pulling at this load, and even in my dream it clearly appeared to have something to do with my work finishing up this book. It was tough going, but I looked around and found that I was in a whole group of people, friends and associates, who were walking along with me on this expedition. It felt good to know that I was part of a group, that I had a whole bunch of people with me, even though I seemed to be the one doing the pushing and pulling.

Returning now to my waking life, I realize that I am not only part of a group, but that in fact a great deal of the pushing and pulling has actually been done by others, in addition to myself and sometimes instead of myself. And with their help something has actually been accomplished: This book has been completed and published (whereas in the dream I don't remember ever getting to where I was going).

So let me gratefully acknowledge help from a number of different directions. First, this book is based on long dream series and collections of dreams from several sources as well as my own dreams and those of my patients. I first want to thank one of the pioneers in sleep and dream research, the late Dr. Charles Fisher, who was responsible for my becoming interested in sleep research many years ago and who supplied me with some unpublished dream material that appears in this book. Other important dream series were provided by Debora Munczek and by my friend and colleague Mary Dombeck. Also, thanks to a number of anonymous donors of long dream series who have given me the honor of sharing their carefully collected, very personal dream material. I am grateful also for unpublished research material—unpublished studies and unpublished groups of dreams—supplied to me by Inge Strauch, Francine Roussy, Barbara Meier, and Deirdre Barrett.

Portions of this book derive from many meetings with a fascinating group of colleagues interested in boundaries in the mind as well as in dreaming and imagery. Members of this group, including Deirdre Barrett, Jon Earle, Frank Galvin, Bob Harrison, Bob Kunzendorf, Maureen McCormack, Rachel Rosen, and Len Solomon, helped me greatly with several chapters of this work.

My recent collaborators Patrick McNamara and Michael Zborowski have nudged my thinking in new directions, as have my collaborators in scoring and examining dreams, Nancy Grace and Rachel Rosen. A number of dream researchers have read portions of this book or papers on which it is based and have made very helpful clinical comments. These include Rosalind Cartwright, David Foulkes, Milton Kramer, and Inge Strauch. Eva Hartmann read the manuscript a number of times and suggested some significant changes. Jon Hartmann helped me by unearthing some literary references I had trouble finding. Larry Hartmann helped me a great deal in writing one of the papers on which this book is based. Special thanks are due Anthony Shafton, author of the wide-ranging and marvelously indexed book, *Dream Reader*, who made his bibliography available to me in electronic form. And heartfelt thanks to one of my oldest friends and best critics, the author/educator Marlene Griffith, whose incisive comments produced important improvements.

Finally, I could not have done all this without the dedicated help of Lisa Minassian, who checked and rechecked, found references, and helped get everything on the computer, and Vanessa Tibbitts at Plenum Trade, who improved the manuscript tremendously by getting rid of a lot of my too technical and too detailed writing.

Dreams
and
Nightmares

THE NEW THEORY
ON THE ORIGIN AND
MEANING OF DREAMS

Chapter One

THE NATURE OF DREAMING (OVERVIEW)

Some people (alas!) have no interest in dreams. They may ask, "Why should I worry about dreams? I seldom remember my dreams. How could something be important if we forget most of it anyway? And what I do remember is often junk."

Here are my answers, elaborated in this book. First of all, we all dream, and we spend a surprising amount of our lives dreaming. Depending on definitions, we spend 5–15% of our lives dreaming. That's 10 years for those of us who live a long time! There must be something important going on here.

Great things can happen in dreams—great discoveries in science and in art. The French chemist August Kekulé discovered the structure of the benzene ring in a dream. Elias Howe invented the sewing machine based on a dream. Robert Louis Stevenson reported that his novel *Dr. Jekyll and Mr. Hyde* came to him directly from a dream. Mozart claimed that many of the themes for his music came to him in dreams, and Tartini wrote a well-known violin sonata that he says he simply transcribed from a dream in which he heard the devil playing it for him on a violin. Every morning we awake from an important state of our minds in which we spend a great deal of time and which can sometimes help us accomplish great feats. Yet we understand so little about it. Psychologists have learned much about the details of our waking thoughts and activities, but little about our dreams. Once we start examining dreams, they turn out not to be junk at all.

There are two main theories or groups of theories followed by dream researchers and clinicians at present. One derives from Sigmund Freud's thesis that every dream when truly understood represents the fulfillment of a wish. Second, there is a group of modern biologists who suggest that dreams are random, more or less meaningless products of brainstem activity during sleep. They believe that, in our dreams, our higher brains are trying to make sense of what is really meaningless stimulation. I believe both theories are wrong.

Based on years of research work and clinical work with thousands of dreams, I am saying that what those of us who love our dreams have always believed is basically true. We consider it obvious that our dreams are meaningful, or that at least some of our dreams are meaningful and not random nonsense. On the other hand, we find it hard to believe that every one of our dreams is a disguised fulfillment of a wish—especially, as Freud insists, of a childhood wish. My studies—starting with dreams of severely traumatized people, and going on to dreams of people in very stressful situations, and then gradually moving through various defined situations toward everyday dreams—show that our dreams indeed deal with our emotions and our emotional concerns. Specifically, dreams deal with them by making a pictured metaphor of our concerns. And the dreaming process is useful to us. Dreaming cross-connects or weaves in new material, which helps us adapt to future trauma, stress, and the problems of life.

APPROACHING THE DREAM

When I consider the world of my dreams, I realize how little I know. Despite many years of working clinically with my patients' dreams and helping patients understand themselves, and despite years of research examining the biology of sleep and dreaming, I still know little about the basic nature of dreams—the "what"—or the possible functions of dreaming—the "why."

The works of Freud and Jung on dreaming, and their many followers as well, have taught us a great deal, but what I have learned from them is chiefly the extremely important art of *making use of dreams.* Dreams are, as Freud states, the "royal road to the unconscious"—a road to greater knowledge about a patient or about oneself. But this does not tell me what dreaming really *is.*

Likewise, work from my own laboratory and many others on the biology of REM and non-REM sleep helps us to understand the essential biology of the underlying sleep state (REM sleep) that is the best, though it turns out not to be the only, substrate of dreaming. This very basic and essential knowledge still fails to satisfy me in terms of the nature of dreaming and certainly tells me nothing of its functions. What I plan to do here is start afresh with a look at the vast array of the picture—stories we call dreams in an attempt to decide just what dreaming is and what it might be doing for us. I will make use of material I have gathered over many years: about 5,000 of my own dreams, over 10,000 dreams in long dream series ("dream logs") supplied to me by various dreamers, several thousand patients' dreams, and dreams from numerous research studies conducted by myself and by others. I have found it especially useful to start with dreams after trauma or dreams in stressful situations when we know quite clearly what must be on the dreamer's mind. The study of such dream series has led me to some new ideas about the nature and function of dreaming. Since my conclusions are in many ways related to those of other recent workers, I would like to call this a contemporary theory of dreaming.

Let me begin with an overview of what we will discuss. I will lay out the general concepts first and explain them further in the following pages.

1. First, dreaming brings a lot of material together. Dreaming is a process of making connections; it makes connections in what I shall call the "nets of the mind." (But so does waking!)
2. Dreaming allows us to make connections more broadly and more inclusively than when we're awake, because dreaming avoids the "tightly woven" or "overlearned" regions of the mind (such as those concerned with reading, writing, and arithmetic).
3. The connecting process is not random. It is guided by the emotions and emotional concerns of the dreamer. As most of us have always known, we dream of what is important to us. Dreams are

not at all "crazy" or arbitrary; this is especially evident when you know the dreamer's emotional concerns.

4. The dream, especially the most striking, vivid part of the dream, pictures or provides a *context* for the emotion. In other words, dreaming *contextualizes* emotion.

5. Because of its broader connection making, dreaming is especially good at noting similarities and creating metaphor. Dreaming makes use of our visual/spatial picturing abilities and provides an *explanatory metaphor* for the dreamer's emotional state of mind.

6. Finally, this broad making of connections serves a purpose. The making of connections simultaneously smoothes out disturbances in the mind by integrating new material—"calming a storm"—and also produces more and broader connections by weaving in new material. It does not simply consolidate memory, but interweaves and increases memory connections. These new connections, or increased connections, are what make dreaming useful in problem solving, as well as in scientific and artistic creation.

Let's discuss each of these statements briefly and try to make them more meaningful. Later chapters will expand on these questions further.

Connections in the Nets of the Mind

Although I will attempt in the following pages to present in detail the particular aspects of a mind net as I view it, for now let us simply remember that all of our thoughts, feelings, memories, and images apparently depend on the function of our brains and chiefly on the surface of the brain—the cerebral cortex. The cortex is basically a widespread net or network of nets composed of small units. What I mean is that aside from certain large neurons—"cables" carrying excitation into the cortex or away from it—the bulk of the cortex is made up of somewhat similar-looking small neurons. There are several billion of these neurons, which are like nerve cells elsewhere in the body except that they have unusually numerous connective elements—short, branched axons and dendrites—that allow them to connect with numerous other nearby neurons. Thus the cortex is basically a vast network of small similar units. Though there is still some disagreement about this, I would say that our minds in fact consist of these connections. It is the pattern of connections among units, not the units themselves, that differentiate one mind from another, and differentiate my mind before and after I have learned a new fact or had a new experience.

Therefore, connectivity is just about all there is in the mind, asleep or awake. As we go through life doing things, learning things, excitation spreads through the net in various ways. Different portions are lit up or excited, and connections are gradually strengthened or weakened. The basic principle is probably close to the one first outlined by the Canadian psychologist Hebb suggesting that connections are gradually strengthened as they are used, and presumably gradually weakened when they are out of use or neglected. In this sort of net the only thing that can happen is that patterns of units are lit up and connections are made. Although this will occur both in waking and in dreaming, I suggest that there is a difference between the two states.

Dreaming Makes Connections More Broadly, More Inclusively, than Does Waking in the Nets of the Mind

Dreaming makes connections especially broadly. This is based in the first instance on a simple "clinical" survey of my own dreams and my patients' dreams. Many dreams are relatively dull: The same kinds of things happen in these dreams as in waking life. Overall, however, a bit more can happen in dreams than in waking. We can occasionally fly. We occasionally find ourselves in houses that are an interesting mixture of different houses we have known. Once in a while we build strange structures that no one has seen before. We meet people we know who live far away or who have died, or who are not known to us in our waking lives; in fact, sometimes we meet monsters or mythical creatures. In all these senses, dreaming makes connections in a broader fashion than ordinary waking thought.

For some, dreaming obviously makes beautiful and interesting connections. But even those who believe dreaming throws things together in a more or less random fashion must admit that a dream image somehow connects a great deal of material from our memories, imaginations, etc. Dreaming makes connections between recently experienced material and old memories; it often puts together or combines two different people, two different places, or two different parts of our lives. Freud refers to this process as condensation. Thus we often dream of a setting that is a bit like our present home but also a bit like an older one. My dreams may take place in Boston, but it's also New York.

This tendency of dreaming to make connections very broadly or widely has been frequently noted. For instance, the existentialist Erik Craig writes, "While dreaming we entertain a wider range of human possibilities than when awake; the 'open house' of dreaming is less guarded."[1] Elizabeth Campbell says, "Anything can happen in a dream. There are no boundaries."[2] Many have simply called dreaming "hyperconnective."

Though dreaming is broader and in a sense more exciting and wilder than waking thought, I also want to call attention to the fact that it is only *somewhat* broader. We may at times fly in dreams, but we usually remain ourselves or a creature very much like ourselves. Hardly ever are we a mosquito or a hurricane (though I have heard one such report). Nor are we molecules of water, or mathematical formulas. We are usually ourselves or perhaps someone or something we can identify with easily. We experience a world roughly parallel to our usual visual-spatial one, though as noted, with some broader or wilder elements.

Furthermore, dreaming avoids the most "tightly woven," "overlearned" portions of the nets. My research shows that we dream very little of well-learned familiar tasks such as reading, typing, writing, or calculating, even when we spend hours per day of our waking lives on these tasks.

The Connecting Process is Not Random; It is Guided by the Emotions and Emotional Concerns of the Dreamer

I believe the dreaming process is not random. Some would agree that dreaming makes connections broadly but would say that dreaming makes connections all over the place—that it is basically a random process. I do not think so, based on a great deal of research beginning with my own work on dreams and nightmares of people who have experienced an acute trauma and are now recovering from it. The advantage to studying dreams in such a situation is that we know what is on the person's mind. We know what is really grabbing his or her attention—what the meaningful concerns must be.

I have been able to collect long dream series from a number of people who experienced a trauma such as barely escaping from a fire, being raped, or having someone killed next to them. These series clearly show that dreams make connections between the traumatic event and other material, such as old memories, including memories of past trauma. The connections appear to be guided principally by the emotions or emotional concerns of the dreamer.

After a severe trauma, the dominant emotions are obvious. A woman who was brutally raped had the following series of nightmares over the next few weeks:

> I was walking down the street with a female friend and the woman's 4-year-old daughter. A gang of male adolescents in black leather started attacking the child. My friend ran away. I tried to free the child, but I realized my clothing was being torn off. I awoke very frightened.
>
> I was trying to walk to the bathroom when some curtains began to choke me. I was choking and gasping for air. I had the feeling I was screaming, but actually I didn't make a sound.
>
> I was making a movie with Rex Harrison. Then I heard a train coming right at us, louder and louder; it was just about upon us when I woke up.
>
> The dream is all in color. I'm on a beach. A whirlwind comes and envelops me. I'm wearing a skirt with streamers. The whirlwind spins me around. The streamers become snakes which choke me and I wake up frightened.

Although this woman's nightmares incorporate some details of the actual rape experience (the rapist, about 18 years old, entered her window through curtains and threatened to strangle her with the curtains), she is dreaming mainly about an emotion—terror (a child is attacked; she is choked; a train rushes at her; a whirlwind envelops her; snakes choke her).

Several people in my series who escaped from fires dreamed first about fires but then reported dreams of tidal waves or of being chased by gangs of criminals. Alan Siegel, a clinical psychologist in California, has reported similar findings in victims of the Berkeley, California, fire of 1991.[3] Why dream about tidal waves or gangs of criminals when you have just escaped from a fire? Obviously the dream images do not come from the actual sensory input experienced in the fire but are guided by the dominant emotions of terror, fear, or vulnerability.

After trauma, I find there is often a progression in which dreams such as the above first appear to picture or provide a context for terror, fear, or vulnerability. Somewhat later they may deal with guilt or shame—for instance, survivor guilt.

> In my dreams, most of the time I am getting hurt in some way by my brother or I get hurt in an accident while my brother is safe [in actual fact, the dreamer's brother died in a fire from which the dreamer escaped].

This young man dreams of guilt, not directly of fires.

Contextualization of Emotion

I hope it is clear, at least in these very pure instances immediately after trauma, that dreams are by no means crazy. Though unexpected dream images may occur, they appear to be picturing, or as I would say, "contextualizing" (finding a picture context for) the dominant emotion of the dreamer.

My co-workers and I have found a large number of very clear "contextualizing images," especially in dreams after acute trauma but also after a death or time of grief. For instance, here are some of the more dramatic examples we have found in our collection of dreams:

> Fear, Terror:
>   A huge tidal wave is coming at me.

A house is burning and no one can get out.
A gang of evil men, Nazis maybe, are chasing me. I can't get
away.

Helplessness, Vulnerability:
I dreamt about children, dolls—dolls and babies all drowning.
He skinned me and threw me in a heap with my sisters; I
could feel the pain; I could feel everything.
There was a small, hurt animal lying in the road.

Guilt:
A shell heads for us (just the way it really did) and blows up,
but I can't tell whether it's me or my buddy Jack who is
blown up.
I let my children play by themselves and they get run over by
a car.

These examples indicate what I mean by "dreams contextualize emotion." When there is a clear-cut powerful emotion present such as fear, vulnerability, or guilt, dreams find a context, a way to picture it.

The situation is especially clear soon after trauma, but I contend that the same thing occurs in all dreams. I examine in the following pages dreams in stressful situations (but without actual trauma) that lead, though less dramatically, to the same conclusion. Dreaming contextualizes the dominant emotion or emotional concern of the dreamer. We can see the same pattern in a situation such as pregnancy, which is not always stressful but certainly involves clear emotional concerns. Pregnant women, especially women in their first pregnancy, have dreams about their bodies or other things changing shape and size, dreams that contextualize their concerns that their shapes are changing and their worries as to whether will they will still be attractive. Later in pregnancy they picture small animals of all kinds, and then usually bigger animals as the pregnancy progresses. Toward the very end of pregnancy women often wonder, "Will I be able to be a mother?" They begin to have dreams and nightmares which picture this concern. For example, one woman reports:

I have some babies out in the garden. It's kind of like they are
plants and I suddenly realize I have forgotten to water them.

This same pattern can be seen in any number of other situations when the emotional concern is obvious. For instance, as a very simple example, which we examine in detail later, three different patients on beginning psychoanalysis or long-term psychotherapy had similar dreams that went approximately as follows:

> I am walking along a mountain path with steep drop-offs on each side. It is a bit dangerous. There is a large, shadowy figure accompanying me—I am not quite sure whether this figure is good or evil.

These patients are obviously contextualizing the fear and concerns involved in beginning a long treatment with an unknown therapist or "guide."

Physical illnesses are also sources of emotional concern. Dreams often portray these concerns very vividly, sometimes even before the waking patient is aware of the illness. A man awaiting vascular surgery on his leg, and afraid of losing the leg, has dream images of defective tools or other defective objects in 11 of 14 recorded pre-operative dreams (see Chapter 3).

I suggest that this is the basic pattern for all our dreams but that we can see it most clearly after trauma or in one of the specific, somewhat stressful situations in which we know just what is on the dreamer's mind. Here, in the examples we have considered, the meaning is quite clear; no detailed "interpretation" is needed. I suggest that more typical "ordinary dreams" may sometimes seem confused because there is no one totally dominant emotional concern that clearly guides the formation of the dream; we are complex beings with a number of ongoing concerns, some of which we may not even be aware of. It is this factor that makes ordinary dreams difficult to understand and makes them appear to require detailed interpretation. When one does take the trouble, with or without a therapist, to obtain detailed associations, amplifications, etc., to arrive at the *meaning* of the dream, this process of interpretation often turns out to be a process of gradually arriving at an emotional concern of which we may not have been entirely aware.

What I am saying is quite consistent with what most of us who love dreams and work with them have always known: We dream

about what's important to us. I am trying to specify how we do this—
i.e., providing a picture context for the emotion—and I am trying to
place it in a framework involving the nets of our minds.

Dreaming Makes Connections More Broadly than Waking, Notes Similarities, and Creates Metaphor

I have suggested that dreams make connections more widely,
more broadly, than waking and that the connections are guided by
emotion. Dreams contextualize emotion. But what form do these
connections or contextualizations take? Obviously they do not, or
only very rarely, take the form of verbal narratives or mathematical
formulas. Dreams are almost always pictures (moving pictures), and
I would say that, in a broad sense, they are picture metaphors. I am
speaking of metaphor not simply as one of many rhetorical devices
but as a general tendency to note similarities between different do-
mains. This is in accordance with contemporary theories of metaphor.

A group of modern linguists and philosophers has made us
aware that metaphor is constantly present, not only in our speech but
also in our thought. The linguist George Lakoff, in his contemporary
theory of metaphor, points out how our everyday thought and
speech—even when we are in no way being poetic—is pervaded by
metaphor.[4] For instance, the broad metaphors "life is a journey" and
likewise "love is a journey" are ubiquitous: "I am stuck," "our goals
are in sight," "we are spinning our wheels," "it should be smooth
sailing from here on," "I have to bail out of this relationship," etc. All
of these familiar phrases are metaphorical. It is hardly surprising
then that in dreams, too, a journey by car frequently represents a
relationship, and that in general dreaming makes use of many of the
same metaphors.

We are indeed using metaphor much of the time even when
awake. Perhaps this does not occur when we are calculating or
typing or engaged in other very tightly structured types of focused,
directed activity. When we speak to each other as above, when we
daydream, image, or fantasize, we cannot help making use of metaphor, and I suggest that we are especially good at producing metaphors when we are dreaming since this is when we are best at

making connections. Making connections most broadly and widely means noting similarities between one thing and another, producing picture metaphors.

Although in poetry metaphor can be of many different types, the kind we use often in our speech and thinking is what I call explanatory metaphor. Metaphor is used to explain something: a "first term" or "target" (such as life, love, death, jealousy) that is somewhat abstract or problematic is explained by a "second term," "vehicle," or "source" (such as a plant, a journey, a departure, a green-eyed monster) that is simpler or more easily pictured. In exactly this sense, I believe that dreams are explanatory metaphors. The dream explains metaphorically the overall state—especially the emotional state—of the dreamer, or at least part of the dreamer's mind. Again, this is easiest to see in the clear-cut examples we have noted after trauma. "I am drowning in a tidal wave" is a metaphorical description for the emotional state of the dreamer experiencing terror and vulnerability. "A mountain has split; there are pieces lying around and I must make arrangements about it" is a metaphoric description of the state of mind of a man whose powerful and beloved mother has just died.

Some dreams in illness can be seen in the same way. The most dramatic example I know is described by Oliver Sacks in *Awakenings*,[5] his series of case studies describing patients with the serious neurological illness Postencephalitic Parkinsonism. One patient had a vivid dream that she was turning into a statue or castle; indeed she had a viral encephalitis that affected her brain in such a way that within a few weeks she became a living statue, unable to talk and almost unable to move until "awakened" by the drug l-DOPA some 40 years later.[5] As we shall see, most modern approaches to "dream working" make use of this metaphoric process using various techniques that enable the dreamer to discover his or her emotional concerns pictured metaphorically in the dreams.

I am not claiming that every piece of every dream must be understood as explanatory metaphor. What I have discussed here, as well as in previous sections, applies best to the major or most striking visual features of a dream. Any long dream also has portions that seem to serve mainly to provide continuity in a relatively straightforward way. Following a suggestion by author Bert States, we might speak of metaphoric and metonymic elements in dreams.[6] The metonymic elements would be the less striking elements, pulled along by their proximity or past connection to a metaphoric element. But the metaphoric elements are the ones we will chiefly want to focus on.

Functions of Dreaming

I have outlined above my views about the fundamental characteristics of dreaming and how dreaming differs from waking—in other words, the basic nature of dreaming. But is this simply the way things are, or does dreaming have a function? Does it play a role in maintaining the human organism? In brief, I believe dreaming does have a function that can be related to, but is not the same as, the function of REM sleep (rapid eye movement sleep, the biological state in which most dreaming occurs). Starting again with my material on dreams after trauma as the trauma is resolving, I suggest that dreaming has a quasi-therapeutic function. Dreaming, like therapy, is the making of connections in a safe place, as we shall discuss in detail. Both good psychotherapy after trauma and dreaming first provide a safe place for work to be done. In therapy the safe place is much more than the physical setting; it involves the safe "boundaries" of the therapeutic situation and the gradual trusting alliance formed between patient and therapist. In dreaming—especially in REM sleep—the safe place is provided by the well-established muscular inhibition that prevents activity and the acting out of dreams.

Once a safe place is established, the therapist allows the patient, especially the traumatized patient, to go back and tell her or his story in many different ways, making connections between the trauma and other parts of the patient's life and trying to integrate the trauma. Dreaming performs at least some of these same functions—since its nature is making connections broadly in a safe place. As connections are made between the terrible recent event and other material, the emotion becomes less powerful and overwhelming and the trauma is gradually integrated into the rest of life. Thus, dreaming appears to have a quasi-therapeutic adaptive role that can be seen most easily after trauma; though again, I believe that trauma is a paradigm and that dreaming has the same therapeutic function, though less easily discernible, at other times as well.

What happens in terms of the nets of the mind when we dream is the spreading out of excitation or "reducing computational energy"[7]— in other words, the subsiding of storm waves. Presumably, this is useful in allowing the net to function better, in a more harmonious state. But the effect is not purely "energetic"; the spread of excitation or energy occurs by forming cross connections that inevitably alter the future functioning of the net. The trauma, or any disturbance, is cross-connected, "woven in" by dreaming as numerous new connections and contexts are provided. This process is likely to be useful for future functioning since a new trauma or disturbance will be less serious, will produce fewer "storm waves" since appropriate contexts and cross connections are already present. In the future a trauma will produce relatively less of the reaction: "Help! The world is ending," "This is the most horrible thing that has ever happened," "How can anyone survive this?," and more of "Yes, this feels bad but it's a bit like . . ." or "I've dealt with something like this before."

Thus, I suggest that the broad making of connections and contextualizing has a function that can be seen first as restorative in an immediate sense of spreading excitation or calming a storm, and secondly as producing changes in memory networks that are adaptive for the future. These changes in the networks are not a consolidation of memory but a broadening of memory through cross connections—an increase in connections, a weaving in of new experience.

This suggested function of dreaming is compatible with views proposed by a number of others who, starting from very different data bases, have all suggested some kind of adaptive, integrative, or problem-solving function of dreaming.[8] I believe all these views are somewhat similar to what I have proposed above. We are in basic agreement, at least about certain *functions* of dreaming, and I hope that my proposal of cross connections in neural nets may be helpful in relating these viewpoints.

Critics skeptical about any function of dreaming often question how dreams can be important if most of them are forgotten. I suggest that remembering the individual dream images is not what is essential—though sometimes, of course, a remembered dream image can be extremely important in learning about oneself in therapy or in producing a work of science or art. What is important is probably the making of cross connections in the net, the redistribution of weights, etc., as we have discussed, all of which can occur whether or not the actual dream content is remembered. Of course, our thoughts and theories about dreaming—including the present one—are necessarily based on examination of the subset of dreams that have been remembered.

Although dreaming should not be confused with REM sleep, nonetheless, most of our memorable dreams come from REM sleep, which is the ideal place for dreaming activity to occur; thus, a theory of the functions of dreaming should at least be compatible with the functions of REM sleep. The function of dreaming proposed here in terms of making connections and cross connections is at least compatible with the view that REM sleep, especially in young organisms, helps to develop the nervous system[9]—evidently by making or organizing new connections. It is also compatible with the view that REM sleep functions in the "repair, reorganization, and formation of new connections in amine-dependent forebrain systems,"[10] summarized as "knitting up the raveled sleeve of care." And it is consistent with a great deal of work supporting a role for REM sleep in certain kinds of learning.[11]

Uses of Dreaming

In the last section I outlined what I consider to be the most basic function of dreaming in terms of making broad connections, and as I mentioned, this function continues whether or not we consciously remember a specific dream. A dream remembered, however, can have additional functions that I would prefer to call *uses*, which are quite familiar to us. For example, a young woman dreamt, "My boyfriend turned into my father," and found this a very useful insight that she had not previously noticed and that helped her in thinking about her relationship. This sort of thing happens all the time and can be used by the dreamer with or without the help of a therapist. One study found that over one quarter of dreams by college students trying to "incubate" a problem included at least a partial solution to the problem, as rated by a group of judges.[12]

In my opinion these are examples of ways in which dreams can be immensely useful in what is perhaps our most important task—self-knowledge. We are all familiar with the many examples of works of art and scientific discoveries attributed by their creators to a dream.[13] In my view, the role of dreaming is an important one, though sometimes a small one—one new connection or one new image. It is obvious that the great preponderance of problem-solving and creative work in science and art is performed in the waking state—though the work often dips into reverie and daydreaming, the more dreamlike parts of waking. I believe that works of art are seldom created totally in dreams. For instance, though Robert Louis Stevenson claimed that the story of *Dr. Jekyll and Mr. Hyde* came to him in a dream, I think it most likely that the dream provided one striking new image—presumably a respectable doctor turning into a hideous monster—and Stevenson's well-prepared waking mind and story-writing skills took over from there.

I am suggesting that the contribution made to these works by dreaming is a new connection derived from the broader and more autoassociative[14] connecting found in dreams; the waking mind does the rest. However, this apparently small contribution—one new connection—may be exactly what is needed. There are many instances of athletes who found themselves trying out a small, new variation of their technique (a different golf grip, for instance, or a different skating technique) in their dreams and then found it crucial in waking; and there are examples of inventions depending on one small, new "twist"—Elias Howe's sewing machine needle with the hole at the tip is the best-known example.[15] Along these lines, it does not seem unreasonable to suggest that our ancestors may have used the new connections made in their dreams to develop new types of tools, weapons, or chariots—major and minor innovations that played a major role in our world.

Chapter Two

THE CLEAREST CASE

Dreams after Trauma

> I was right back there in Vietnam. The shells were flying. Just the
> way it really was. Then the shell came right into the hole we were
> hiding in. I couldn't tell whether it hit me or my buddy. I woke
> up terrified.

This was dreamt repeatedly by a young man whose buddy had in
fact been killed next to him in Vietnam.

> I dreamt he was there again, the rapist. Except I think there were
> two of them in the dream. I couldn't get away. There was some-
> thing wrapped around my eyes and it seemed to be happening
> in an apartment I lived in years ago.

This was dreamt by a woman who had been brutally raped two
weeks earlier.

Obviously, when something terrifying has happened to us, we
dream about it, and the dreams bring in other, related material from
our lives. However, things are not quite that simple.

J. H. is a 21-year-old man who remembers dreams almost every
night. He has had occasional nightmares since childhood. He says his
dreams are more vivid and more nightmarelike when there is stress
or a traumatic event. He recorded a series of dreams after a trauma at
age 14. He was traveling to Washington, D.C., with his parents and
was inadvertently locked into a room from which he could not
escape for most of a day and night. He became terrified, screaming,

developing all kinds of fantasies about what was happening to him. He summarizes what happened over the following eight to twelve weeks:

> I then had many dreams and nightmares about this event. I was always locked in, enclosed, and trapped in some way, but the dreams gradually changed. Sometimes I was trapped in a room like the actual one, sometimes in a very different situation. I also dreamt of being caught in a fire and of drowning in a tidal wave. Sometimes my parents were there, sometimes scenes from my childhood entered into the dreams. My dreams were playing with the theme of my being trapped in a room and bringing in all kinds of things from my life, from stories I'd read, and from my imaginings.

This young man is dreaming about what actually happened to him, but also about fires and tidal waves. I have several series of dreams from adolescents and young adults who barely escaped from fires in which their houses burned down. Two of them dreamt, "A huge tidal wave was coming for me. I didn't know whether I could get away." Very similar dreams of tidal waves have been reported in survivors of the Berkeley/Oakland fire of 1991.[1] One week after a brutal rape a woman dreamt, "There was a huge tank coming right at me. I was stuck. I couldn't get away." I have a large number of dreams of this kind in my files. People who have been through a fire do not dream only of fires, but of tidal waves, of being chased by gangs, etc. These dreams do not deal with the details of the actual event experienced, but with the emotion—the terror or fear. The dream deals with a powerful emotion by finding or putting together a picture context to represent that emotion. The frequent nightmare image "I'm overwhelmed by a tidal wave" is a perfect picture content for the emotion "I feel terrified, vulnerable." The theme I will develop is that dreaming makes connections among all the material in our memories; dreaming makes connections more broadly and widely than does waking; and it is driven by the emotion of the dreamer. In other words, dreaming makes connections guided by the dominant emotion, and the chief way it does this is what I call "contextualization of emotion"—finding a picture that provides a context for the emotion.

DREAMS AND NIGHTMARES AFTER TRAUMA

If we want to approach the questions of the basic nature of dreaming—what is really going on during dreaming—and of the functions of dreaming—what is dreaming doing for us (if anything)—I believe the best place to start is with dreams after trauma, dreams during the period when a traumatic event is resolving. It is the best place because we know exactly what is on the dreamer's mind in an emotionally meaningful sense.

This is not the case in the usual studies of dreams in which, say, 50 dreams are collected from college students, or perhaps 10 dreams from each of 10 college students, and then various analyses are applied. Such studies are useful in answering certain questions, such as how many characters a typical dream has, whether we dream more about men or women, etc. But it is very hard to make much sense of the individual dreams. They appear to consist of a hodge-podge of material from the dreamer's life. Even when students are asked about their "chief concerns" at a given time, it is very difficult to find any relationship between these concerns and the dream content. (For instance, a recent, well-controlled study[2] failed to find any clear relationship between dream content and students' chief concerns.) Some have concluded from such results that dream content is more or less random, not connected particularly with anything, even a "chief concern." I feel that, though emotional concerns are important, such results are not surprising. First of all, students may have many concerns on their minds at the same time. Secondly, they may not even be aware of their main concerns at a given time. For instance, a student asked in a study about three major concerns typically lists such things as plans for the weekend, worries about money for next year, the possibility of acquiring a new girlfriend or boyfriend. But if he is asked some years later to look back on this time of his life he may then say, "Well, of course my main concern was to make a break with my parents, to see whether I could become my own person, to be less influenced by my dominant mother." And it may very well be this concern, which was unconscious or at least not listed at the time, that might have been an influence on the student's dreams rather than the concerns he actually listed.

In any case, I think an optimal starting point is a series of dreams occurring after a serious trauma has occurred, as in the examples at the beginning of this chapter. Here there is absolutely no doubt as to what is on the dreamer's mind in an emotionally meaningful sense, and this should allow us to see what is happening in the dream (assuming a series of dreams—the longer the better—have been recorded). One problem, of course, is that most people do not routinely record their dreams. Even those who do often find their lives disrupted enough in the period after a trauma that they may stop doing it just when, from the research point of view, we would have needed the material most. Thus one rarely finds detailed series of recorded dreams after a trauma. Much writing on posttraumatic dreams and posttraumatic stress disorder in veterans, for instance, depends on the veteran's recall years later of what was dreamt about in the period following trauma, and we know that such memories are far from reliable.

It is not easy to obtain appropriate material to look at. However, over the years, working both as a clinician—a psychiatrist and psychoanalyst—and as a researcher obtaining material from dreamers and from other professionals in a number of settings, I have been able to collect 40 long series of dreams from people who experienced a trauma, where I could examine what happens in the dreams as the trauma resolves.

I want to emphasize that what is most important in my endeavor is to find series of dreams in someone who is *recovering from* trauma rather than someone who is "stuck" and has the constant repetitive dreams found in posttraumatic stress disorder (PTSD). I have studied the latter situation as well,[3] and I will discuss PTSD later, but I think we will be able to examine better what is really going on in dreaming if we can look at dreams after a trauma in a relatively "normal" (nonpathological) situation where the trauma appears to be resolving and the person is gradually "getting over it." The dream series I have collected are very individual and difficult to compare. They vary in length from six dreams to over 1,000 dreams in periods following trauma; the dreams came chiefly from the weeks and months following a trauma, but in some cases the collection period extends as long as five years.

I have conducted some quantitative studies using this material, but first I and several other clinicians simply looked over the material to get a sense of just what was going on. In some cases, but not all, we had additional material available, such as associations to dream content or the dreamer's further notes as to what had been happening after the trauma. One initial finding that emerged from scanning all these dreams was that although the trauma itself does occur in the dreams, dreams very seldom replay the trauma exactly as it occurred. The literature on dreams frequently speaks of dreams replaying the trauma exactly, and this certainly may occur on occasion, but in the series available to me there was no instance of an absolutely exact replay. The dream, even if it occurred only a few days later, often did include the trauma but already involved some distortion or change, bringing in material from other parts of the dreamer's life. Studies by Brooks Brenneis, a Michigan psychoanalyst, have come to similar conclusions.[4]

I believe that previous authors who have spoken of exact replay most likely relied on memories obtained years later in which the dreamer was often likely to generalize and say, "Yes, I dreamt about it just the way it happened," without actually recalling it in detail. Also, past reports were often based on cases of posttraumatic stress disorder in which there is indeed a repetitive dream dealing with the trauma. However, even in the cases of PTSD that I have studied in detail, the dream, though repetitive, is not usually a repetition of the trauma exactly as it happened, but involves at least one important change. The change is often in the direction of "who was hurt" or "who was killed, him or me?" The typical situation in wartime is that the dreamer was a survivor while his buddy was killed. In the dream the situation is similar except it is the dreamer who is killed or wounded or about to be killed or it is unclear who the victim is; in other words, an element of "survivor guilt" appears; this will be discussed further below.

In any case, the dreams and nightmares in these series often involved the trauma, though not exactly as it happened. What was most striking was that the dreams obviously appeared to make connections between the trauma and other parts of the dreamer's life, and the connections often involved not the detailed physical events of the trauma, but the emotions experienced, as in the examples we considered in the last chapter. It is obviously the emotion of terror and fear, not the actual event experienced, that is being portrayed when the fire victim dreams of being caught in a tidal wave or the rape victim dreams of an oncoming train. Here are some other examples in my series of nightmares after trauma that picture or "contextualize" the feeling of terror:

> I'm on the roof of a garage or something like that; this huge whirlwind comes and sweeps me up in it. I am absolutely helpless; I am swept away. I wake up terrified.

> I am trapped in an elevator. I am not sure whether I am alone or others are with me, but no one can help. We are falling faster and faster and are about to hit bottom.

> These little animals like squirrels or rabbits have been run over on a road and they are lying there dying. I am watching but I also seem to be one of them.

> This woman is standing there helpless and a man comes along with a knife or something and is cutting her face to pieces. Help!

> I am swimming underwater. I have to get up through some sort of tower. I am scared. I am suffocating. I don't think I am going to make it.

> I am with a bunch of people in the lobby of some kind of a building all made of glass. Something breaks the glass and it all starts falling on us. We are all being cut to pieces. There is nothing we can do.

In none of these cases was the dream picturing anything that had actually happened to the dreamer. The dreams appear to be picturing the emotional state of the dreamer: "I'm terrified," and often also, "I'm vulnerable."

After the sudden death of someone close, the emotion that is experienced is not terror, but overwhelming grief. Dreams find a way to picture this emotion too. A man whose greatly loved and very powerful mother had recently died dreamt,

> A mountain has split apart. This huge mountain has split apart and there are pieces lying around. I am supposed to make arrangements to take care of it.

A woman whose mother had just died dreamt,

> There was an empty house, empty and barren. All the doors and windows were open and the wind was blowing through.

Another dreamt,

> A huge tree has fallen down right in front of our house. We're all stunned.

These dreams are portraying not the actual details of the events, but the emotion experienced by the dreamer.

Sometimes after the acute fear or terror subsides, the dreams continue for quite a while to portray a feeling that could be called vulnerability. This is closely allied to fear but seems to be somewhat less intense. The dreams often portray someone or something other than the dreamer as victim, and the dreams are not always described as nightmares with an awakening in fright.

> I dreamt of a small, hurt animal just lying in the road bleeding.

> There were these shellfish creatures, like lobsters or crayfish maybe, with their shells torn off. They were just lying there white and pink and very exposed.

> There was this light yellow-white membrane, sort of like a skin, stretched taut. I could feel it, and these huge birds and things were diving down and pecking at it. It felt very painful.

> Several of us were wandering around on this huge plain. We were all lost and helpless. There was storm and rain beating on us and we had no place to go. We were all lost.

In the earliest dreams after a traumatic event, terror and fear usually predominate. Sometimes these are followed by dreams of extreme vulnerability; then survival guilt surfaces. "Why am I alive, while he/she is dead or injured?"; "I deserve to have died." Survivor guilt is an extremely common emotion felt after a trauma, and not only in a wartime situation. For instance, a young woman, one of whose best friends had injured himself in a fall from her roof and was now a paraplegic in a wheelchair, dreamt a number times that she herself was in a wheelchair. She felt guilty and was taking her friend's place, as it were, suffering for him. I have numerous such examples, and similar dreams are recorded in fire survivors, rape victims, and others.

Here are some examples of dreams that appear to contextualize the feeling of survivor guilt:

> I dreamt that my brother and I got into a bad fight and my brother was beating me up.

> I dreamt of a fire somewhat like the one we were really in, only the house was different, and in the dream my brother and everyone else escaped. I think I was still in the house getting burned.

The two examples above were dreamt by a young man whose brother had actually been killed in a fire from which the dreamer had escaped.

> I am opening up body bags containing guys who have been killed in the last battle. I open up the last body bag, look inside, and the body is me! I wake up screaming.

This is close to what actually happened in Vietnam. He had opened body bags and the last bag contained his buddy.

Or the very common "ordinary guilt" (as opposed to "survivor guilt"): "I must have been responsible for this event; I must have done something to bring this on."

> I keep dreaming that I had left the stove on and the house caught fire.

> I dreamt I had left my children locked in on the third floor and forgotten about them.

Various other emotions, such as grief and anger, sometimes come up, too, either alone or mixed with the previous more usual emotions. Gradually, guided by the sequence of emotions, the trau-matic event is connected up, woven in, placed within whatever contexts are available in the dreamer's memory systems.

A PROGRESSION OF EMOTIONS

The dreams certainly seem to be picturing or contextualizing the emotional state of the dreamer, and the dreams change somewhat as the emotional state changes. Perhaps this is all that happens, but it is tempting to go further and examine this picturing and connecting process with the view that like everything else in the body, making connections might have a function—that it might be useful in some way.

One can envision the process after trauma as a series of emotion-generated questions and answers. First comes absolute terror: "The world is ending! This is the most horrible thing that has ever happened to anyone! How can I or anyone survive this?" The nightmares and dreams attempt an answer along the lines of an internal dialogue such as,

> Well, let's take a look at what happened. It is a terrible event, yes, but is it unique? Let the emotion flood your mind, and let's see what images it calls up. Let's picture this feeling of terror. Let's look at other terrifying situations, other catastrophes. . . . Awful, yes, but it's part of a whole catalog of human disasters. All are horrible, but sometimes people seem to survive. In fact, does this remind you of anything else? Let's look at other times when you felt terrified. Not quite the same? No, but let's keep looking; wasn't there some similar feeling? And you survived. In fact, you seem to be surviving this time. Let's see what else comes to mind, even if it makes little sense just now.

Terror lessens; the basic human fears of annihilation, separation, and loss emerge. These fears may then be pictured and connected in dreams.

Next, perhaps survivor guilt comes to the forefront:

> Yes, I seem to have survived, but he was blown up. How come I survived? And did I really? Maybe I'm the one who's dead. I'm a

much worse person than he was. I certainly deserve to have
died. . . .

Then answers in dreams begin:

> Well, let's keep picturing it, working on it. This isn't the first time
> you've been in a difficult situation. Let's see what happened
> before. Weren't there other times something like this . . . with a
> feeling like this? Let's look at those, even situations in your
> childhood, or maybe a similar event involving someone else.
> What about you and your brothers or sisters? Haven't you and
> they been through a lot? Maybe not just siblings; how about pets,
> animals, stories, picture books? Things that stick in your mind. It
> may take awhile but let's look at all that. Let's put it in perspec-
> tive. Is it always you who's unhurt while others are hurt? Aren't
> there a whole lot of such experiences, real or maybe imagined,
> that were important for you? It seems that sometimes you were
> hurt, sometimes others were. There are all sorts of possibilities.

Another common scenario involving guilt:

> I was attacked, I was hurt/burned/raped. But it was all my
> fault. I'm a horrible person. I brought it all on. I deserve to die. . . .

> Wait a second; let's look at it. Let's look at what happened; let's
> look at what else in your mind is connected to it, what else
> produced this kind of feeling. It doesn't seem clear that you
> caused it all; isn't it like when you were much younger . . . and . . .
> yes you blamed yourself then too, but give yourself a chance to
> make some more connections. Let's see what else is there. You
> were in a complicated, difficult family situation. . . . Now here's a
> place where it looks like your father/mother didn't treat you
> well, didn't protect you. The more we look, the less clear it is that
> the fault is all yours. Let's go on. . . .

The way I have outlined the progression of emotions above is of
course speculative and shamelessly anthropomorphic. I have put it
this way to begin to suggest that this process of connection and
contextualization may indeed be useful or functional, as we will
discuss later.

What happens following a trauma as it resolves is that gradually more and more "usual" dream material is introduced along with the direct or metaphorical representations of the trauma. Eventually, usually within weeks or months, dreams return to their normal patterns, whatever those may be. In some persons the normal pattern is to remember very few dreams; in these cases it is only after traumatic events, stressful situations, or illnesses, perhaps, that dreams are remembered at all.

The dominant emotion of the dreamer—first, terror and fear in these cases, and then often survivor guilt, other types of guilt, grief, etc.—also leads the dreamer toward other material in his memory associated with the same emotions. Thus, trauma often "rekindles" memories of an older trauma, and the dreams often refer to older traumatic situations involving the same emotion. For instance, I interviewed a woman recovering from a recent rape whose dreams related to the current incident but then also rapidly brought in material from a near-rape in adolescence.[5] In a case described by Ramon Greenberg,[6] a World War II veteran had a nightmare that recurred a number of times of a severed human head lying by a roadside in war-torn Europe. This scene filled him with horror and anger, and he would wake up sweating. Although he had been through battles in Europe and had seen atrocities committed, he could not recall anything actually happening involving a severed head. It was only after working for awhile in therapy that he remembered a scene from his childhood that was associated with the same emotions of horror and anger. He had kept a pet guinea pig in a cage; one day the guinea pig disappeared. Several days later he suddenly discovered the severed head of his guinea pig in a stew his mother had prepared. The family was short of money and his mother was attempting to add meat to their diet. Apparently his wartime experiences had revived this old horror/anger, and the nightmare put them together (condensation). For this man, the horror and anger he had felt as an adult could best find a context by bringing up this old scene from childhood.

The material in our dreams is always personally relevant, though the dream is perfectly capable of concocting scenes that did not actually happen to us. As we will discuss later, our memory nets are not filing cabinets containing index cards describing exactly what happened, but rather patterns of connection weights allowing us to reconstitute or re-create past scenes—though sometimes not precisely as they happened—and also to combine them and create other imaginary scenes. Our memory nets allow us to remember (to re-create roughly) not only what happened to us, but also our concerns about what happened, our wishes as to what could happen, our fantasies, etc.

CONTEXTUALIZING IMAGES

I call the process we have discussed above "contextualization of emotion." My collaborators and I have started to quantify this concept, since one can sometimes fool oneself by simply picking striking examples to make a point. Tidal wave dreams certainly occur after trauma, but can't they occur at other times too? Do just as many such dreams occur in an average person on an ordinary Thursday? We have developed a scoring system for "contextualizing images" (of which the most clear-cut examples are the tidal waves, fires, etc., above). Each judge is asked to look through the dream report for a striking image, specifically "a striking, arresting, or compelling image, not simply a story, but an image that stands out by virtue of being especially powerful, vivid, bizarre, or detailed." The judge tries to picture the imagery of the dream as described in the dream report and to score an image that stands out powerfully, if there is one. He or she is not asked to think of an emotion at this stage, and it does not matter whether any emotion is mentioned in the dream report. After deciding whether there is such an image or not, the judge is then asked to assign an intensity scale from 1 to 3. Actually, the scale runs from 0 for "no image" through 3, "one of the most intense images you have come across." Finally the rater is asked, "what emotion is most likely to be contextualized" from a list of 18 emotions. We found that different judges working independently had quite good agreement (intercorrelations).

In an early study two scorers trained in this procedure then scored a group of 135 dreams as to whether they contained a contextualizing image, what its intensity was, and what emotion it seemed to be contextualizing. Sixty-eight of the dreams came from the weeks following trauma (from 10 different dreamers), and 67 were ordinary dreams or at least dreams in a period with no known trauma. The results of this preliminary study show that dreams in the period following trauma were scored as showing significantly more contextualizing images, more intense contextualizing images, and involving the emotions of terror, vulnerability, and guilt.[7] More recently a number of dream series after trauma have been scored individually and compared with nontrauma dreams. In our most severe case, eight dreams were available in the three weeks immediately following a rape. In this case the two judges agreed on all eight: all were rated *yes* (a contextualizing image present). The average intensity score was 2.53, much higher than the average in nontrauma dreams (about 1.0–1.2). The emotions scored were fear, terror, and vulnerability.

A 31-year-old man lost a good friend in the Oklahoma City bombing. His 12 dreams in the weeks after the bombing were scored as all (100%) containing a contextualizing image, with an intensity score of 2.54. This same man's dreams in the period before the bombing had 58% containing a contextualizing image, with an intensity score of 1.17. Ten such series have been scored so far.[8] We also found that, as predicted, contextualizing images were more frequent and more intense in dreams than in daydreams.[9] These quantitative studies suggest that contextualizing images can be scored reliably and that indeed they are more frequent and more intense in dreams after trauma. Later I will discuss further the role of emotion in dreams and the way we can visualize this process of making connections in the networks of our mind in a way that contextualizes emotion.

MAKING CONNECTIONS IN A SAFE PLACE

Having seen this sort of regular sequence of connections and contextualizations repeatedly, I have no doubt that this is at least a general outline of what happens after trauma. But a further question, which I cannot answer so definitely, is whether this is functional. Is this simply something that happens in dreaming—a bunch of connections get made and emotions are contextualized—or is this somehow useful to us? I believe that probably the process is a functional one, though it is not easy to prove this. We will examine in the next chapter how a similar series of events occurs in dreams after stressful events that do not qualify as trauma. What I want to call attention to now (see also Chapter 8) is that what occurs in dreams after trauma is quite similar to what occurs in good psychotherapy following trauma. In other words, dreams may be therapeutic.

The period following trauma is one of the times when therapy or counseling is most clearly indicated. Someone who has just been through a serious traumatic event of any kind is often advised to obtain some therapy or counseling if at all possible to "help deal with it." What happens in such psychotherapy? This has been written about for many years from a number of different standpoints, but there are good recent summaries.[10] There is agreement that the process involves, first of all, providing a safe place for the victim. A safe place does not refer simply to a comfortable quiet room without intrusion. It refers more to the sense of safety provided by the therapist, the gradually increasing conviction of the patient that she is not endangered, that the therapist is working entirely for her and will not hurt her, that she will not again be taken advantage of, that she will be allowed to explore feelings and options at her own pace, and so on. Once this feeling of safety is established, and this may take some time, the patient or victim is then allowed to tell the story of the trauma in any way she wishes and as often as she likes. As the story is told, associations and connections are made. Other traumatic events are brought in. Powerful feelings emerge—terror at first, and then, very often, guilt, shame, and so on. The process of psychotherapy after trauma can be thought of as "making connections in a safe place."

I suggest that dreaming allows very much the same process to occur. A "safe place" is provided by the bed, and in REM sleep, where most dreams occur; it is provided additionally by the muscular paralysis of REM sleep which completely prevents the dreamer from running around screaming, shooting people, etc.[11] In this safe place, dreams appear to make connections in similar ways, as we have discussed above. In fact, the fantasied "conversation" a few pages back between the terrified, traumatized dreamer and his "dreaming process" is not unlike what happens in psychotherapy. In this sense dreaming can be seen as our own built-in form of counseling or psychotherapy. I visualize this process as being functional or helpful in several related ways. As I have indicated above, dreaming moves the dreamer from the position of absolute terror ("This is the most terrible thing that has ever happened to anyone. How can anyone survive?") to a series of connections ("This is somewhat like such and such" or "In a similar case [similar emotions] I did such and such or someone else did such and such" or "People do survive; I survived."). At the end of this series of connections the new material is woven in, and is less dangerous. One could visualize the situation after trauma as the surface of the sea in a typhoon that with time gradually subsides to a quieter surface. As the mind calms, there is a weaving in of new material. Thus, using different metaphors we could think of a cloth being rewoven with a new thread, or we could imagine a kind of electrified net in which there was excitation going off in one section, excitation that gradually spread out to other portions of the net.

Of course dreaming is not our only resource. While awake, too, we try to deal with and make sense of traumatic material. But our minds function somewhat differently in waking: We are more focused and directed, we think somewhat more narrowly (see Chapter 5), we tend to "keep things in their places" more, and thus traumatic material may often be dealt with by being kept out of the way, or walled off, rather than being integrated. I visualize dreaming as being another form of dealing with emotional material, somewhat different from waking in that connections are made more easily, more widely, and more broadly. Making these broad connections not only helps to quiet the traumatic "storm" by spreading out the excitation, but is also useful in other ways. It can be seen as helping with memory storage in terms of cross-indexing—making more connections between new material and older material—and sometimes, as we will see, the new broader connections can in themselves be extremely useful. Making new connections can mean seeing things in a new way.

POSTTRAUMATIC STRESS DISORDER

So far, we have concentrated on what is probably the simplest case: what happens after a single trauma in an individual who has not been severely traumatized previously and who is gradually recovering. We have tried to follow what happens in this "ideal case" during normal recovery and integration, and this is the case we consider a paradigm—a model—to let us examine most clearly what happens during all types of dreams.

However, life is not always so simple or so benign. First of all, even after a single severe trauma or series of traumas, recovery and healing do not always progress perfectly along the lines we have discussed. In severe cases, classic PTSD develops. The symptoms of PTSD include not only nightmares and flashbacks about the traumatic event, but also avoidance of any situation or feeling associated with the trauma, and sometimes a general detachment or reduced responsiveness known as "psychic numbing." Here the sequence is stopped short. The patient is stuck with repetitive posttraumatic nightmares, which are classically described as repeating the very earliest stages—picturing the trauma as it occurred. However, as discussed above, the nightmares most often actually repeat a slightly later stage of the process with an added element of survivor guilt: "Was it him or was it me?" For instance: "Then I open the last body bag and the body inside is me; I wake up screaming." The actual traumatic scene with this one amendment then becomes the repetitive traumatic nightmare.

When this situation becomes chronic, the entire process we have followed seems to become "stuck." Dreams are no longer making any new or useful connections with other materials of life. In children, play also becomes repetitive and "stuck" at such times.[12] And, in fact, psychotherapy frequently does not help greatly either. Clinicians have repeatedly noted that patients with established PTSD and chronic repetitive nightmares resist psychotherapy, find becoming involved to be too painful, and seldom benefit greatly from treatment. These patients have developed a different style of existence, involving walling off the trauma and avoiding anything that might remind them of it, avoiding emotional relationships that might bring up painful memories, and in fact avoiding emotion generally. They are in a sense walling things off and avoiding connections of any kind; they have developed "thick boundaries" (Chapter 13). Such a style is not easily compatible with the making of connections in psychotherapy. And in my experience these people do not report dreaming much, aside from the repetitive nightmares.[13]

DREAMS AFTER TRAUMA AS A PARADIGM

Finally, I want to take a large step and suggest that what we have examined in these nightmares and other dreams after trauma, as the trauma resolves, is prototypic and that in fact the same process occurs in all dreams. You may feel that what we have discussed so far is a very specific and rare situation—dreams after a serious traumatic event—and luckily for many of us, this is true. However, this is the case mainly for those of us living in relatively safe circumstances, in relatively safe countries, and in the last few centuries. In other words, it is an accident of place and time. I suggest that for most of the history of mankind life was much less safe and predictable and that traumatic events—something terrible, frightening, unpredictable—happened considerably more often. Even now, there are many parts of the world in which trauma and terror are daily occurrences. Those who have worked with survivors and victims in these areas speak of almost constant nightmares and frightening dreams, and there are many people who live in high-crime areas in advanced or "civilized" countries whose situation is not that much different.[14] I have interviewed a number of children and adolescents from inner cities who speak of being shot or being attacked or being chased by frightening aliens as a very frequent occurrence in their dreams.

In these situations in the past and in the present, dreaming may be doing on a fairly regular basis just what we have discussed. Even when we are not leading traumatized lives, I suggest that the pattern we have examined after trauma is a paradigm, an illustration of what happens all the time, though often it may be less clearly visible. In other words, we can visualize our minds as always in some sort of emotional turmoil, though the emotions are usually less dramatic and less obvious than after trauma. And our dreams are always finding a picture context for ("contextualizing") these emotional concerns.

Of course, trauma itself is not necessarily an all-or-none concept, and it is not necessarily the same thing for different people. An identical external event may be very traumatic for one person and much less so for another, depending on personality structure and past experiences. For this reason I have tried to collect material after especially serious trauma that would be expected to be a problem for just about anyone. I cannot imagine anyone escaping from a burning house or being raped and then treating this situation with complete equanimity. However, there are many situations, such as breakup of a relationship, a sudden change in employment, finding out one is unexpectedly pregnant, which some may feel to be seriously traumatic— and their dreams deal with the situation accordingly—while others take the same situations much more in stride. Here I have a great deal of material, too, but it is less clear-cut and obvious since so much depends on knowing the inner dynamics of the particular person. Some of this material will be considered in the next chapter, where we will consider dreams in situations that are not obviously traumatic but that can still be defined in terms of an obvious emotional concern. From there we will move gradually to more "ordinary" situations.

When I say that dreaming contextualizes an emotion, I am oversimplifying somewhat. In the examples we have examined, I have usually chosen the most striking image, and this is also what our judges have been rating. There is almost always a background narrative as well as one or more striking contextualizing images. As we get away from posttrauma to more ordinary situations, the background material, presumably from elsewhere in the dreamer's life, may become relatively more prominent in the dream and may obscure or overwhelm the simple contextualizing images. I am not implying that this "background" is unimportant. I would agree with Freud that every element in the dream is determined. It comes from somewhere in our lives. Even in our archetypal dream of being overwhelmed by a tidal wave or chased by a monster, the dream usually contains more than this simple tidal wave or chase; the "more" obviously comes from somewhere in the dreamer's world, and following it up can be very revealing.

However, in one sense I do insist that the central image (contextualizing image) is the most important part of the dream. Such an image is found to be present more often, and scored as more intense by judges on a blind basis, in dreams from the period following trauma, and I believe it leads us most directly to the underlying emotion or concern. This in turn has implications for working with dreams (and dream interpretation), as we will see later.

Chapter Three

FROM DREAMS IN STRESSFUL SITUATIONS TO ORDINARY DREAMS

Let us move gradually from the extreme case of an acute trauma, where we are quite certain of the person's emotions and concerns, along a continuum toward the average, "ordinary" dream not associated with any obviously unusual events or powerful concerns. First, still fairly close to trauma, we can examine "stressful situations" that do not quite qualify as trauma, in the sense that they disrupt or tear apart the mind, but nonetheless are obviously emotionally disturbing. These would be, for instance, the death of someone close or other kinds of loss, getting through a divorce, or having a dangerous surgical procedure. One special situation, pregnancy (especially a first pregnancy), is worth examining, since whether or not we call pregnancy a "stress," it certainly involves powerful and relatively predictable emotional concerns. In all these situations we may not be as sure of the person's emotional state as immediately as after trauma, but we certainly have some knowledge of what is going on. Similarly, we can examine the dreams of certain patients in psychotherapy or psychoanalysis whose lives appear to be dominated by one powerful emotion or concern.

DREAMING IN STRESSFUL SITUATIONS

Charlie is a 25-year-old man who suffers from severe muscular/skeletal problems. He lives in his parents' home and has felt anxious and guilty for some time about his inability to earn a good enough living because of his illness. Recently life has become even more difficult for him since his father fell from a roof and became paralyzed. The father is now paraplegic; he was actually quadriplegic for a time but is beginning to regain some ability to move his arms. The young man and his mother are trying desperately to take care of the ailing father while keeping their own lives and jobs in order, but it is obviously a great stress for everyone. Charlie reports:

> I dream all the time about my father. Interestingly, it's not exactly his real injury and the actual things that happened to him, but it's always something parallel to that—something picturing the same kind of thing. For instance, I see him badly hurt in a flood and swept away; I'm unable to get to him. I picture him in a house on fire; he can't get out and I am not able to help him. He is lost or suffering somewhere and I can't find him. I never feel I have done enough for him. The dreams very clearly show me my guilt feelings in all kinds of ways.

I know Charlie quite well, and I completely agree with his summary. He is going though a painful time characterized by his feelings of guilt and inadequacy, and his dreams picture (contextualize) his feelings.

We have seen in the previous chapter that in dreams after trauma, as the trauma resolves, the dominant emotions of the dreamer (first terror and fear and then often vulnerability, guilt, and others) guide or organize the connecting processes of dreaming. Dreams after trauma may appear to represent a rare situation. However, for many, now and in the past, trauma is an almost constant presence and their dreams reflect this. But however common or uncommon it may be in our lives, I suggest that trauma can be seen as a paradigm, or a simplest case, in which we can see most clearly what happens in dreams, and that other situations probably follow the same pattern though it may be more difficult to discern.

In someone who has just experienced a severe traumatic event, we can be quite certain of the dominant emotions even without knowing the person's life in great detail. Of course past experiences, day residues, etc., are not irrelevant; they are, in fact, what is swept up by the emotion to form the pictures of the dream. I believe if we move on from trauma to somewhat less dramatic situations, we can still see the same patterns (as in Charlie above), though not always quite as vividly.

A very detailed study was conducted by psychologist Louis Breger of two different highly stressful situations, one of which involved a collection of dreams in the sleep laboratory from several persons who were about to have major cardiovascular surgery.[1] One of these men, "Al," was a 64-year-old retired veteran hospitalized because of vascular blockage in his legs producing considerable symptoms. He was scheduled to have surgery to remove an aneurism found in the femoral artery in his leg. Al was an active, outgoing person who "created the impression of being tough, experienced, and independent, and of having little room in his life for fear or weakness." He continually emphasized that the anticipated operation did not make him worried, fearful, or anxious in any way. He did not expect any pain or problems, stating, "Oh, I know there will be some soreness, but I don't think about those things." His dreams, however, clearly picture his concerns. Here is the first dream he reports, a few days before surgery:

> My daughter and I was talking about a quarter of beef. You understand? . . . Now . . . the funny part of it is . . . this quarter of beef had been delivered apparently and we were talking about cutting it up . . . to preserve it you know. This ex-boss of mine she come in the picture. She discussed that with me and with the daughter too how this meat should be cut up. There was a kind of heated argument there about how that meat was gonna be cut I think between me and my ex-wife . . . we were, uh . . . more or less, arguing which way it was going to be cut. But then it turned into a surgical . . . rather than a hospital, it turned into an operation, a surgical conversation, something like that. They were me and one of them guys in that room over there, it seemed like my ex-wife moved out of the picture but Jack and my daughter and I was discussing or talking about one of those guys that had a surgery over there and how they cut them, and then this pocketknife. I had a pocketknife and was examining to see if there was any blood on it, you see? And the blood was all cleaned off of it. The handle was left but all three blades fell out of it. . . .

And here are several dreams from the next few days, still before surgery:

We was working on a stove you know. Well it was a boy there . . . and this stove, we got it all back together. You know we had it all apart to clean it. We got the stove built in there but it wouldn't tighten up . . . on this side. There was a bolt like on each side. So we took it out tryin' to get the other side to fit. You see, we had tore it down . . . and then it seemed like we remembered we had tore that stove down the year before, quite some time before that and had the same trouble there. Then we remembered that we . . . kinda hammered that hole in and we done that and we got the screw back in and it seemed like we just picked up one piece of the stove and just push it down in there. I don't know what the heck we was going to do with it. We talked about this bolt in the stove.

We was all just standing there looking at this other engine and . . . we lined the switch, it seemed like the switch . . . it was a funny thing. They had to come off this private road onto ours and them switches weren't a standard switch, we had to dig some rocks out of the ground . . . and throw this switch over. And I was doing that, I was helping . . . I can't tell you what a switch is, instead of them just being flapped over and locked down to the padlock they was flapped over, the ends of two pipes together and there was a piece of this crooked zigzag piece of iron that was run first in one pipe and then the other so you couldn't lift the one out. But anyway, it was a complicated thing and so we got down there and was digging them things out of them pipes so we could throw the switch for them guys so they wouldn't have to stop . . . it took a little time and they hadn't used that switch it seemed alike for years and naturally the sand and dust had blowed into these pipes and it was all rusty.

Obviously, these dreams about beef being cut up, about stoves and engines that need fixing, are about Al's current emotional concern. Eleven of Al's 15 preoperative dreams dealt in some way with concern about his perhaps defective body and concern about what was happening to him. Here the dreamer is not quite as overwhelmed as in the dreams we have examined occurring immediately after trauma, but despite his denials he is certainly upset and under a great deal of stress. We can see his dreams as contextualizing emotion, but here it is not as clearly one simple emotion as is the case after trauma. In Al's case it may make more sense to speak of contextualizing his emotional concerns. His dreams picture worries about his body, about defects in his body, and about whether he is going to be injured or disabled further by the surgery. It becomes clear through interviews that Al is a very physical and active man who likes to deal with a problem by jumping in and trying to fix it. For him, undergoing surgery is especially stressful because it represents complete passivity. Thus his dream also contextualizes the concern that he is losing his status as an active, powerful male and becoming simply a passive piece of meat that is being cut up, or a malfunctioning piece of equipment.

In addition to examining people undergoing surgery, Breger's group[1] also examined a more complicated stressful situation in which students participated in a session where they took turns being the "focus subject." In this position, one student was the center of attention while everyone else in the group pointed out his problems and issues to him. It is difficult to do justice to the complex material gathered in this study without presenting a great deal of background. Just one simple example: The very first dream presented is from a young man (Hal) who has just been the "focus subject"; he feels attacked and is somewhat hurt by the criticisms made by the other group members. That night he dreams:

> I was in a swimming pool . . . all the water dripped out . . . I was swimming along . . . then there was nothing left . . . everything disappeared. . . . I was alone in the pool . . . no lifeguard . . . no nothing. Everything just dropped out right underneath me. Roger and the two girls [group members] were there. . . . We were having a great time and suddenly the water and the people disappeared . . . I was just wallowing on the bottom . . . crying out. It scared me . . . I could feel myself falling. Not hurt physically . . . I just felt damaged or bruised. . . . I wasn't bleeding or anything.

Here several related emotions are presented, but clearly Hal's dream is portraying his feeling of loss of support and his feelings of anxiety and loneliness.

A well-known psychologist and sleep researcher, Rosalind Cartwright, has been doing a series of studies on people going through a painful divorce.[2] Here, too, the dreams clearly picture or find a context for the dreamers' concerns. For instance, Tony had just been left by his wife of 19 years. She had been dissatisfied with the marriage for a long time, and left him to have an affair with another woman! She had taken their younger child with her and left Tony with his two older boys. The first dream Tony reports is:

> I was in a small boat, a 15-man rubber raft. I was trying to paddle ashore, and a storm came up and caught us in a sort of open sea. It was some kind of military operation that had something to do with a submarine that dropped us there. It was a big raft, but only two other people were there with me. The raft was being tossed around. It was an amphibious infiltration. Something artificial about it, life a mock-up of a battle being filmed in a tub. It was dark and stormy and the raft was spinning and the water was boiling.

This dream scene is a complicated one. Some of the imagery in the dream comes from Tony's experiences in Vietnam years before. To the artificial "mock-up" aspect he associates that this is the way his marriage was; his marriage was a "sham situation." But chiefly the dream appears to be picturing his emotional situation; he is "at sea" with his two boys. He is being tossed around in a storm and there is an obvious sense of danger.

In fact, this sort of image is extremely common. I have over 50 examples in my files from people undergoing stress of various kinds in which the dream imagery involves one of the following: "I am in a raft (or a boat) being tossed around on the sea." "I am lost." "I am wandering through buildings and can never find where I am going." "I am walking around (or driving) in this desolate area; I can't find my way; there's no one to help me." Clearly such dreams at times of stress picture feelings of vulnerability, of confusion, of feeling lost or hurt.

I recently saw a charming young woman, June, whose life had become incredibly stressful in the past few years. She seemed to be very normal psychologically, but had a serious medical illness: childhood-onset diabetes. Her diabetic condition had become worse so that June was now almost entirely blind and had severe pains that made it hard for her to sleep and impossible for her to function in her professional position. She had to give up her job, but had one remaining consolation. She and her husband had no children, but she had befriended and helped to care for the young child of a woman friend who was having difficulties caring for the child. June became almost an adoptive mother for the youngster and derived great satisfaction from this relationship, which kept her going despite her serious illness. For unknown reasons, the young child's mother suddenly decided that she wanted her child back and would not let the child have any contact with June. June felt devastated, developed a depression, and felt that there was little left to live for. At this time, she told me that her dreams changed; lately her dreams all seemed to be about "fecal matter," as she put it to me delicately; fecal matter, human and animal, all over the place. She was puzzled and somewhat embarrassed by these dreams, but with a little discussion it became obvious to both of us that her dreams were simply picturing her obvious and justified emotional concern, "too much shit. There's just too much shit in my life."

It must be clear from these situations that there is no clear dividing line between a trauma and a stressful situation. A trauma is the most sudden, unexpected, disturbing type of event that can happen. The stressful situations we have discussed are not quite so disturbing but fall somewhere between trauma and ordinary life. Overall, my impression is that dreams in these stressful situations can be understood quite similarly to the dreams after trauma. There is at least one difference: In the stressful situation, the dream imagery appears to be capturing or contextualizing a strong *emotional concern* or group of concerns (how will this affect my body, my abilities?) rather than one simple overwhelming emotion such as terror.

Our judges (see Chapter 2) also score contextualizing images in stressful compared to nonstressful periods in the same persons. Early results show that the stressful periods appear to be characterized by more intense contextualizing images than the nonstressful periods. The stressful periods are scored somewhat like the posttrauma periods discussed previously, except that the "emotions contextualized" are different: Whereas the posttrauma dreams scored a preponderance of terror, fear, and vulnerability, the stressful period dreams were scored as portraying these emotions, and also a wider range, including vulnerability, guilt, shame, and grief.

What we are doing by examining stressful situations is finding
another place where we know more or less what must be on the
person's mind, though not as clearly and strikingly as after trauma.
We can then easily move on from clear-cut trauma and clear-cut
stress to other situations that may not obviously qualify as trauma or
stress, but in which we know the dreamer's primary concern.

PREGNANCY

Dreams of pregnant women provide a situation in which there is
a series of somewhat predictable emotional concerns that can perhaps be traced in dreams. I have a few series of such dreams, and
dreams in pregnancy have been studied in more detail by other
researchers.[3] The dominant concerns early in pregnancy generally
revolve around "What is happening to my body?," which includes
"Will I still be attractive?" The dreams reflect this through changes of
shape and increases in size of the self and other objects or animals;
the dreams also involve large, disfigured creatures. For example, one
woman reports:

> I was attending some kind of show or concert. I was real fat; I
> looked like a blimp. The guys were all laughing and admiring
> these really cute girls on stage. No one paid attention to me.

Later, concerns arise about what will this thing, this baby, actually look like, which then leads to innumerable dreams of small and
then large creatures—sometimes monsters or strange, ill-formed
things—portraying these concerns of the dreamer.

> I go out the back door of my house and I see in the neighbor's
> yard their pet dog with many small black animals. They are a
> triangular shape, a kind I never saw before. They are playing
> with some rats on a little hill of dust.[4]

> There, sitting between my legs, was this naked little boy . . . his
> face was like an old man's and there were fangs coming out of
> his lips.

And toward the end of the pregnancy, the woman's primary concern becomes whether or not she'll be able to handle birth, motherhood, and child-rearing.

> Our apartment was invaded with mice, lizards, rabbits, kittens, puppies. They were coming in the windows and front door. I couldn't stop them and they were messing up everything.

> Someone left a box full of baby chicks on our doorstep. I was busy with my small son and they died before I had time to take care of them.[5]

These dreams clearly picture the woman's concerns that she'll be overwhelmed and not be able to take care of everything.

Here, as in the dreams during "stressful situations," the dreams picture or contextualize not a single emotion but rather a series of powerful emotional concerns: first, "Will I still be attractive?," then "What will this thing inside me be like?," and finally, "Will I be able to take care of this thing?," "Will I be able to love it, to be a good mother?" The similarity to the stressful situations we previously discussed is obvious.

Clearly, not all dreams of pregnant women are the kind we have just discussed. Some series of dreams in pregnancy I have examined include a lot of very ordinary dreams, and occasionally there are dreams dealing with trauma or with concerns completely different from those of pregnancy. This is hardly surprising, since pregnancy is not the only thing of importance in these women's lives. My impression from the series I have examined is that dreams clearly contextualizing concerns about pregnancy occur more often in the case of a first pregnancy, and in relatively peaceful surroundings where the woman is focused on the pregnancy, where it is the most important thing in her life. There are fewer clear dreams picturing these concerns if it is a fourth or fifth pregnancy, or if the pregnancy is only a minor detail in the woman's complicated and traumatic life.

PEOPLE IN THERAPY

We sometimes are in a position to know the dominant emotional concern of a dreamer quite well even in someone who has not been in an acute trauma or an obviously stressful situation and who is not pregnant. This can occur, for instance, in a patient we have gradually come to know. I recently treated a mother of two young children, a professional woman who was for the most part satisfied with her career and her family and as far as I could tell was an excellent wife and mother. However, in one way her life was not going well. She was dominated by an obsessive emotional concern that could be described as longstanding guilt, especially guilt about not being a good mother. Her parents, for pathological reasons of their own, had always been extremely demanding and critical. No matter what she did or how well she did it, she was always made to feel that she could and should have done much better. She internalized this parental attitude and became at times acutely unhappy during her childhood and adolescence—always feeling guilty that she had done something wrong or had not measured up to an external or internal standard. When she left home for college, her life improved considerably. She actually had many intellectual and social talents that she found (to her surprise) were appreciated outside of her home. She began to relax and enjoy life. She finished college, worked on a career, and married a man with whom she was in love. Everything appeared to be going beautifully until the births of her two children. Becoming a mother herself revived her early concerns about her inadequacy and brought back memories of her parents' criticisms, especially her mother's. At this time she developed almost constant anxiety dreams and nightmares, all dealing with a similar theme:

> My children are lost in a storm; I can't find them.

> I leave my son alone and a big cat is clawing him, killing him.

> I'm at a hotel by the seashore. My two children are off in separate rooms and the tide is coming up fast. I wake up panicked that they'll drown.

She has told me over 45 dreams of this kind. Even without the benefit of her associations, I think it is clear that the dreams are about her feelings of guilt and more specifically, they are contextualizing her emotional concern, "I'm not a good mother; I'll never be a good enough mother."

This woman is an example of what generally occurs when there is one dominant emotion or emotional concern. Dreams find a way to portray that emotion or concern and contextualize it repeatedly in what is often a fairly clear manner. I could give many examples from patients in therapy in which a known dominant emotional concern is portrayed and readily decipherable.

There are also certain situations in therapy that can produce more or less expected emotional concerns even in very different people. As a simple example, we have already considered the patients who, on beginning psychoanalysis, had similar dreams about walking along dangerous mountain paths. Another dream I have heard several times from different patients goes:

> I come to your office for an appointment, but the door is locked and there are workmen painting the walls or something. It seems you've moved away.

These dreams, instigated by something that makes the patient worry that the therapist might abandon her or him, picture a common concern called "fear of abandonment."

Carl Gustav Jung reports that a young woman who had seen two analysts before him, had the same dream at the start of each of her three analyses:

> She came to the frontier and she wanted to cross it, but she could not find the customhouse where she should have gone to declare whatever she carried with her.

The young woman is clearly concerned about the "baggage" she is bringing with her. After starting analysis with Jung, she had another similar dream of the frontier, but this one continued:

> She had only a small bag with her, and she thought she would pass unnoticed. But the official looked at her and said: "What have you got in your bag?" She said: "Oh, nothing at all," and opened it. He put his hand in and pulled out something that grew bigger and bigger, until it was two complete beds.

Because of this dream, Jung was eventually able to work with her on her concerns about sex and marriage. "She was engaged and would not marry for certain reasons, and those beds were the marriage beds. I pulled that complex out of her and made her realize the problem, and soon after she married."[6]

RECURRENT DREAMS AND NIGHTMARES

Recurrent dreams are reported by a sizable percentage of college students and are usually described as frightening or negative in tone.[7] Such dreams also provide an opportunity to examine how dreams deal with emotional concerns. One 20-year-old woman had a recurrent dream off and on since a major disruptive change in her life at age 14, when she left her mother's house to live with her father and stepmother. She dreams:

> It is pitch black and like a vacuum. There is a vague feeling of dizziness. A large, hairy [masculine] hand reaches out and pushes me into my closet. The door cannot be opened. The hand sets the closet on fire and I suffocate and die in the heat and smoke.[8]

Obviously, a feeling of terror and painful emotional concern is being pictured, though we are not provided more details.

I have spoken with three women who had recurrent dreams of violence and murder—people stabbing or shooting one another—including dreams in which the women committed violent acts themselves. These dreams were surprising and disturbing to the women, who were middle-class professionals or housewives living fairly peaceful lives and who considered themselves to be opposed to and incapable of violence. It turned out that all three had had abortions some years before, and the dreams appeared to be picturing their concerns about this. In fact, two of the three, the recurrent dreams stopped after the women became aware of the connection and explored their unresolved feelings about the abortions.

I have studied approximately 100 persons who suffered from lifelong frequent nightmares (50 of these have been described in detail previously[9]). Most of them did not describe their dreams as exactly recurrent dreams, but nonetheless they dreamt repeatedly about the same themes. The dreams usually began in childhood and involved being chased by a monster or a strange wild animal. As the dreamers grew up, the chaser was more likely to be a large unidentified man, a group of frightening people, or a gang. One reported the following dream:

> There were these evil people who were after me. I could never see them clearly, but I knew they wanted to kill me. I kept running into a house, locking the door. They would come crashing through the door. I would then run up the stairs, lock another door. They would crash through the door again. I would keep running, becoming more and more frightened, but would never quite get away from them until I woke up drenched in sweat.

Such dreams were frequent, described as fantastically vivid and "real," although they were nothing like any actual events that had happened to the dreamer. Here is another from that series:

> I was swimming along in cool, blue water. A strange man swam after me and started slicing me with a knife. It was all in brilliant color and I could feel everything. I felt the cool water and the hot pain of the knife slashing into my arm; I saw my blood spreading out in the water and I could see slices of my flesh drifting off away from me. It was very real. I could definitely feel the knife and feel the pain in this dream.

Detailed interviews with these nightmare sufferers led to the conclusion that most of them did not have a single acute trauma in their childhoods; rather they had thin boundaries. "Thin boundaries" refers to a lack of separation between areas and processes in the mind, and also a lack of walls and defense. Everything seems to "get through" to people with thin boundaries. They may be sensitive in a positive sense, empathic and creative, but they are also oversensitive and vulnerable. They often feel "there is too much coming at me all at once." We will discuss boundaries in more detail in Chapter 13.

In any case, traumas that might have seemed minor to others had a great impact on those people. In their later nightmares, they appeared to be repeatedly picturing (contextualizing) fears and vulnerabilities they had experienced in childhood and which in some way had remained with them, even though their adult lives were often quite peaceful. These emotions were easily reactivated by any situations in their adult working lives or their relationships that somehow reminded them of their childhood fears or vulnerabilities.

In fact, having some nightmares is not unusual. Almost all children have occasional nightmares, usually involving a theme such as being chased, at some point in their lives (most frequently at age 4 to 6). I believe we can understand these dreams as picturing or contextualizing the inevitable vulnerability of a small child in a world run by large, much more powerful creatures—adults. In some very sensitive people (those with thin boundaries), this pattern seems to continue unabated into adulthood.

PHYSICAL ILLNESS

Physical illnesses are obvious sources of emotional concern. Dreams often portray these concerns very vividly, at times even before the waking patient is aware of the illness. The man we discussed previously, awaiting vascular surgery on his leg and afraid of losing the leg, had dream images of defective tools or other defective objects in 11 of 14 recorded preoperative dreams. This man was of course aware of his illness and the planned surgery, though while awake he claimed to have no worries about it.

Vasily Kasatkin in Russia[10] and psychologist-author Patricia Garfield in the United States[11] have collected large numbers of dreams related to physical illness that portray the dreamer's concerns about the illness. The dream images range from very realistic/anatomic to more metaphoric. For instance, Garfield said a dreamer suffering from hemorrhoids reported: "I was impaled by a sharp pole in the anus."

A patient with a severe peptic ulcer dreamt his house was on fire. A patient with acute appendicitis dreamt of being wounded in the stomach in a war. A dreamer who had had a heart attack dreamt of four villains shooting bullets through his heart, causing it to bleed. Another victim of a heart attack dreamt of visiting a spouse's grave and feeling hands squeezing his throat and chest. A patient with a sore throat dreamt of a pink stairwell covered all over with scratches.[12]

Dreams sometimes make one aware of bodily problems and may picture (contextualize) these concerns before the waking mind becomes aware of them. Kasatkin reports several patients' almost identical dreams:

> I dreamt there was a crab or something like a crab clawing at my stomach.

According to Kasatkin, these patients were unaware of any illness at the time of the dream, but they turned out to have cancer of the stomach diagnosed some weeks or months later.

Patricia Garfield describes the dream she herself had 10 days after a painful wrist injury that she had been told was only a sprain. She had a long dream involving secrets and "seeing the whole picture." One part of the dream was:

> I seem to be with a group of people outside a large hotel where a man—one of the two other people who also understand the secret—is explaining about a problem that a man has a break in something. As I watch him make a diagram on a clipboard, I have a revelation: "Don't you realize?! *That's my broken arm!*" I say.[13]

This dream made her almost certain that her painful arm was broken after all. And indeed this was confirmed by further X-rays a few days later.

Neurologist Oliver Sacks described a man who had just had a heavy leg cast put on. The patient dreamt:

> A heavy man had stepped with agonizing effect, on his [the patient's] left foot. Politely at first, then with increasing urgency, he asked the man to move, and when his appeals were unheeded, he tried to shift the man bodily. His efforts were completely useless, and now in his dreams, in his agony, he realized why: the man was made of compact neurons—"neutronium"—and weighed 6 trillion tons, as much as the whole earth. He made one last, frenzied attempt to move the immovable, then

woke up with an intense viselike pain in his foot, which had become ischemic from the pressure of the new cast.

Sacks also described the dreams of some of his neurological patients, for instance, patients with severe migraine:

> Thus the phospenes (sudden sensations of light) of migraine are commonly dreamed of as firework displays, and one patient of mine often "embedded" his nocturnal migraine auras in dreams of a nuclear explosion. He would first see a dazzling fireball with a typical, iridescent, zigzag margin, coruscating as it grew, until it was replaced by a blind area with the dream round its edge. At this point he would usually wake, with a fading scotoma, intense nausea, and an incipient headache.[14]

In all these instances, the dreams picture, or find a context for, the patient's disturbing bodily sensations. And sometimes they appear to pick up or notice a small disturbance that the waking mind has not noticed. The dreaming mind is thus in this respect more sensitive.

Several women have reported to me that they regularly have violent dreams a few days before their menses begin. In these dreams they are being hurt in some way, attacked, or killed. Sometimes they take part in violent acts, too. They are aware of no symptoms or very mild premenstrual symptoms when awake, but perhaps their dreams are picking up a disturbance as the lining of the uterus begins to tear.

INCORPORATION OF EXTERNAL STIMULI INTO DREAMS

The situations we have considered above all involve large emotional concerns or physical disturbances occurring naturally in the course of life. We can also examine external stimuli during sleep—minor but identifiable disturbances that can be considered at least temporary "emotional concerns." Consider a common occurrence—the ringing of an alarm clock. Sometimes this simply awakens the sleeper; sometimes, however, when the alarm sounds during REM sleep and for one reason or another it is not loud enough to waken the sleeper, the sound is incorporated into an ongoing dream. (This incorporation of the sound led Freud to posit that a function of dreaming was to preserve sleep—to allow the sleeper to continue sleeping rather than being awakened by the alarm.[15])

From our present point of view, what is of interest is that the dream immediately finds a context for this mild disturbance. The alarm may be recognized as such within the dream:

> I dreamt that the alarm went off. I turned it off, got up, got dressed and went to work. It didn't look like my regular work, though. After a while I realized there was something wrong and I must be dreaming and then I actually woke up.

Even more often the dreamer will perhaps not recognize the exact nature of the sound but notice some disturbance and find a context for it. Thus, during an ongoing dream:

> Then I hear a doorbell or something ring and I go downstairs and find my old friend Joe at the door. I start a long discussion with him, we walk outside. Finally I wake up and realize my alarm has been ringing for quite a while.

This phenomenon has been studied in the sleep laboratory and we can examine a whole body of literature on incorporation of external stimuli into REM dreams.[16] The stimulus such as water on the skin, sound, or tightening of a blood-pressure cuff on the leg produces a small emotional concern in the mind nets of the sleeper. The "storm" or emotional concern is a minor one compared to the ones we have considered previously, but its known source makes it more traceable. When incorporation of the stimulus occurs (rates vary from 9% to 75%), the dream does not accurately report the stimulus ("I dreamt that there was a blood-pressure cuff on my leg"), but contextualizes the emotional concern. For instance: "The dream protagonist found his leg to be paralyzed and unmovable despite his strongest attempts."[17] Or, in an early study, several of the sleepers who had water squirted onto their skin pictured this mild concern by dreaming of sudden rainfalls and leaking roofs.[18] I consider these stimuli, like the physical pains and illnesses, as producing an emotional disturbance (even if a minor one) that is then pictured (contextualized) in the dream. This view is more consistent with our other data, and more fruitful than positing that one object (a cuff) is translated into another (a rope or weight). This is discussed further in Chapters 6 and 9.

"Ordinary Dreams"

In the many situations reviewed above, we have fairly easily been able to discern a dominant emotion or an emotional concern from the content of the dream without a great deal of background information and without obtaining free associations to the dream, but this is not always possible. Using our image of a storm at sea, we have looked first at regions where there are huge storms and perturbations on the surface and then gone on to consider less tempestuous seas, but where there is still at least one clear concern ("storm"). Often, however, the sea may already be fairly calm, without a great deal of storm activity, or there may be a number of very minor storms in a number of different places. In such situations the processes we have discussed can be difficult to discern.

Thus ordinary or "everyday" dreams may actually be the most difficult to understand even though they have been the starting point of so many studies. As mentioned in Chapter 2, there is laboratory research attempting to relate dream content to students' concerns, usually with inconclusive results. The concerns are usually minor concerns dealing with plans for the weekend, dating, or an exam. In other words, they are not powerful enough to produce a simple, dominant emotional image in the dreams.

Thus if we now move on to more ordinary or everyday dreams— collected in one of many studies, or if we pick our own most ordinary dreams—we may find the dream confused with no single dominant image of the kind we have discussed. There is no one dominant emotion or single strong emotional concern; rather, it is an ordinary day, there are many small concerns, and no one of them completely takes over the production of the dream. Or there may be important emotional concerns such as "How can I escape the influence of my powerful mother?," but these are not obvious without detailed knowledge of the dreamer.

In a human being with an intact central nervous system, I believe it is impossible for there to be no emotional concerns whatever. More likely, there may often be a number of active concerns, with no one of them so dominant as to single-handedly guide the formation of the striking dream images we saw after trauma. Here what is produced is an "everyday dream." No single, obvious emotional concern stands out, although some underlying concerns, wishes, and worries always exist. This is where various techniques of "dream interpretation" are useful. As Freud suggests, one can associate to each element of the dream or, as per Jung, one can amplify certain images, or one can use any number of interpretive techniques, all of which will usually lead to the emotional concerns of the dreamer.

In other words, I believe that it can indeed be very useful to obtain associations to each element of the dream, as Freud recommends, but I see this as simply one approach to determine the principal emotional concern or concerns of the dreamer. In many situations, as we have seen, the emotional concern is fairly obvious and no detailed interpretation is needed.

For our present discussion, in which we are trying to understand the basic nature of dreaming, this is as far as we need to go. We have discovered one or more emotional concerns that are pictured or given a context by the dream. Of course if the dreamer is a patient in therapy or if we are dealing with our own dreams and want to learn more about ourselves, we can do much more: We can continue the associative or other interpretive process to help discover why a particular dream element appeared at the time, how one emotional concern may relate to another, and so on.

When there are several competing concerns, we tend to dream of the most important one. For instance, in one sleep laboratory study, Trenholme et al.[19] compared women going through a difficult divorce with a control group of women of the same age whose lives were fairly stable. The researchers found that the women going through divorce had more dreams involving threat and anxiety, portrayed in any number of different ways, but that they dreamt relatively little about the laboratory situation. The women in the control group, on the other hand, had many dreams about the laboratory study—

hospitals, wires, technicians, research, etc. The two groups were experiencing the same laboratory conditions, but clearly for the control women this was a relatively major concern, perhaps the most important thing they were involved in at the time. For the divorcing women the same laboratory situation was probably a small, unimportant annoyance, a relatively minor concern.

When there are several different concerns that might be considered approximately equal (the death of two parents, for instance), the dreams tend to deal especially with the unresolved concerns. Albert, a middle-aged man, had a stressful and rather tortured relationship with his father ever since childhood. The father was brilliant in his own right but dogmatic and a bit eccentric. He never seemed to accept or appreciate what his very intelligent son did at school, brought home, worked on, etc. Albert continued to feel criticized by and not understood by his father right up to the time of the father's death. He had a number of striking dreams after his father died in which the father came back but was half dead, a kind of ghost or ghoulish creature, which made Albert very uncomfortable. As it happened, Albert's mother also died a few years later. Albert had a much more peaceful relationship with his mother. In the months after her death he had one striking dream in which he saw her as if alive but glowing and apparently very happy, and his feeling was that he knew that she was all right. The greater frequency of dreams about his father, as well as the dream content, obviously reflects Albert's continuing concerns and conflicts about his father, contrasting with much less conflict and relative acceptance concerning his mother.

In summary, I believe we can see dreams after trauma as a paradigm: The same processes occur in all dreams, though they are less clearly discernible. Dreams make cross connections to calm the storm—to distribute excitation or smooth out the net (Chapter 5)—guided, in the simplest cases, by a powerful emotion or more commonly an emotional concern. In the clearest cases, after trauma, the dreams need little interpretation to discover the emotional concern. As we move to less dramatic situations, with smaller disturbances in the net and multiple emotional concerns, it is harder to see what is going on, and some form of interpretation is helpful.

Dreams Are Not "Crazy"; the Broad Concerns, at Least, Are Clear

There is a widespread view that dreams are "crazy" or "psychotic" or make very little sense.[20] Oddly, this view is shared by those who feel dreams are some form of random, meaningless process, and by those, like Freud, who feel there is an underlying meaning (latent dream thoughts) that have become distorted, disguised, and censored, so that on the surface the dream ("manifest dream") appears to be a "meaningless mental product."

Obviously, I do not agree with this viewpoint. The many dreams we have considered in the previous chapters do not appear crazy. A person who has just escaped from a fire and is terrified about the fire dreams about variations on the fire; surely this is not crazy. And if that same person dreams about being overwhelmed by a tidal wave or an onrushing train, we can hardly call this crazy, random, or meaningless. At least it makes perfect sense if we consider dreams as contextualizing emotion. Likewise, in the other dreams we have considered when there is one clear-cut emotion, viewing the dream in this light makes it quite meaningful, or at least makes good sense of the basic theme or dominant imagery of the dream. In this overall sense the dream is often quite clearly and obviously related to one or more emotional concerns, even if these do not account for all the details of the dream. The major image and major theme often make a lot of sense, though the details may seem confused.

I think this approach is useful even in everyday dreams, ones not resulting from trauma or stress. For instance, let us take a well-known example, Freud's dream of Irma's injection, which is perhaps the best-studied dream in the modern world.[21] Freud provides the reader with a lengthy "preamble" about his medical colleagues and about his patient Irma—treatment has been "partly successful." On the day of the dream Freud's friend and colleague Otto told Freud that Irma was "better but not quite well." The dream:

> A large hall—numerous guests, whom we were receiving.
> Among them was Irma. I at once took her on one side, as though
> to answer her letter and to reproach her for not having accepted

my "solution" yet. I said to her: "If you still get pains, it's really only your fault." She replied: "If you only knew what pains I've got now in my throat and stomach and abdomen—it's choking me"—I was alarmed and looked at her. She looked pale and puffy. I thought to myself that after all I must be missing some organic trouble. I took her to the window and looked down her throat, and she showed signs of recalcitrance, like women with artificial dentures. I thought to myself that there was really no need for her to do that. She then opened her mouth properly and on the right I found a big white patch; at another place I saw extensive whitish grey scabs upon some remarkable curly structures which were evidently modeled on the turbinal bones of the nose. I at once called in Dr. M., and he repeated the examination and confirmed it. . . . Dr. M. looked quite different from usual; he was very pale, he walked with a limp and his chin was clean-shaven. . . . My friend Otto was now standing beside her as well, and my friend Leopold was percussing her through her bodice and saying: "She has a dull area low down on the left." He also indicated that a portion of the skin on the left shoulder was infiltrated. (I noticed this, just as he did, in spite of her dress.) . . . M. said: "There's no doubt it's an infection, but no matter; dysentery will supervene and the toxin will be eliminated." . . . We were directly aware, too, of the origin of her infection. Not long before, when she was feeling unwell, my friend Otto had given her an injection of a preparation of propyl, propyls . . . propionic acid . . . trimethylamine (and I saw before me the formula for this printed in heavy type). . . . Injections of that sort ought not to be made so thoughtlessly. . . . And probably the syringe had not been clean.

Having presented this dream, Freud insists it is completely meaningless: "No one who had only read the preamble and the content of the dream itself could have the slightest notion of what the dream meant." I do not agree with this statement, at least concerning the broad meaning of the dream. Applying what we have learned about dreams contextualizing emotions or emotional concerns, we can quite easily guess, without associations or detailed interpretation, that this dream expresses Freud's concerns about his professional life. Obviously he is concerned as to whether he is truly helping his patients, and he is especially concerned about his reputation and his status among his peers.

Freud, after presenting the dream, supplies 15 pages of free associations, starting from each element of the dream, and those associations do indeed explain quite convincingly most of the specific details he has dreamt about. His overall conclusion after the entire dream analysis is that the dream expresses the wish that, if his patient is not cured, it is not Freud's fault but someone else's, and so his reputation can remain intact. I would say this wish fits very well with our easily discerned, broad, emotional concern. I am not saying that the additional associations are useless: They shed light on the dream and the dreamer in many ways. And I would agree that the dream story is a bit odd (by waking standards). But it is only the details and their juxtapositions that sound crazy relative to our focused, waking thought and require analysis to understand. The main concerns are fairly clear.

I do agree with Freud that the dream is completely determined and that every element and detail of the dream comes from one or more places in the dreamer's head; in fact, Freud has provided a brilliant instruction manual as to how to arrive at these origins by means of free association.

What I am discovering is that the simplest cases—the person overwhelmed by a tidal wave and similar dreams—do not require interpretation of this kind at all. The emotional concern is obvious, however, if the dream gives other details, for instance, "My friend Judy, looking like my aunt as well, and I were walking along the beach when a tidal wave came and engulfed us," one can certainly use free association to try and determine why Judy rather than another friend appeared in the dream.

I have emphasized, perhaps overemphasized, the dramatic aspects or portions of a dream—the handling of traumatic or new material—in the past two chapters. Another important part of the nature of dreaming is the background, the continuity, the tendency for the dream to follow a plot or a script. We can see this both following the introduction of some new, emotional material (the tidal wave) and when there is no such obvious material. In fact, in studying this sort of background scripting it becomes clear that dreams generally deal with visual-spatial imagery and follow a more or less predictable script, so that elements of the dream can to a certain degree be predicted from previous elements.[22] A perusal of this research, however, reveals that the basic mental dream-processing system—picturing, scripting, etc.—is not very different from what occurs in waking, and we can most parsimoniously suppose that the same kind of processing system is involved in both. I will not discuss this aspect in detail since it appears to involve a system active in producing dreams, daydreams, and background waking as well, and is not specific to dreaming. I have instead emphasized what is special about dreaming—the increased connection making in dreams guided by the dominant emotional concern of the dreamer.[23]

Clearly, in some dreams the emotion or emotional concern stands out as extremely prominent, whereas in other dreams the connection making will be most prominent, with very little obvious emotional concern. At one extreme we have the tidal wave dream after trauma, and at the other end we have the ordinary or everyday dream when the emotional concerns may be smaller or more distant or less known to us. In these latter cases the broad connection making of dreams may be all that is noticeable and the dream may sometimes appear to be simply a hodgepodge of flotsam and jetsam thrown together from various places in our minds.

Chapter Four

THE ROLE OF EMOTION IN PRODUCING DREAMS

DREAMS ARE GUIDED BY THE DOMINANT EMOTION OR CONCERN

The series of dreams we have examined after trauma and in many other conditions suggest that the dominant emotion or emotional concerns of the dreamer are what is most important in guiding or determining the images in the dream. As we have noted, the dreams of a young person who has just escaped from a fire, for instance, seem to show associations along the line of fire, producing tremendous terror or fear, leading to images of that fear such as tidal waves or chases by gangs of Nazis. Sometimes the fear then leads to images of previous terrifying experiences, or imagined experiences—dealing with accidents, death, illness, or other such events. Then the process continues to incorporate themes of guilt; questions arise such as "Why am I alive and why is he dead?" or "I deserve to die, too." The dreams picture other times involving the dreamer and his brother (for instance), dealing with who got hurt, who got punished, etc. The dreaming process is guided by the emotions of the dreamer rather than simply by the sensory input or the dreamer's waking thoughts.

It is important to point out that this sort of associative chain based on emotion (which I have found repeatedly in these dream series) is not at all obvious—it is by no means the only way our associations can develop. The human mind has numerous ways of creating associations or associative chains. For instance, starting from

61

fire (the house burning down), one could associate fires of different kinds—forest fires, fires in a fireplace, fires in a wood stove, roasting marshmallows over a campfire, etc. However, I have never seen this sort of sequence in the dream series I have collected. We can also associate to the sensory aspects of a fire—the color, for instance. Fire—red, orange, yellow; warm, yellow beaches; yellow or red sports cars; brightly colored clothing; clowns; etc. Again, I have not seen such chains of associations in dreams. We are capable of engaging in associations to sound ("clang associations")—fire, tire, wire, mire, etc. We can produce scientific conceptual associations—fire, burn, oxidize, add oxygen to a compound, recombine chemically. We can consider the various related meanings of the word "fire"—"fire off a memo," "fired from a job," "on fire with desire," etc. And we can form various poetic or spiritual associations to fire—cleansing fires, purifying fires, hellfire, the Phoenix rising from its ashes, etc. Our minds can and do employ all these possible and permissible chains of association, but strikingly, such chains do not appear at all in the series of posttraumatic dreams I have examined. I have not seen a single dream series after a fire, a rape, or an attack that developed along one of these associative lines. Instead, what occurs repeatedly is the development of images along the lines of the *emotion* or *emotional concern* of the dreamer; thus, images appear first related to terror, then to fear, vulnerability, guilt, etc. In these situations, the dream images, insofar as they associate at all to the disturbing material, deal with the emotional aspects of the disturbance. They *contextualize the emotional concern.*

Of course, an emotional concern does not have to involve the terror resulting from a trauma. We started our discussion with this example because I believe it is the simplest case in which we can most readily see what is happening. Many different emotional concerns can be pictured in dreams, as we saw in the last chapter. We noted that an emotional concern can be anything that is disturbing the system. An emotional concern is a kind of perturbation in the nets of the mind (see next chapter), which is then gradually alleviated, reduced, and woven in. In this sense, an emotional concern can involve something as simple as "What is that annoying, buzzing noise by the bed?" to physiological states such as hunger or sexual desire, to more emotional, interpersonal problems, for example, being dumped by a girlfriend or discovering your husband is having an affair. Concerns can also include important life problems such as, "How can I keep my children from being eaten by tigers or falling off trees?" to "How can I get this invention of mine to work effectively?" to broad spiritual problems—"Who am I?," "What am I doing here?" (see later). Any of these problems, assuming they are not simply intellectual ideas being played with but are truly emotional concerns, can guide the images that appear in dreams.

Even the emotional concerns "in the air," that is, the emotional concerns of an entire society or nation, make their way into dreams. The author Charlotte Beradt has published a whole collection of dreams from people living in the Third Reich that capture the emotional state or concern of the populace.[1] A 60-year-old factory owner, whose factory was functioning normally under Hitler, but who felt definite discomfort living under a totalitarian regime, reports a typical dream:

> Goebbels was visiting my factory. He had all the workers line up in two rows facing each other. I had to stand in the middle and raise my arm in the Nazi salute. It took me half an hour to get my arm up, inch by inch. Goebbels showed neither approval nor disapproval as he watched my struggle, as if it were a play. When I finally managed to get my arm up, he said just five words—"I don't want your salute"—then turned and went to the door. There I stood in my own factory, arm raised, pilloried right in the midst of my own people. I was only able to keep from collapsing by staring at his clubfoot as he limped out. And so I stood until I woke up.

Beradt's book is a compilation of dreams of this kind; unfortunately, she tells us little about the identity or situation of most of her dreamers, nor does she elaborate on her methodology in choosing the dreams. We do not know whether most of the dreams cited were dreamt by Jews or others in acute danger, by Nazis, or by "ordinary Germans," though Beradt's introduction suggests that she was collecting dreams from a wide range of people, including a lot of ordinary Germans. It is hard to draw any firm conclusions, yet remarkably, the overwhelming majority of the dreams portray a helplessness, vulnerability, and discomfort in the dreamer. The emotional tone of the society seems to have powerfully influenced its citizens' dreams.

NIGHTMARES IN CHILDREN AND ADULTS

It may be worth pausing at this point to consider an entire category of dreams characterized by powerful emotion—a very important category, known as nightmares—to see whether our formulations help us make sense of them. I am not discussing night terrors—frightening, early-night events producing arousal—but rather the long, frightening dreams leading to an awakening that generally turn out to come from long REM periods late in the night.[2] Many of the dreams we have considered after trauma are obviously nightmares. They often end with a feeling of fear and awaken the dreamer. Indeed, fear and anxiety appear to be the overall most common emotions reported in dreams.[3]

Let me try to apply the notion of dream images contextualizing emotion in a thought experiment. Suppose that in my waking life I find myself in a strange situation that I do not completely understand. I am relatively small and helpless, just learning my way around, and find myself surrounded by much larger and much more powerful creatures. These large creatures appear to be benign and even friendly toward me much of the time, but I cannot be absolutely sure. Sometimes the large creatures change and become angry, scream, push me around, hurt me; perhaps they hurt me without meaning to, but how can I be sure? Sometimes they do seem to want to hurt me. Sometimes the large creatures force me to follow rules or do things that make no sense to me. Sometimes they yell and scream and fight with each other, and I am worried about being caught up in these struggles I do not understand. And furthermore, I am completely dependent on these large creatures for food, comfort, love. Suppose they abandon me, stop caring for me? Or suppose they realize how angry I am sometimes at them, or at my baby brother? Suppose they punish me in some terrible way?

What sort of dreams, what sort of contextualizing images might I have under such circumstances? I think we would have to predict that at least some of my dreams would attempt to contextualize this vulnerability, uncertainty, and fear. There would surely be some dreams of being in danger, or of being chased and perhaps hurt by some large creature or monster ("monster" implies exactly that—a large, powerful, dangerous creature). There might also be dreams portraying the more specific fears of abandonment and punishment.

I am of course describing, roughly speaking, the world of a small child. Some children live in a family world that is very frightening even by our adult standards. Yet I would say that every two- to five-year-old child who is just developing the cognitive structures to realize who is who, who's safe and who's unsafe or unpredictable, and to realize how relatively powerful all the adults are, is bound to have some of this sense of vulnerability. Indeed, nightmares of being chased or attacked by monsters or strange animals are extremely common among the dreams of three-, four-, and five-year-olds. Estimates of nightmare frequency vary and depend a great deal on how the information is obtained. Sixty percent to 80% of adults report having had nightmares in childhood.[4] Studies of children vary in their estimates of frequency but agree that nightmares are especially frequent at the ages of three to six.[5] My own impression based on clinical and research work is that nightmares of some kind are pretty much ubiquitous in children of that age, though some children admit to them more readily and are more willing and able to talk about them than others. In my clinical experience and that of others, the most common themes are being chased or hurt.

Sometimes the nightmares seem to portray (contextualize) a general fearfulness and vulnerability, but often if one knows the child one can also pick out more specific fears. For instance, Harry was three and a half years old when his youngest brother was born.[6] Just before his brother's birth he became aggressive, began hitting his brothers and sisters, and became angry at his mother and her large stomach and told her he was going to open up her stomach and cut up her new baby. About a month after the baby's birth, Harry began to have nightmares from which he awoke in terror. He dreamt that someone was coming to hurt him, that monsters were after him, that a large woman was coming to kill him. Here the nightmares clearly seem to be portraying a very specific fear of punishment for his aggressive wishes.

In any case, here is a whole large class of dreams that to some extent are predictable based on an expectable realistic sense of vulnerability in young children. As the child grows up, the situation changes, and nightmares, especially nightmares of being chased by monsters, etc., usually become less prominent. However, there is great individual variation in what happens during nightmares, based on both external and internal factors.

Some children live in truly dangerous worlds that do not become less dangerous as they grow up. They are surrounded by trauma and stressful situations that produce contextualizing dreams along the lines we have indicated and that also connect to and rekindle the old feelings of vulnerability from childhood. Some children are luckier in that their external life indeed becomes smoother, more predictable, and less traumatic. But internal factors are tremendously important as well. The entire life of a child in the latency years (the grade-school years) can be thought of as learning one's way around the world, learning the rules, learning to be less vulnerable. Some children do this especially rapidly and solidly. These children become the adults I have spoken of as having "thick boundaries".[7] They are tough, or at least well-protected, and they have learned to handle or ward off or keep away danger. As adults they tend to have few or no nightmares. Sometimes the process goes further and these people may become somewhat rigid and hardened. They not only have no nightmares but most of them recall few of their dreams.

At the opposite extreme, some children as they develop maintain much of their childhood openness and vulnerability. These people, who have "thin boundaries" (we'll return to boundaries later), remain more sensitive and more flexible—often more open, more creative, and also more vulnerable as adults. They tend to remember a lot of dreams and may continue to have nightmares. In fact, I have studied a large group of persons who describe themselves as having frequent nightmares occurring for many years, usually for as long as they can remember.[8] Although a few of these people had traumatic childhoods, most of them turned out to take ordinary traumas of life—such as the birth of a sibling or loss of a pet—extremely seriously. Somehow they developed very thin boundaries so that they were sensitive in many ways. Everything "got through" to them. Their adult world too, though not grossly traumatic, constantly produced hurt and injury, and they appeared to have nightmares whenever something in their current lives was very painful and reminded them of their extreme childhood vulnerability, which was still present to some extent.

In any case, I am suggesting that some feeling of vulnerability is inevitable in childhood. We all tend to contextualize this vulnerability in dreams and thus to have nightmares, though there are great individual differences in the intensity of these nightmares and the extent to which they continue into adulthood.

EMOTION INSIDE AND OUTSIDE DREAMS

Our focus here has been on the dominant emotion of the dreamer and how this affects the dream. There are other ways of looking at emotions in dreams which are of less immediate concern to us. First, one can study emotion *in dreams*—in other words, emotions recorded by the dreamer. There are in fact a number of studies of emotions in dreams. The incidence—the percentage of dreams in which emotions are actually mentioned—varies a great deal depending on whether the instructions or the interviewer asks about emotions. For instance, in laboratory-collected dreams when there is no specific concern about emotions, they are mentioned in dreams only about 25% of the time or less.[9] However, the incidence rises to almost 75% if the dreamer is asked in detail about emotions.[10]

The dreams after trauma, in stressful situations, etc., discussed earlier, sometimes mentioned emotions but frequently did not. Our judges scoring "contextualized images" in dreams make their decision and choose the emotion they believe is contextualized without regard to whether the dreamer mentions any emotion in the dream report. Thus, our dream of "I was overwhelmed by a tidal wave" is rated as contextualizing fear and terror whether or not the dreamer goes on to say, "I woke up terrified." Nonetheless, when an emotion *is mentioned* in the dream, it might be important to know whether it is the same as or similar to the presumed underlying (contextualized) emotion; certainly it would be troubling if the emotions were completely different. Therefore I asked two judges who had already scored a number of dreams for contextualizing images, to go back and check whether or not an emotion was mentioned in a dream and if so whether it was the same as (or very similar to) the underlying contextualized emotion. Of a total of 748 dreams scored in this way, there were 212 that actually mentioned an emotion and had been scored as containing a "contextualizing image." Of these 212, there were 140 in which the mentioned emotion was rated as the same as or very similar to the emotion previously rated as contextualized, while only 72 mentioned a "different" emotion (out of 18 possible emotions). Thus there was some consistency: When emotion was mentioned in dreams it was most often identical or very similar to what had been judged as the dreamer's underlying emotion.[11]

There is still another way to consider emotion in dreams: Does the dream produce an emotion after you wake up? Does the dream have an emotional effect on the dreamer? This is a separate issue but a very fascinating one, which we will discuss later. We will see that some dreams have very profound effects on the dreamer, quite similar to the effects of a work of art.

What is emotion, anyway? On one level we all know perfectly well, but at the same time it has been very hard for cognitive scientists, neuroscientists, and neurologists to fit emotions into their schemes of the brain and mind. In Chapter 5 I will discuss emotion in terms of the nets of the mind. For now, I would say that emotion is the force that guides or drives our minds; it is the guiding force that gets us moving and moves us in a particular direction. Based on our genetic makeup and on our past experiences, our emotions tell us rapidly and powerfully whether something is "good" or "bad" or something to be approached, explored, or avoided. Emotions are needed to lend value to our thoughts and enable us to make decisions.

Of course this is true all the time, in waking as well as in dreaming. The way we experience the world is constantly influenced by our emotions. There seems to be no absolutely objective viewpoint; no two people see the world in exactly the same way, nor does one person under certain emotional conditions see the world in exactly the same way as he does under other emotional conditions. The same bushes along the same bicycle path I have passed many times look different to me depending how I am feeling inside. The literary device known as "pathetic fallacy," in which a storm rises up in the landscape when a character is experiencing stormy feelings, is not really a fallacy. We could consider it another instance of "contextualizing emotion," played out—and perhaps exaggerated—in the dreamlike creative space of the author. But in fact our emotions always color the world for us; a depression actually colors the world gray, while someone in a powerfully happy mood can see "la vie en rose."

Here is a large-scale, real-life example. A well-known mountain range in Wyoming is called the Grand Tetons. Historians tell us that it was named by French trappers who had come upon these mountains in their westward treks over the plains. "Grand Tetons" comes directly from the French: "les grands tétons," which means "the big breasts." To most of us coming upon those mountains the resemblance is far from striking. However, for the French trappers, who were of course all males and had been traveling through the woods for weeks or months without having seen a woman, the image was probably much more compelling. Their emotional concerns influenced and formed the image of the mountains before them!

I am using emotion and emotional concern in a very broad sense here, including simple feelings such as hunger, thirst, and bodily needs, as well as deeper or higher-level concerns. Some "hardheaded" types consider emotion to be a sideline, something that should not interfere with one's thinking—it can only "throw you off." But this is actually far from the case. Emotion of some kind as a guiding principle is totally necessary to us. When emotion, including emotional interest, is absent, we are in a terrible state, sometimes called "volitional apathy." There are many medical forms of this and none of them is pleasant. For instance, in Alzheimer's dementia there may be a loss of interest in everything. A patient with Parkinson's disease not only has tremors, but experiences a difficulty in "getting going," in the sense of initiating motor activity, and also a general apathy, a difficulty in getting going emotionally. In someone who is seriously depressed, there is not a total lack of emotion, but an all-pervasive darkness and sadness that prevents other emotions from coming up. In all these situations, the patient is severely limited, and sometimes may seem to be a human body with barely a spark of human spirit inside.

In other cases, simple emotion is present, but there is something wrong with the linkup of emotion to the cognitive nets of the mind. This is true, for instance, in patients with subtle damage to the frontal lobes of the brain. These people are not depressed or apathetic; they are able to experience emotion such as joy or anger, they look and act normal in most ways; in fact, they perform adequately on just about all standard psychological tests. However, there is something wrong with their judgment. They do not have the emotional conviction to make a decision; they spend hours deciding whether to eat at one restaurant or another, or trying to decide which of the many tasks on their desks they should do first, so nothing gets done. They have lost their sense of priority or guidance, which we can see as emotional guidance of thought. Despite their normal appearance, they are unable to guide their lives meaningfully, and their lives fall apart.[12]

In all these senses, emotion is of obvious importance. It is in fact our major guiding force at all times, though we do not always appreciate it. As we have seen, it can even influence our view of a mountain range. However, in focused waking activity, we are often caught up in our small day-to-day tasks, caught up in our over-learned activities—reading, writing, figuring things out. This is when emotional forces have the least effect on our thinking. When we are more relaxed, involved in reverie or daydreaming, emotion plays a greater role, and its role is probably greatest when we are actually dreaming. We will discuss this continuum from focused waking to dreaming in the next chapter. But again, there may be a complex mix of emotions making the effects difficult to discern. And there is a quantitative side: An emotion has to build up to a certain level in order to make itself felt.[13]

UNRESOLVED EMOTIONAL CONCERNS

Even if we accept the general principle that dreams deal with the emotional concerns of the dreamer, this by no means allows us to predict exactly what dream content will appear: There's obviously a great deal involved in forming each dream that we do not fully understand. However, the principles we have discussed make it possible at least to begin to predict dream content in certain instances. For example, based on my experience, I would predict that someone who has just been through a severe trauma will almost certainly have a dream of a tidal wave, whirlwind, onrushing train, or something of that kind in the following days or weeks. Likewise, if a four-year-old child—the age when nightmares are frequent in any case—has been somewhat more frightened than usual, I believe we could predict with fair confidence the child will have a dream of being chased by monsters or frightening animals at some time during that period.

However, when there has been no recent severe trauma or stress, we are faced with a dreamer who presumably has a number of emotional concerns or problems to be solved and a tremendous number of possible ways to picture these concerns. Here we cannot go very far in predicting a specific dream. It is tempting to give up and simply speak of random activation of material in memory, but I do not believe we need to give up quite so readily. Although we cannot predict exactly what will occur in a dream, there are certain principles that become evident as we examine large numbers of dreams. Among emotional concerns, I believe the evidence suggests that we dream about those that have not been adequately dealt with during waking; if we speak in terms of problem solving, we dream about problems that have not been adequately solved—solved in a total or emotional sense. In other words, it is the *unresolved* emotional concerns that affect our dreams.[14] Thus, a nagging problem that has been pushed out of waking consciousness or not thought about a great deal is most likely to appear in a dream.

For instance, as I mentioned in Chapter 3, I know three different women who for some time had violent dreams in which they were committing murders or some other violent crime. Since their lives were not in the least violent, such dreams most likely indicated guilt on their part. It turned out that all three of these women had abortions a number of years previously. In waking life they had dealt with the abortions in different ways: One of the women said she had simply pushed it out of her mind and never thought about it. The two others did not speak of it that way. They did think about the abortion sometimes, but decided it had definitely been right for them, and what use was it to worry about it. In two of the three cases the dreams stopped entirely after the women made the connection with the abortion and dealt with it in some way. One of these women said that the simple realization that the dreams were related to guilt about the abortion was enough stop the dreams. The second woman had to do more waking work in accepting that she indeed had a great deal more feeling about her abortion than she had previously admitted. The feelings included guilt and other negative feelings about herself that she had not readily wanted to admit; her waking work on the feelings involved accepting that she was not as "perfect" as she had tried to be, that her emotional life was not completely in control, and so on. In coping with these issues she shifted her views of herself, and the dreams finally stopped. The third woman, who is not a patient of mine, tells me that her nightmares are still present but are changing somewhat, and she feels they may be related to other guilts dating back to before the abortion.

Thus, when an emotional concern is appropriately worked on and understood, it no longer acts as a major force in the production of dreams. As we have discussed, many children—perhaps all children at some point—have nightmares in which they are chased by monsters or strange animals. These nightmares presumably picture or contextualize their fearful emotions, their not being quite in control of their world, which is their major unresolved concern at the time. Many parents have found that discussing fearful material with their children, helping them face the dream images, discussing the monsters, relating them to various daytime fears, will reduce the anxiety and the nightmares.[15]

This relates to Jung's notion of "compensation" in dreams.[16] By this term Jung implies that portions of the personality that are repressed or not significantly expressed in waking, are the ones that appear in dreams. There has been a great deal of discussion and argument as to whether the relationship of dreams to waking life is basically one of "continuity" or "complementarity." In many ways, what I have discussed about dreams after trauma or stress can be considered a kind of "continuity." The dominant emotion or emotional concern of the person continues into sleep and influences the dreams. However, what we have just discussed suggests that compensation may also play a role. Among the emotional concerns active in the mind, it is those that are not adequately dealt with, which are perhaps pushed away or repressed in waking, that are more likely to make their appearance in dreams. In some cases—for instance, my friend's "punch dreams" discussed in note 13—the dreams, though making connections of their own, appear to be nudging waking consciousness into taking a role in dealing with the problem.

POSITIVE EMOTIONS

It has not escaped my attention that throughout the last chapters we seem to be dealing mainly with what we can call negative emotions or emotional disturbance. I have nothing against positive emotions (in fact, I love experiencing them myself), but somehow they have not appeared a great deal in the material I have examined. To some extent this is because we are purposely starting with dreams after trauma, and at times of stress, which are perhaps bound to have a negative tone. But it has also been reported by several authors that in general dreams have more of a negative than a positive tone.[17] Indeed, since we are talking of portraying concerns or disturbances, perhaps it is inevitable that negatively toned emotions should predominate.

I have made an effort over several years to obtain series of dreams from people who have experienced a happy event rather than a trauma—for instance, a wedding or an unexpected reunion with a loved person after many years. I have even tried to get dreams from lottery winners, but have not been successful so far. I do not have many long series as yet, but so far my finding has been that even when people experience a happy event, they are more likely to dream about problems associated with it than the pure happiness of the event itself. A woman who gave me a series of dreams in the period surrounding a happy wedding found herself dreaming several variations of this dream:

> It was a wedding scene, but I was in terrible shape. I had rags on instead of a wedding dress. I was totally embarrassed. I was preparing for the wedding, but I couldn't find anything. I kept going through different rooms, corridors, and I kept not finding anything I needed. I felt totally unprepared for the wedding. It was like my old dreams of exams at school.

Two other women's dreams about a wedding were very similar. If this pattern holds up, perhaps it should not disturb us too much, as we are speaking of dreams portraying unresolved emotional concerns, and perhaps simple happiness is unlikely to constitute an emotional concern. Nonetheless, there is no question that happiness and positive emotions find their way into dreams. I do not know whether they qualify as emotional concerns, but maybe a truly powerful emotion of any kind does have an influence on the nets of the mind. A woman's dream report goes:

> I was out camping somewhere. I saw some kind of flashes. I saw these absolutely beautiful shooting stars everywhere. It was like a fireworks display, only better. I just watched. It was an ecstatic experience.

Or a dream of my own:

> I was showing people this beautiful golden sculpture. I can see it very clearly outdoors in bright sunlight. I had either made or discovered this marvelous glowing abstract sculpture, formed of thick, golden tubes. It was about eight feet high and I was pointing it out to people. Everyone seemed to love it.

In this chapter we have examined the ways in which the dominant emotion of the dreamer guides the dream imagery and to a great extent forms the dream. We have seen this especially prominently in nightmares. We have discussed how emotion guides or influences our cognition all the time, but perhaps least when we are engaged in detailed, focused waking tasks, and most when we are dreaming.

And we have noted that among our emotional concerns it is often our active, unresolved concerns that make their way into our dreams. In the next chapters we will examine how our view of dreaming can make sense in terms of the networks that make up our minds, and how the emotion-guided making of broad connections leads to metaphor.

Chapter Five

THE NETS OF THE MIND

We have discussed in the preceding chapters how dreams make connections—especially connections between traumatic or other new material and older material—guided by the emotion of the dreamer. But what does "making connections" really mean? This will depend on how we picture and understand our minds, especially the functioning of our cerebral cortex, which, with some help from the rest of the brain, constitutes everything we call mind.

At present I believe we need to think of a complex net made up of simple units. There is always a danger in picturing the mind according to our latest technological advances, a practice that has led to many images such as the "hydraulic" or "steam engine" model of the mind, which was soon succeeded by a calculating machine or simple computer model and now by a network model, which may perhaps prove as ephemeral as the rest. Nonetheless, since we inevitably think in terms of visual models, I believe we require some such image to hang our thoughts on. At this particular point, I believe the best model involves a net or perhaps a network of nets. In fact, models employing net images have proliferated lately. Such model nets are sometimes called "neural nets" in the hope that they will correspond with the actual structure of the cerebral cortex. More often they are now referred to as "connectionist nets" described by computer models, assuming a large number of simple "on-off" units with variable connection strengths between them. Information consists of the strengths of those widely distributed connections (parallel distributed processing).[1]

There is certainly some relationship between these connectionist nets and brain structure. In fact, the cerebral cortex—the physical structure of most of what we call the mind—consists of a complex neural net composed of close to 10^{11} (100 billion) neurons, with as many as 10^{14} synapses, or connections between the neurons. The net concept depends not only on the physical and microscopic appearance of the cortex but also on a number of lines of evidence, for instance, the increasing certainty that memories are widely distributed, that there is no one "place" for a given memory.

Although the models are imperfect, it is already clear that these connectionist or "parallel distributed processing" models approximate much more closely the way our minds actually function than do models based on the familiar computer, which relies on rapid serial processing. However, this is not saying much. There is no way that our minds are computers in the usual sense of a serial computer such as a PC. It is evident that our desk-top computer is incredibly better and faster than we are at certain tasks, such as calculation, rapid checking for errors, rapid word searching, precise graphic displays; but much worse than we are at such things as "guessing creatively," finding a particular memory—someone's name or face—using very incomplete information, understanding language even if full of mistakes, or dreaming up a work of art.

Even very simple connectionist net models with only a few tens or hundreds of interconnected units have shown success in modeling certain aspects of how humans learn simple tasks. For instance, such a net can model quite well the way we learn to form past tenses of regular and irregular English verbs,[2] or performance on the Stroop color-naming test.[3] In fact, several researchers have attempted to apply certain aspects of connectionist net modeling to the process of dreaming.[4]

I have suggested "connecting" and "cross-connecting" as basic aspects of dreaming,[5] but without specifying any particular mechanism in the nets of the mind. In what follows I envision nets that derive from, but need to be more complex than, the connectionist nets specified so far. But I hope to maintain the elegance and simplicity of the assumptions of the model: The entire net is constructed of simple units and the connections between units. The term "unit" is used to suggest that for modeling purposes we need not worry about any internal structure. A unit is simply a mechanism, a thing with a number of inputs and outputs. Its sole function is to add up incoming excitation; when this reaches a certain level, it produces an output. A great deal can be done by simply modeling groups, or small networks of such units, on a computer. And of course it is hoped that the cerebral cortex, made up of large numbers of individual, small neurons, will turn out to act somewhat like these connectionist nets made up of individual units. All that occurs is a flow of excitation in the nets determined by connection strengths between units; the use of the net determines and changes connection strengths so that they are slightly different each time the excitation has passed. Memory resides in the totality of all the connection strengths in the net. A given mental "event"—a specific thought, fantasy, or dream image— represents the excitation or lighting up of some widely distributed grouping of units.

Of course, the net in our cortex is not a randomly organized net, and it is not a smooth, undifferentiated net. The net has portions in the occipital cortex that are connected more closely to the visual system and other portions related to other sensory systems. Also, as I conceive of it, the net has "denser" portions—areas that are more "tightly woven" than others, involving well-rehearsed or over-learned material. In part, it is a trained net or an entrained net, as we shall see. I will present below a rough sketch of how I think we can conceptualize dreaming and other cognitive activities in terms of the nets of the mind. I will not include any sort of mathematics, although some consensus is beginning to emerge about the kinds of mathematics that may describe such nets.[6] I will rather try to describe what is going on using a number of metaphoric pictures. We will speak at times of woven and torn cloth, of stormy and calm seas, of discharging electrical grids, each image approaching a truth but probably not capturing it exactly. I have found from experience that different metaphoric pictures appeal to or make sense to different readers, so please accept and make use of the ones that appeal to you and do not worry that you are missing something important if some of them do not make sense to you. I only hope to give some sense of my thinking on dreaming and the nets of the mind. If the picture does not appear to have perfect resolution, if it does not appear quite clear or precise, this is acceptable to me and in fact may present an accurate picture of our incomplete and still developing knowledge.

DREAMING AND WAKING

In the sort of net we have discussed above, all that can happen, whether we are awake, asleep, or dreaming, is the lighting up of certain patterns of units and the strengthening or weakening of the weights on certain connections; in other words, we make connections all the time. However, I believe there is an important difference: Dreaming connects more broadly and more widely than does waking; in this sense dreaming can be considered "hyperconnective." Figure 1 illustrates part of what I have in mind. This is a highly simplified rendering in two dimensions of a few aspects of the net using a "spread of excitation" model. I suggest that in waking there is a tendency for linear development of specific imagery, usually guided by a specific task or goal. For instance, thinking of something like a house, my waking mind seldom pictures a generic house; rather, it is looking for a particular house to answer a specific question: "Where did I live in 1980?" The entire pattern lights up, representing not just any house but a specific house in my memory and in fact the specific house in which I lived in 1980. The excitation follows a set pattern; it remains in a "groove," with relatively little "spread" (Fig. 1a).

In dreaming, I suggest the progression is less specific and less focused. The pattern representing "house" may be lit up, but then rather than only moving to a specific house, the excitation process also spreads "laterally" to patterns representing other houses and other similar structures—hotels, institutions, etc. (Fig. 1b). Waking—and for now I am speaking of focused waking thought, the sort of waking thought that is furthest from dreaming—tends to stay in a sort of "groove" or "rut," whereas dreaming thought tends to wander and combine widespread material. The setting for a dream can often be a generic house or a combination of several houses. In looking over 100 of my recent dreams in which I had very carefully

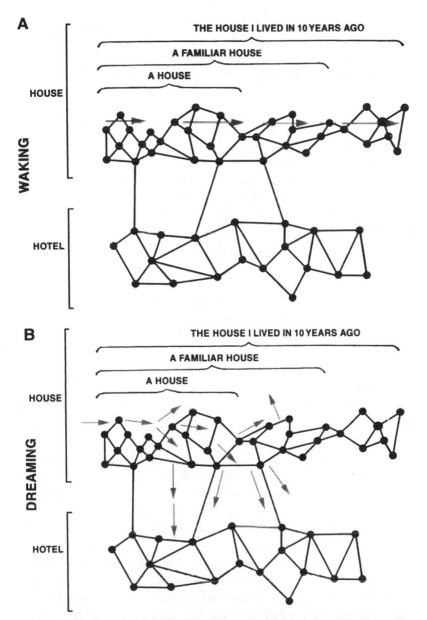

Figure 1. The spread of excitation in a schematic two-dimensional model of a portion of our neural nets. In waking, excitation spreads in a more direct, linear fashion, leading to a specific image. In dreaming, there is more lateral spread, leading to generic images and condensed images.

noted details of the setting, I found that the most common settings (over 60%) involved a kind of generic house (or room or outdoor area)—for instance, a house that was partly my house and partly a different, unknown house, a room that was partly a lobby and partly a lecture hall. Freud's best-known dream likewise starts with a generic setting: "A great hall . . . ."[7]

The idea that in dreams we connect material more broadly or more loosely than in our waking thought is also consistent with what we know about our dreams on an everyday basis. We dream about settings, characters, and actions that may be a bit "far-fetched"—that remind us of waking material, but are stretched somehow. We dream not only of ordinary creatures, but also of monsters and chimeras. We walk and run, but sometimes we also fly. We may dream of someone who appears to be two or more different people in our lives. Freud has described this aspect of dreaming very beautifully as "condensation"—putting together two or more underlying thoughts or other items into one dream image.[8] Some of the brief dreams we examined earlier, such as "I dreamt of a man who looked like my boyfriend, but was also my father," are condensations in which, as we noted, the dream is connecting a little better than our waking thought, "seeing connections" that were not quite apparent during waking. Existentialists have called attention to the fact that we are more open—especially open to more possibilities—in dreaming.[9] Thus, it is hardly a new idea that in some sense we make connections more broadly during dreaming.

The biology of REM sleep—the biological substrate of most dreaming—also supports this characteristic of dreaming as opposed to focused waking thought. I suggested as early as 1973, based on a number of pharmacological studies, that dreaming represents the functioning of the cortex without the influence of the neuromodulator substance norepinephrine.[10] This has since been confirmed, extended, and elaborated using studies of single neurons and other techniques.[11] The action of norepinephrine on the cortex has been summarized as producing "inhibitory sharpening,"[12] and this can readily be mapped onto Figure 1. Waking thought (Fig. 1a), with its direct, straight-line spread of excitation, illustrates inhibitory sharpening, produced by high levels or norepinephrine. Broader connections in dreaming, more condensation, and more generic rather than specific images (Fig. 1b), mean less inhibitory sharpening produced by the very low levels of cortical norepinephrine found in REM sleep.

Figure 2 presents, again very roughly, a model of the cortex seen as a simple, two-dimensional net, with some more tightly woven regions representing well-learned tasks and processes, characterized by complex but well-established connections for rapid processing of information. These are related to functions and learned abilities such as reading, writing, and calculating, and to special skills such as drawing or playing a musical instrument.[13] Recent imaging studies are beginning to demonstrate reliable patterns of activation in a number of cortical regions corresponding with activities such as reading and calculating; however, the anatomical locations need not concern us here. Outside of these areas are more "loosely woven" regions in the nets, regions less related to a specific ability or process. This is a land populated by images or moving pictures and by

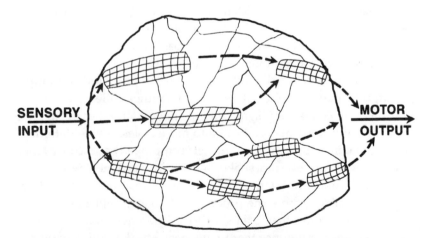

Figure 2. A portion of the nets of the mind in the human cortex represented schematically, showing a few tightly-woven regions corresponding to well-learned, rapid-processing abilities and functions, surrounded by more loosely woven regions. Focused waking thought involves a relatively rapid movement from input to output using the tightly woven regions as indicated by the arrows, whereas dreaming involves the more loosely woven regions. This is, of course, oversimplified in many ways. There is likely to be a gradation, rather than simply two types of regions.

metaphor (as we shall see), which has relatively little direct connection to sensory input or motor output.

I suggest that typical focused, goal-directed waking thought makes use of the relatively more tightly woven portions (on this diagram), which involve rapid processing, leading from sensory input to motor output or to some definite "result" or "solution"; dreaming makes connections more widely, especially in the "loosely woven" regions. In fact, our dreams mostly avoid the rapid-processing areas and functions (see below). In this sort of picture, focused waking is more a hunt, and dreaming is more an exploration. Figure 2 suggests two different sorts of "regions" in the brain, but this is of course schematic and oversimplified; there is probably a whole gradation, from regions with the most organized, overlearned pathways to regions with the least-used, "far-out," bizarre (or original) connections.

To supplement this quasi-anatomic view, we can consider "modes of processing" rather than regions. Focused waking thought follows a relatively straightforward A-B-C-D sequential mode of processing, aimed at reaching a goal. Dreaming uses a more parallel, less focused, less directed mode. Many kinds of connectionist nets have been modeled, but they can be subdivided roughly (Fig. 3) into two categories: feed-forward nets and autoassociative nets.[14] A feed-forward net consists of units in a number of "layers," which act on each other unidirectionally; interaction "flows" forward from input to output. In an autoassociative net (sometimes called an attractor net) the connections are symmetrical; there is no clearly defined input or output; the net "settles" into more or less stable patterns. I suggest that in focused waking the net is employed as, or constrained into acting relatively more like, a feed-forward net, whereas in dreaming it functions relatively more as an autoassociative net. Here we are visualizing the same process of "broader connections" as a shift in mode rather than as a shift to a different "region."

The reader will notice that I have been speaking of waking in a kind of caricature as purely focused, waking activity. Actually I believe that there is a whole continuum on the dimensions we are discussing, from the most focused waking thought through relaxed, somewhat looser thought, to reverie and daydreaming (which begin to resemble dreaming), and finally to dreaming itself, as we will

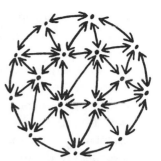

A Feed-Forward Net   An Autoassociative Net

Figure 3. Two basic types of connectionist nets. The idea is that our neural nets can assume both of these forms. The net is constrained into acting relatively more as a feed-forward net in focused waking, and acts more as an autoassociative net in dreaming.

discuss later. In many ways, one can engage in relatively "dream-like" thought even while awake. This has in fact been demonstrated by numerous studies of daydreaming and mental activity under relaxed, isolated conditions.[15] I have artificially broken off the focused waking end of the continuum to make the distinction between waking and dreaming most clear.

What We Don't Dream

The view of dreaming I have outlined suggests that we dream relatively little about the rapid, input/output processing activities (or the well-learned activities) that occupy the tightly woven portions of the net and use the most serial A-B-C-D processing—such as reading, writing, and arithmetic (the "3 R's"). Thus, we can postulate that dreams should contain very little actual reading, writing, typing, or calculating.

This was tested first in a preliminary study in which two judges examined 129 written dream reports from several studies and rated whether there was or was not an instance of actual reading or writing (word-by-word reading or writing, or calculating) in the dreams. The two scorers agreed perfectly on all dreams: They rated no instances of reading, no instances of writing, and one instance of probable calculating.

In a larger study, questionnaires were mailed to 400 people known to be very interested in dreams, most of whom were very frequent dreamers. On the questionnaire they were first asked to rate how frequently they dreamt about reading, writing, typing, and calculating on a 5-point scale from "never" to "all the time—it's in most of my dreams." They were also asked how much time they spent on these activities in waking. This part of the study showed that 90% of these frequent dreamers (reporting an average of 6.8 dreams per week) answered "never" or "almost never" to each of the four questions, even though they reported spending an average of six hours a day in these activities. In the second part of the questionnaire they were asked, "Please estimate how prominent each of the following activities is in your dreams as opposed to your waking life," concerning each of six activities: walking, writing, talking with friends, reading, sexual activity, and typing. They rated each activity on a 7-point scale from 1 ("far more prominent in my waking life; occurs little or not at all in my dreams") to 7 ("far more prominent in my dreaming life").

The results were very clear-cut (Fig. 4). Writing, reading, and typing showed an average rating close to 1 ("far more prominent in my waking life . . ."), whereas the other three activities were rated between 3 ("slightly more prominent in waking") and 4 ("equally prominent in waking and dreaming"). Interestingly, this was true of all three of the "control activities"—walking, talking with friends, and sexual activity—although these activities certainly differ considerably from one another.[16]

These results appear to confirm the view that we dream very little of rapid-processing serial activities such as the 3 R's. The results are at least consistent with the view that dreaming involves the less structured, less tightly woven portions of the nets. There are other possible explanations for the results, though I do not find them quite as satisfactory.[17]

Aside from the 3 R's, but perhaps related, there are a number of styles of mental functioning that we use a great deal in waking thought but which apparently occur very rarely in dreaming. Espe-

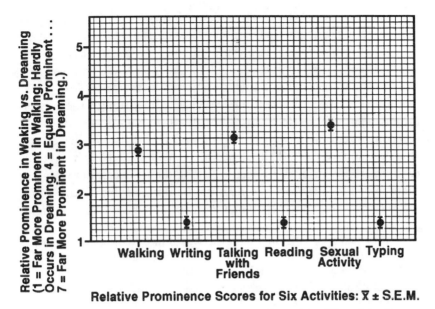

Relative Prominence Scores for Six Activities: $\bar{X}$ ± S.E.M.

Figure 4. The relative prominence of six activities in waking life and in dreams. Results of the questionnaire study (see text) summarizing 250 completed questionnaires. The scale on the left runs from 1: "The activity is far more prominent in my waking life; it hardly occurs in my dreams," to 7: "The activity is far more prominent in my dreams; it hardly occurs in my waking life." For each activity the graph plots the mean plus or minus the standard error of the mean.

cially striking is the lack of sequential thinking—1, 2, 3, 4, 5. The simplest form of this is making lists, for example, "What shall I take with me this weekend?" (toothbrush, soap, underwear, boots, etc.), or "Who do you think are the greatest writers of all time? Make a list." Or, "List your favorite movie stars." All this does not occur at all in dreams. I have not done as formal a study of this as of the 3 R's, but an associate and I have each scored 100 dreams looking for lists of this kind and have agreed that there were no dreams containing a listing of four or more items. I believe this is not because lists are verbal and dreams are pictures. When I list favorite paintings or places or movie stars, I definitely see them. The list is often highly visual and there is no reason why the dream could not also picture a sequential list, but this appears to happen rarely or not at all.

Not only are lists themselves absent from dreams, but this is true of other forms of sequential mental processing as well—for instance, sequential testing of possible explanations for a phenomenon, such as occurs constantly in our waking lives. Let's say that, while awake, we see an unusual light low down in the distance. We think, "Hmmm. . . . It could be a plane's headlights, though there is no airport nearby. Perhaps a car is lost in an unusual location. Could someone have built a campfire over there? Or maybe an alien space-ship has landed, etc."; then we rapidly consider the facts in favor of each possibility and try to decide among them. Dreaming does not seem to include any sort of sequential thinking of this kind. Nor do we see simple extended chains of logical, "detective-style" thought:

> If he had spent the night here, he would have had to come in through this door; that means he would have made tracks in the snow; perhaps we can find some evidence of that. And then he would probably have used the bathroom and perhaps would have taken something out of the refrigerator. And he must have slept somewhere. Is there any sign of a bed having been used, etc.?

Again, such an extended chain is rarely if ever found in dreams.

Overall, we do not find in dreaming the solid A to B to C to D connections that are found readily in, and which constitute part of the essence of, ordinary focused waking thought. Along these lines, it is not a coincidence that people who are very solid, down-to-earth, and sequential (people we have spoken of elsewhere as having thick boundaries) tend to recall few dreams and to be relatively uninterested in dreams; on the other hand, people with thin boundaries, who are less oriented to sequential thinking, find themselves in a more "dreamlike" frame of mind even when awake, often engage in reverie or daydreaming, are also more interested in and more involved in dreams, and recall more dreams (see Chap. 13).

A WAKE–DREAM CONTINUUM

For some purposes it is useful to consider waking and dreaming as two totally different modes of mental functioning. For instance, the perceptual rapture (the complete involvement in one's visual or sensory experience) characteristic of some dreams seems very different from ordinary, plodding waking thought. Likewise, the "out of one's control" feature of dreaming, the lack of free will[18] in all ordinary (nonlucid) dreams seems totally different from waking. Yet for most purposes I think it is more fruitful to consider dreaming to be one end of a continuum, or perhaps one end of several related continua (Fig. 5). The continuum runs from (at the left end) focused waking thought—doing arithmetic or solving a well-defined problem—through looser, less tightly structured waking thought, through reverie and daydreaming, to dreaming at the right end. At the left end of the continuum we are dealing with words, mathematical symbols, and perceptual input from the world, while at the other end (dreaming) we are dealing with almost pure imagery. The left end of the continuum is characterized by strings of sequential or logical relationships, "A leads to B leads to C," or "if A then B"; at the other end of the continuum everything is connected, and usually connected using imagery, which can be considered as picture metaphor, as we will discuss. Toward the right-hand end there is less of a sequence of elements and more of a combining in images. In terms of our connectionist net model, we have a complex net that is constrained (pushed) into functioning as a feed-forward net during focused waking but that "relaxes into" an autoassociative net when we move toward daydreaming and dreaming.

Categories, boundaries, and divisions characterize our mental processing at the left end of the continuum, whereas less solid boundaries, a loosening of categories, and a merging or condensation of material characterize the right end. One way to summarize these changes along the continuum, which may allow us to relate all this to the biology of the mind and to approach it through a study of complex systems, is to think of the mind nets (as in Fig. 2) composed of tightly woven, well-learned regions as well as more loosely woven surrounding areas. What we have spoken of as the left-hand end of the continuum can be seen as activity taking place within a tightly woven region or along a short chain of such regions, while the right-hand end (dreaming, etc.) involves activity less within and more across or outside of these specific regions.[19]

Variable	Focused waking thought	Looser, less-structured waking thought	Reverie, free association, daydreaming	Dreaming
What dealt with?	Perceptual input: math symbols, signs, words	Fewer words, signs; more visual-spatial imagery		Almost pure imagery
How?	Logical relationship: if A then B	Less logic, more noting or picturing of similarities, more metaphor		Almost pure picture metaphor
Self-reflection	Highly self-reflective: "I know I am sitting here reading."	Less self-reflective; more "caught up" in the process, the imagery		In "typical dreams" total *thereness*, no self-reflection
Sequence of ideas or images	A→B→C→D	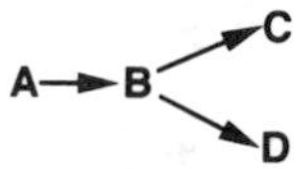 A→B, B→C, B→D	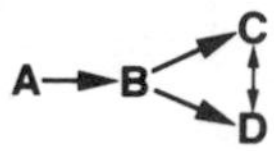 A→B→C, B→D	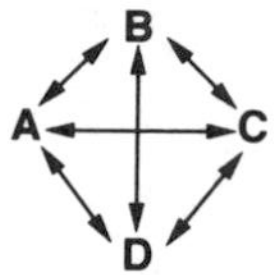 B, C, A, D (fully interconnected)
Processing	Relatively serial; net functions chiefly as a feed-forward net	Net functions chiefly as	Net functions more as an autoassociative net	
Boundaries	Solid division, categorization, thick boundaries	Less rigid categorization, thinner boundaries		Merging, condensation; loosening of categories; thin boundaries
Subsystems	Activity chiefly *within* structured subsystems		Activity less *within*, more *across* or *outside of* structured subsystems	

Figure 5. A wake–dreaming continuum.

I realize that I have collapsed a number of separable continua into one general scheme. There are many research projects investigating these continua separately and showing that they are not necessarily the same continuum. Thus, it is not absolutely necessary that sequential A-B-C-D thinking should predominate in words and mathematical symbols. It is certainly possible as a thought experiment to use images in a purely sequential fashion. Likewise, it is possible to use words in a completely loose and dreamlike sense, a kind of word salad. Such relationships are possible but I think unusual. My only excuse for attempting to combine or collapse all these continua is that in my experience and investigations this appears to be roughly how the mind works. We tend to shift in a total sense toward the left or the right end of the continuum rather than dissociating the strands.

EMOTION AND THE NET

The picture of the mind developed in the last few pages may seem a bit static—like a woven piece of cloth or a grid of little light bulbs lighting up at different times. But of course we all know that the mind is hardly a flat, untroubled place. The guiding metaphor I want to use here is not Freud's picture of the mind, with wild horses pulling in different directions, or a clash of conflicting forces. It is rather something like the surface of the sea in which there may be storms or even typhoons, but also calm regions and calm periods.

In this picture, traumatic events and the other powerful emotional situations we have discussed produce upheavals on the surface; then various processes play a role in calming or smoothing the surface. These processes involve various forms of reconnecting or interconnecting as in psychotherapy and also (I suggest) in dreaming. In this sort of spatial metaphor, the calm, relatively smooth surface is a theoretical ideal of the relaxed, untroubled state, probably unreachable, but perhaps approached temporarily by trained meditators, or in "transcendent" states.

In general terms, we are somewhat more "relaxed" and the sea is somewhat calmer in the morning than in the evening, and this may be related to the functions of sleep, especially REM sleep.[20] In some sense we are constantly going through phases of increased tension, worry, and concern, and then phases of relaxation, but the process is obviously complex and multilayered. Even when we have achieved a solution to some minor problem and are more relaxed, underlying worries or concerns and our old personality configurations and "complexes" may still disturb us. I believe that dreaming plays a part in achieving a calming of the storm, usually without our conscious awareness.

I realize that in this chapter and the previous ones I have talked chiefly of powerful, negatively toned emotions such as terror, fear, helplessness, and guilt, in part because these are the ones that occur most clearly after trauma and are thus most easily tracked into dreams. What about our many positive emotions? As mentioned, I have been trying to obtain series of dreams from people who have experienced something truly happy and joyous, such as a wedding or falling in love with someone new and wonderful. So far, my impression is that even when a happy event such as a wedding occurs, there are always worries, concerns, and not-so-happy feelings associated with it; and in the dreams I have collected, it appears easier to see these partly negative feelings or concerns portrayed than the positive ones.

This should not surprise us in terms of our model of the nets of the mind. We have pictured a disturbing emotion as a storm or a disruption in the net—a force acting on the net. It is not as easy to picture a truly positive emotion: Shall we imagine an unusually flat and calm sea? But no, this image would more likely represent a lack of strong emotion. Perhaps a very smooth, flowing current would come closer. In any case the situation is far less clear with respect to positive emotions. In most cases positive emotions do not appear to impress themselves on dream content as clearly, though we examined in the preceding chapters a few dreams that appeared to be expressing chiefly joy or amazement.

SUMMARY

We have considered a broad outline of a net, or network, picture of the mind. Within the overall nets of the mind we visualized regions that are more tightly organized, regions that involve well-learned or overlearned material (Fig. 2). The basic idea is a very widespread net that can undergo perturbations of various kinds that correlate with trauma, stress, and various emotional concerns.

At the simplest level, the net, visualized as a broad, connectionist net or perhaps a grouping of connectionist nets, is always disturbed, always trying to settle into a relatively stable pattern—a place with the least disturbance or agitation—referred to mathematically as the lowest "computational energy." However, the sea never becomes absolutely calm; the process is never quite complete because there is always another series of influences on the net. The net is pushed by new input and new emotional concerns of various kinds, producing excitations and disruptions.

The conditions we have discussed in the preceding chapters, ranging from trauma, to stressful events, to other situations associated with powerful emotions or emotional concerns, to needs such as hunger and thirst, and even to external stimulation (the disturbing sound of an alarm clock, etc.), can all be seen as more or less powerful disturbances in the net. Trauma associated with terror can be seen as a widespread disturbance. Particular emotional concerns such as "I really need to figure out how to get out of this relationship" or "I have to solve this one remaining problem in order to complete my invention" are more localized forces or "storms" acting on the net. They can influence thinking, waking imagery, and, of course, dreams.

I realize that this attempt to connect dreaming with the incompletely understood nets of the mind is sketchy and cannot at this point be fully convincing. We will return to the biological aspects of cortical functioning later, in Chapter 11. In the next chapter we will discuss metaphor in dreams and how the view just explored about nets in the mind can help us make sense of metaphor. We will see, for instance, that a car is like a truck but also like a personal relationship.

Chapter Six

METAPHOR

Three different patients beginning psychoanalysis or long-term psy-chotherapy reported very similar dreams:

> I was walking on a narrow mountain path with steep drop-offs on either side; it seemed kind of dangerous; the path was foggy; I could not see ahead very well. There was a large, shadowy figure walking with me; I was not sure whether this figure was good or evil.

I have heard somewhat similar dreams many times. The dreamer is portraying a current concern—starting therapy—and making use of the common metaphor, "Life is a journey," or more specifically, "This particular part of life (therapy) is a potentially dangerous journey."

Without even noticing it, we constantly use such metaphors in our speech, our thinking, our fantasies, and our dreams. Metaphor is not simply a figure of speech but a basic foundation of our thought and mental functioning. This view has been developed and explored in detail recently by George Lakoff and his associates.[1] Even in our everyday practical speech, we are "stuck," I'm "loaded down," this relationship is "going nowhere," he is "spinning his wheels."

Dreaming makes use of many metaphors that we use frequently in speech as well as in stories, poems, and other works of art, and it also creates new metaphors to convey meaning. I will argue that the dream connects, or brings closer together, subsystems of the memory

95

nets, revealing similarities that the dreamer may not previously have noticed. Dreams do this by taking the form of pictured metaphor.

One woman found her boyfriend intelligent and attractive but also extremely dogmatic and rigid. She was at some level aware of these same traits in her father, although she had never consciously noted the similarities between the two men. Her sleeping mind, with its thinner boundaries and less rigid categories, brought these characteristics together, and she dreamt: "My boyfriend turned into my father." This very common kind of dream image could be called an example of condensation—simply combining two things into one. One could argue as to whether it is truly a metaphor, but this simple "noting of similarities" is at the heart of metaphor.

Another woman told me this dream: "Joe [a boyfriend] was a werewolf. He turned into a wolf in my dream." In thinking about her dream, she realized that Joe, whom she found in some ways powerful and exciting, also struck her as unreliable and possibly vicious or dangerous. Indeed, he showed many of the characteristics she (like many of us) had stored as part of her memory image for a wolf. A dream made this connection for her. Here we have caught the dream on its way to producing a standard metaphor: "Joe is a wolf."

In most cases the metaphor is already fully formed and the dream image only presents the second term or vehicle of the metaphor: "This big, gray wolf was running loose in my apartment, tearing up my things. Its jaws were tearing into this special pink pillow I've had ever since childhood." The woman who had this dream thought it over, let herself make connections, and decided that it clearly referred to a relationship in which she was currently involved.

METAPHOR IS EVERYWHERE

Metaphor is a fundamental part of our thinking and memory processes. I think of metaphor as basically a noting of similarities. In terms of the nets in our minds, it can be seen as a bringing together of separate subnets. Metaphor is what occurs more and more naturally and prevalently as we move from the serial, highly structured, rapid-processing mental activity of focused waking to the broader, more parallel realms of reverie, daydreaming, and actual dreaming.

Metaphor is ubiquitous. Perhaps the only time we do not employ metaphor is when we are engaged in direct focused activity, such as doing an arithmetic problem or typing (correcting a manuscript, etc.; the mechanical portion of the "3 R's"), or perhaps while we are chasing a deer (supposing we are hunters) and figuring exactly which way to run and in what direction to shoot our arrows. As soon as we get away from this focused waking activity and sit back to think, to wonder, to explain something, and of course, to daydream or dream, metaphor enters in.

We can hardly talk about our lives or our relationships without using one of many metaphorical descriptions, usually some version of "life is a journey" or "love is a journey": "I don't know how I am going to get there from here," "our relationship seems to be stuck," "it's been a bumpy road," "you're just throwing up roadblocks." We can shift readily from a land vehicle to a boat ("lately it's been smooth sailing") or a plane ("I'm going to have to bail out of this relationship").

Even at our workplaces, when we step back for a moment from doing our work to thinking or talking about it, we automatically find ourselves speaking of "workload" (already a metaphor): "I am really loaded down," "the straw that broke the camel's back," "I can hardly see past all this," "there are more regulations coming down the pike," "it's a rat race," "it's a dog-eat-dog world," or, on a more positive note, "I can see the light at the end of the tunnel," "it should be all downhill from here." Thus, our speech and thought are loaded with (whoops), filled with (I can't help it!) metaphor even in talking about everyday concerns. When we broaden our focus (metaphor again!) and try to discuss with someone the nature of life, death, or eternity, we can hardly help speaking in terms of the length of the day or year, the growth of grass, the emptying of flasks, or going on a journey. Soon the air is thick with buzzing swarms of metaphor and there appears to be nothing else in sight. And all this refers to verbal activity—using speech and accomplishing ordinary, waking, goal-directed activities. Thus, we are still in the relatively tightly woven portions of the net. We have not yet entered the land of daydreams and dreams where pictured metaphor reigns.

Nor have I yet spoken of poetry, usually considered the best place to find metaphor, because I was emphasizing that metaphor is everywhere. We can hardly help using it even when discussing our work, our love lives, and our friendships in an ordinary conversation. But of course poetic reverie (a kind of daydreaming) and poetry itself are often characterized by striking, novel, or deeply layered metaphor. For instance, Lakoff and Turner have identified 16 different metaphors describing the course of life in one Shakespearean sonnet (Sonnet 73).[2]

> That time of year thou mayst in me behold
> When yellow leaves, or none, or few, do hang
> Upon those boughs which shake against the cold,
> Bare ruin'd choirs, where late the sweet birds sang.
> In me thou see'st the twilight of such day
> As after sunset fadeth in the West;
> Which by and by black night doth take away,
> Death's second self, that seals up all in rest.
> In me thou see'st the glowing of such fire,
> That on the ashes of his youth doth lie,
> As the death-bed whereon it must expire,
> Consum'd with that which it was nourish'd by.
>   This thou perceiv'st, which makes thy love more strong,
>   To love that well which thou must leave ere long.

Poetic metaphor is known for its newness, its aptness, and to some extent its unexpected or farfetched qualities. But we use metaphor all the time in our explanations. Try explaining to someone, to a child, say, what life is, or death or time or love, and you will immediately find yourself using metaphor or simile.[3] I call this very common use "explanatory metaphor."

Furthermore, all the metaphors we have considered, both poetic and nonpoetic, are based on images. Sometimes the imagery is called forth very vividly, as in Shakespeare's poem, while sometimes the image is vague or so overused that we barely see it at all ("I am loaded down," or "we seem to be stuck," the "foothills"). But the image is always there in the background and the more we get away from the constraints of focused waking, the more this metaphoric imagery emerges.

The Dream as Explanatory Metaphor

We have spoken of the dream as contextualizing an emotional concern. But this process does not occur in words or formulas. The form it almost always takes is picture metaphor—usually visual-spatial metaphor—for instance, a dream we mentioned briefly in Chapter 2, "there was an empty house, empty and barren. All the doors and windows were open and the wind was blowing through," is a beautiful picture metaphor for the state of mind of the dreamer, a woman whose mother has just died. This is not a motivated disguise or an attempt to fool the waking mind. It is simply expressing the state of one's mind in terms of the language available in the neural nets as they function in the dreaming, auto-associative mode—thus, visual-spatial imagery[4] and picture metaphor. In this sense dreaming is explanatory metaphor. What I mean is that the dream is doing (in pictures) something very similar to what we do when we speak of life metaphorically as a road, a plant, a tree, or a fire, or speak of love metaphorically as a journey. We try to explain something important but difficult or problematic in terms of something simpler; we especially try to explain it in terms of a visual image.[4]

Again, this is perhaps easiest to see in extreme cases such as those after trauma as we have discussed. The state, "I am terrified," or "I am absolutely overwhelmed," is metaphorically pictured as "A tidal wave is breaking over me," or "I am in a burning house and can't get out," or "A gang of thugs has me trapped."

Author and psychiatrist Robert Jay Lifton describes a group of veterans discussing their feelings and dreams about the Vietnam War: "I wanted to die clean. It didn't matter if I died—but I just didn't want to die with mud on my boots, all filthy. Death wasn't so bad if you were clean." Another man strongly agreed and told of a repetitive dream he used to have in Vietnam, always with the same terrifying conclusion: "I would end up shot, lying along the side of the road, dying in the mud." There was intense response in the group, as one veteran after another told of similar fears. In their associations it became clear that "dying in the mud" meant dying in filth or evil, without reason or purpose—without nobility or dignity of any kind.[5] The dreams are clearly trying to picture some very painful and difficult emotional concerns.

The same process of explanatory metaphor occurs in more ordinary dreams, also. The complex emotional concern that can be described verbally as "this relationship is in trouble; I don't feel in control anymore; I'm afraid something bad will happen" may be expressed visually (and frequently is) as, "I'm going downhill in a car and the brakes don't work."

This metaphor making can likewise be seen in certain cases of illness when the mind is trying to describe something that is very disturbing physically. We discussed in Chapter 1 the woman who had a terrifying dream that she was turning into a stone castle, but the castle was shaped like her; she was turning to stone. She dreamt this while she was acutely ill with viral encephalitis in the flu pandemic of 1918. Encephalitis can often lead to Parkinsonism, and in fact this woman did develop severe postencephalitic Parkinsonism, which turned her into a kind of stone castle or statue, barely able to move, within a few weeks of the dream. She remained in a frozen state for a number of years until partially cured by l-Dopa.[6]

Indeed, dreams often portray a concern about the body in a metaphor, as we discussed in Chapter 3. A man with a peptic ulcer dreamt his house was burning down. "The burning sensation was being experienced during sleep and stimulated a dream with fire destroying his home." A patient who had extensive pelvic surgery dreamt she saw dead and dying animals on a hillside.[7]

People diagnosed with Multiple Personality Disorder—a form of disassociative disorder, now officially called Disassociative Identity Disorder—may or may not be consciously aware that they have other, disassociated portions of themselves or "alters." But they sometimes dream of these alters. In a survey of dreams in patients with multiple-personality disorder, 19 of 23 had dreams involving multiplicity metaphors. For instance, one patient recorded a dream a while before the diagnosis of Multiple Personality Disorder was made:

> I was sitting in a photo booth trying to get it to take a picture of
> me, but all the pictures that came out showed other people or at
> least faint outlines of other people. In the mirror where you see
> what will come out, the faces kept changing like ghosts.[8]

Some of these patients also had vivid dreams of certain dream characters, for instance, little children who later, according to therapists,
turned out to be the patients' "alters." In all these cases of physical or
mental illness, one can see the dreaming mind trying to picture,
trying to find a metaphor for, a disturbing internal state. The same
making of picture metaphor can also be seen when one is dreaming
about less traumatic situations.

In a study mentioned in Chapter 3, subjects had blood pressure
cuffs gradually inflated on their legs while they were in REM sleep.[9]
Generally they did not dream of pressure cuffs. Instead their dreams
produced metaphoric pictures involving snakes or ropes tying them
down. The dreams seemed to be trying to explain the uncomfortable
state of the sleeper's legs. One middle-aged man had a urinary tract
problem that on one occasion caused him unexpectedly to wet the
bed, so he realized on awakening that the lower part of his back was
actually wet. He had just awakened from a dream of a scene in which
he and others were playing outdoors with garden hoses. Several of
the others had their hoses lined up to make a wall of water right
behind him and he was backing into it, getting wet. In these cases the
emotional concern or disturbing state is a minor annoyance (I feel
uncomfortable; my ankles feel odd; my back feels wet), not a major
upset like some that we have discussed before.

There is an important distinction here between my views and
the views of others who speak of "dream symbolism." I am not
claiming that the dream translates one object or stimulus into another. I am not saying that dreams, for reasons of their own, express a
blood pressure cuff as a rope or snake, or a wet sheet as water
sprayed from garden hoses. I do not believe the dream produces such
simple, object-to-object symbolism. For one thing, while dreaming,
we do not perceive the external world clearly; this is exactly what we
are worst at while dreaming. The dreamer in the study does not
perceive that there is a blood pressure cuff on his leg and then decide

to translate it. Rather I am saying that the dreamer is aware only of a disturbance or annoyance (a minor form of what we have been calling an emotional concern). The dreamer senses an uncomfortable feeling, a sort of tightness centered around his ankles. It is this discomfort, this small emotional concern, that is expressed meta-phorically as, "There are ropes tying me down." In all these cases the mind during dreaming attempts to use a metaphoric picture to de-scribe the current emotionally important state, whether this state is a dimly perceived physical illness, a mental illness, or a state of sleep disturbed by an annoying external stimulus.

Another situation that has been well studied and that provides evidence for such metaphor imagery is pregnancy, discussed in Chapter 3. In early and midpregnancy a woman is often concerned about changes in her body shape and whether these will perma-nently alter her appearance or reduce her attractiveness. The dreams clearly reflect this; for instance, one pregnant woman dreamt of being part of a "girlie show" in a carnival:

> A sexy girl named Wanda danced. Then it was my turn. The barker yelled, "Now here's Colleen. Just look at those curves." I danced out into the spotlight. Everyone began laughing and jeering. My husband Carl was sitting in the front row with his arm around Wanda. I looked at myself and saw that I had this enormous belly. My arms and legs had flabby rolls of fat on them. Men in the audience began yelling, "We didn't come to see the fat lady."[10]

Obviously, she is dreaming about concerns that her pregnancy is making her unattractive and that her husband may prefer someone else. But it makes more sense to me to understand her dream as meta-phorically explaining her concerns than to emphasize a one-for-one symbolic translation such that "her enormous fatness symbolizes her pregnancy." Later in pregnancy a woman is dealing with more indef-inite and unfamiliar bodily sensations and in addition is psycho-logically trying to cope with the idea that there is actually another creature inside her, that she will soon be a mother. The dreams often reflect this metaphorically. For instance, there are any number of dreams of animals: "I was swimming and there were these turtles all over the place. I could hardly see for all the turtles swimming around." Later in pregnancy the animals become larger: "I dreamt the doctor presented a baby to me but it was a puppy. I was sure there was something wrong; it wasn't supposed to be a puppy." Again, we can most easily see this as metaphoric picture of her concerns.

I have again started with trauma, with illness, and with somewhat unusual situations because I believe we can see what is happening most clearly at such times. However, the metaphoric picturing of major concerns is found absolutely everywhere—in dreams of my patients, my associates, and my own dreams. For instance, I constantly find concerns about relationships (obviously a frequent problem) portrayed as dangerous journeys, as on the first page of this chapter. In our present Western culture, the relationship journey is represented especially frequently as a trip in a car: "I am in a car going downhill around some curves. The brakes don't seem to be working. I am afraid I am going to crash." I have heard dreams like this any number of times, and they usually appear to be metaphoric descriptions of a concern about a relationship that is somehow out of control.

METAPHOR IN THE NET: A CAR, A TRUCK, A RELATIONSHIP

Taking seriously the idea that the mind consists basically of a complex net rather than a group of categories, rules, and regulations, leads to some interesting possibilities and some clarification of dream images. Any given "item" or concept is considered to be stored in a widespread fashion in the nets of the mind. Something like a car is presumably stored as a widespread distribution of connection strengths representing the various microfeatures of a car. The microfeatures include, but are not limited to, the parts we can see easily—the wheels, body, hood, trunk, windows, etc.—as well as parts we know are inside—engine, drive shaft, etc. Of course *car* is stored very differently for a mechanic, who knows the insides in great detail, than for someone who has only driven a car and seen it from the outside. The car involves a great deal of visual storage—the facts we have learned about the appearance of a car. The microfeatures that we store also involve sounds. We know what a car sounds like when it starts up, when it is running smoothly and not so smoothly, when it is stalling, and when the brakes are suddenly jammed on. There are also certain smells associated with a car— leather seats, gasoline, spilled coffee. And we have a lot of knowledge about a car in motion—the way it moves, the way it stops, the way it goes over bumps, the way it occasionally skids out of control on water or ice, and the way the brakes act or fail to act. All of these bits and pieces (widely distributed microfeatures) are brought together to form our idea of a car.

Now as a thought experiment let us consider three familiar things—a car, a truck, and a personal relationship. On the face of it, this seems like a totally absurd grouping, containing two very similar items and one that is completely different. It's like two apples and an orange; no, worse than that: two apples and a gorilla. We would have no trouble answering a "similarities" question on a grade-school intelligence test asking us to group which two items go together. In the mappings in our minds, car and truck have a great many features in common; however, they also have some items that are stored differently, and thus we have no trouble differentiating them. Trucks are bigger, rougher, less comfortable, make somewhat different noises, and are used in different ways. We can list a large number of differences.

Now a "relationship" appears on the surface to be something entirely different. After all, it is not a "real thing," not a "hard" object in the world like a car or truck. It cannot be touched or weighed or bumped into in a literal sense. Nonetheless, when we stop to think of it (Fig. 6), a relationship and a car, especially a car in motion, have a number of similarities. At least in our Western, car-dependent culture, we often think of relationships in carlike ways. Relationships can go smoothly or be stuck: "Things are rolling along," "We're really moving," "We're in the fast lane," or "This relationship is going nowhere." "It's going to be a tough uphill climb." "It's a bumpy road." Another relationship may be "on the skids," or "spinning out of control." "The brakes are not working." Clearly there are many ways in which we think of a relationship that resemble the way we think of a car, especially a car in motion or a journey by car. Indeed,

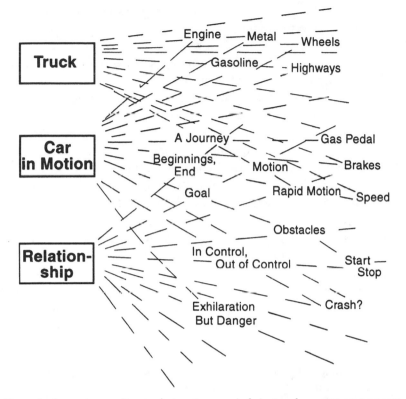

Figure 6. Assuming any item or feature in our minds is stored as a pattern representing its microfeatures, there is considerable overlap between CAR and TRUCK, and also between CAR and RELATIONSHIP. It is not surprising when we are concerned about the personal relationship, we sometimes dream of a car. Of course, a personal relationship can also overlap with a growing plant, building something together, a contest, etc.

this may be one of the major ways we think about a concept such as a relationship and thus a major way in which it is stored in the nets of our minds. Clearly there is considerable overlap between the storage of "relationship" and the storage of "car." Of course this is not the only way something like "relationship" is stored. A relationship is complex, and depending on circumstances there may be overlap between the storage of "relationship" and the storage of other simpler items, such as "building a house," "growing a plant," "an athletic contest," or even "a war."

When we are in a focused waking state we can dismiss all this and speak of it merely as a manner of speaking, or metaphor. Things are kept separate; we have clear-cut (thick) boundaries between real objects, such as cars, and abstract concepts, such as personal relationships. It is a question of separation, of boundaries, of sticking to our A-B-C-D thinking. Hard, real objects are in one universe; concepts such as relationships are in another. Yet the similarities are all there, stored as an overlap of patterns in our nets. I suggest that as we leave focused waking thought and approach reverie, and daydreaming, or especially dreaming (see the continuum, Fig. 5), these separations are less clear-cut; the boundaries become thinner. We not only dream simple condensations—for instance, I have seen many dreams of vehicles that are somewhat like cars and somewhat like trucks—but we also easily cross the category divisions or boundaries. Thus we find ourselves dreaming of cars out of control when what we are worried about is a relationship. Such dreams are very common, for instance, our familiar dream about brakes not working. Or:

> I am in my car which isn't steering too well. It comes to a screeching halt and I get flipped out of it. I think I wake up before I hit anything. It's kind of scary.

> We're in a car. It feels all right at first, but I don't know whose car it is and I'm not sure who's driving. We're in a complicated maze of roads, and we seem to be lost.

What I am saying—and this may be a bit difficult to grasp—is that a metaphoric similarity is a real similarity. In the nets of our minds (and that's all we have), metaphor is real: The similarity between a personal relationship and a journey by car is just as real as the similarity between a car and a truck. If there is enough overlap in our representations of two items, they are related items for us, and the looser "flow" of excitation in dreaming can and often will make connections between them. This happens more easily in dreaming since we have fewer or "thinner" boundaries and less of the logical rules (and category rules) that we maintain in waking. Thus dreaming, when we are processing more broadly and loosely with less emphasis on categories and separations, is absolutely full of metaphor.

"Working with One's Dreams"

A number of authors have recently written somewhat similar popular works on understanding and making use of one's dreams.[11] These are not the old-fashioned and surprisingly still popular dream dictionaries that supply a standard "meaning" for each item in a dream. Rather, each of these authors intelligently follows Freud in recognizing that the dreamer's own associations to the dream are essential and will lead to an individual meaning for that dreamer. Although the techniques described differ somewhat, it is impressive that in the many examples given the dream images almost always turn out to be metaphors for personal or interpersonal concerns of the dreamer. For instance, in one example a man dreams:

> I am carrying my boss on my back piggyback style. I am going downhill with my boss on my back. I am attempting to run, but he is too heavy for me. I am trying to be careful and strong. My boss says, "That's why I like using those five Green Bay Packers." As he says that, implying I am not as strong as they, I stumble and fall on the ground on my belly.[12]

The dreamer quickly realized after the dream how critical and demanding his boss was and, in fact, that the boss resembled the dreamer's father in this way and that the dreamer was always carrying around someone critical and demanding. Such metaphors for problems in relationships, or sometimes metaphors for *intrapsychic* problems—problems or concerns with a portion of the dreamer's self—are found repeatedly, although these authors do not make much use of the term "metaphor." We will consider later, in Chapter 8, the widespread movement known as "dreamworking." This consists of people getting together in a group and sharing dreams, usually with some attempt to clarify and understand the meaning of the dream. These groups are quite disparate in their membership and their background. I have taken part in a number of such groups and I have found that no matter what the orientation of the group, the useful suggestions and interpretations developed by group members and the dreamers themselves almost always turn out to be metaphorical pictures of the dreamer's personal and interpersonal concerns.

THE WAY OUR MINDS FUNCTION

Why should metaphor, which has traditionally been conceptualized as one specific rhetorical device among many, have such a prominent role in dreaming? I would say this is because metaphor has been falsely characterized as merely a rhetorical device. Rather, metaphor is a basic aspect of our mental functioning,[13] as we have noted. I would add that metaphor is especially prominent when we get away from the most focused, precise, rapid-processing activities to states of reverie, daydreaming, and dreaming. In a general sense, metaphor is simply a noting of similarities; we use metaphor all the time, and when we are daydreaming or dreaming it involves picturing the similarities.

Metaphor is learned and understood early in life. A number of studies have shown that children understand metaphor quite easily at the ages of four to seven, when they have not yet mastered the propositional logic that supposedly allows us to explain metaphor, and certainly long before they have any notion of a "rhetorical device."[14] In all these senses, metaphor is by no means a figure of speech, but rather a basic part of our understanding of the world, a part of our being in the world. Far from being only a device used in speech, metaphor may be older, broader, and deeper than speech itself.

Our continuum (Fig. 5) is relevant here. There are forms of pure, nonmetaphoric cognition—perhaps calculation is the simplest form, or the cognition involved in any straightforward pursuit of a goal—escaping from a charging bull or positioning oneself at exactly the right place to catch a fly ball. As soon as we leave these "rapid-processing" regions (the most tightly woven portions of the net), metaphor and usually picture metaphor begin to enter in. There are, of course, individual differences. I am quite a visual person and for me visual-spatial images are present even when I am working on

something as purely cognitive as a logical syllogism. The old paradigm of logical reasoning, "All men are mortal; Socrates is a man;
therefore Socrates is mortal," sounds fairly reasonable in words, but I
am more truly convinced of it when I picture it as a stick figure or
small circle called "Socrates" placed within a larger circle called
"men" or "humans" within a still larger circle called "mortal creatures" (Fig. 7).

As we get away from focused waking activity, our world becomes increasingly metaphorical. To me this seems obvious if we
consider metaphor in the broadest sense as a noting of similarities. I

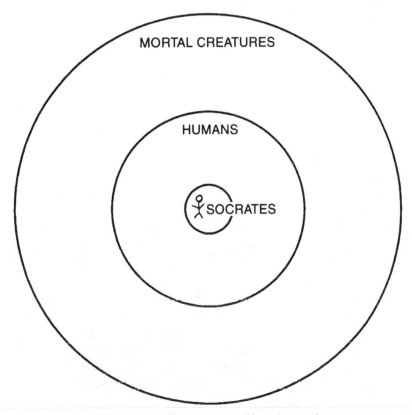

Figure 7. A syllogism in visual form (see text).

would say that while we are thinking in a groove or a rut, noting one thing at a time in a straight-line, A-B-C-D pattern, we do not or cannot note similarities with other lines or patterns. But as soon as we broaden our focus and get out of the straight line or rut, we cannot help noticing that the world is not made up of single, straight lines but is full of connections. We cannot help noticing similarities.

For some it may be useful to consider metaphor in terms of "semantic spaces and subspaces." Several research groups propose that our minds work in a series of "semantic subspaces" dealing, for instance, with separate categories of objects.[15] As a simple example, there appear to be empirically derivable rules as to how we place various mammals in our semantic spaces. Most people locate various mammals in this space using only three dimensions, which can be called size, ferocity, and humanness. In one of many studies exploring this semantic space, subjects were asked to complete the analogy, "rat : pig :: goat : ____)" (rat is to pig as goat is to what?). Given four possible choices, of chimpanzee, cow, rabbit, or sheep, subjects almost unanimously chose cow. Chimpanzee invariably was in last place. In other words we all seem to have a kind of map in our minds for locating and relating different mammals.

We can then imagine another subspace for locating different birds. And we can create some simple metaphors relating the mammal and bird subspaces. For instance, "a wildcat is a hawk among mammals" indicates that the wildcat in the mammalian subspace occupies about the same position as the hawk in the bird subspace (not especially large, but very fierce, and rapidly swooping down on its prey). In this sense, "Mapping is the heart of metaphoric comprehension and appreciation," as Yale psychologist Robert Sternberg phrases it.[16] The distance between subspaces is important. The "closeness" of two semantic subspaces is a determinant of how understandable the metaphor produced will be. More distant subspaces produce metaphors that may be harder to get but more striking or poetic. Thus, "a wildcat is a hawk among mammals" is an understandable but dull metaphor. "A wildcat is an ICBM (intercontinental ballistic missile) among mammals" might be a little harder to understand but is more memorable.

If we wish to make use of semantic subspaces in our present view of dreaming, we could say that the semantic subspaces are somehow less separate or less distant during dreaming; we can move to far-off subspaces more easily. I believe this is simply another way of stating that dreaming makes connections more broadly, contains less rigid categories, or has "thinner boundaries" between regions. The "distance" between these imagined subspaces is a measure of difficulty of access. Access becomes easier as we move from focused waking to dreaming, and accordingly the subspaces seem "closer" as we approach the dream state.

Such semantic subspaces, with each animal represented as a point, are of course abstractions designed to help us conceptualize what is going on. They refer to some kind of distributed subnets within our mind nets. Returning to our mind nets, or neural nets, presumably each animal or bird is represented by a whole, widespread pattern of activation, and we could speak of "subnet" activation patterns representing each animal. Making of metaphor is simply noticing similarities among such activation patterns within different subnets. This leads readily to the similarity between wildcats and hawks, but also, returning to our more real-life concerns, the same process can produce metaphors such as "man is a wolf" or, for that matter, the metaphors we have found in dreams such as "Joe is a wolf" or "Jim is (like) my father."

We can imagine a young woman we previously spoke of thinking about her boyfriend as she goes about her daily life or speaks with friends. She may think or say, "Jim is really wonderful. He is A and he is B and he is C and he is D." She may think or say, "Jim and I have a lot of plans. Tomorrow we are going to do X and this weekend we are going to do Y and next week we are probably going to do Z." She may even try at times to think of Jim's faults or problems as they have shown up recently. "When we went to visit my friend Jane, who's ill, Jim kept talking about himself all evening. Perhaps he is kind of self-centered. But on the other hand he was really helpful when I needed an ally in my arguments with my sister." Jim clearly has a prominent place in one of the subnets in her mind.

This young woman is on reasonably good terms with her father;

she sees him once in a while and frequently talks to him on the phone. From long experience with him, she also knows a great deal about her father's likes, dislikes, habits, and character, and the fact that he is quite self-centered; but all this material is in a different subnet from the material about Jim. In the course of her waking life, the two subnets remain far apart and separate. It is only in a dream (or occasionally in a daydream or reverie) that she suddenly notices similarities and dreams the personal metaphor, "Jim is (like) my father." Or in one specific dream, "I dreamt that Jim turned into my father."

I am suggesting that in dreaming, these subnets somehow appear to be brought closer together. If we follow our discussion of semantic subspaces, it is as though the relationships within each subspace remain unaltered but the distances between the subspaces become less, so that it is easier for us to notice the similarities between birds and mammals, between people (Jim is like my father), and for that matter between people and animals (man is a wolf), or even between objects and body parts (a penis is like a cigar). Thus the complex pattern representing Joe, a particular boyfriend, includes a subnet that is somewhat similar to that stored by the same woman for "wolf." Such similarities can certainly be noticed during waking, but are noticed more readily in dreaming or sometimes daydreaming.

The patterns are somehow brought closer together, and the similarity is more easily noted, during dreaming. This obviously is not a physical shifting of portions of the brain. We can imagine it (Fig. 1) as a less linear and more diffuse spread of excitation, so that connections between this house and other houses or hotels are made more easily during dreaming than during waking. We can also speak of a more direct sort of processing during waking. "Joe," in the woman's waking mind, is caught up in a series of specific trains of thought. "I was planning to see Joe this weekend . . . plans for the weekend . . . plans for next month . . ., etc.," or perhaps, "Shall I stick with Joe or switch to Jack? . . . thoughts about Jack . . . last time I saw Jack . . ., etc.," whereas "wolf" is in a whole different context. "Wolf" is not thought of at all during the daytime, or perhaps occasionally, briefly, while reading a children's story or doing a crossword puzzle. In dreaming, one tends to note the similarities. This can occur to a

certain extent in wakefulness, during reverie or during daydreaming, but is less likely to occur while one is entirely focused on solving
an arithmetic problem. It occurs during waking more frequently in
persons with thin boundaries, persons whose thought is somewhat
dreamlike even when they are awake (Chap. 13).

Of course the nets of the mind are immensely complicated, and I
do not mean to imply simple, one-to-one correspondences. For instance, I have frequently heard dreams about a car going downhill
out of control in which the concern was about a relationship. However, this certainly does not mean that we can equate the two and tell
people, "If you dream of a car going downhill it means you are
worried about a relationship out of control." Concepts other than a
relationship in trouble also have an overlap with cars in motion. I
have examples of persons who were concerned that their lives were
not quite in control, that they were "losing control of their lives," who
also dream about a car going downhill out of control. Sometimes, as
discussed, a technique such as free association or simply thinking
about one's life will make it absolutely clear what emotional concern
is being pictured. Sometimes we will remain unsure. Occasionally
someone who is worried neither about relationship, nor about life
being out of control, may dream of a car going downhill out of
control. We have to admit that perhaps there are also smaller concerns pictured in this way, or perhaps we just don't know enough to
explain this particular person's dream image.

It may seem that we have used metaphor in two different
senses—a simple noting of similarities—"Joe is a wolf" or "Jim turns
into my father"—as opposed to explanatory metaphor such as "this
relationship in trouble is like a trip in a car with poor brakes."
However, I do not believe the two are as different as they appear.
Both of these somewhat different senses of metaphor can be understood in terms of our basic concept of dreaming as making connections, especially in the broader and less structured portions of our
nets. A simple noting of similarities means bringing together portions of the nets in the ways we have discussed. In cases where one of
these portions involves an abstract, complex, or difficult concept, a
noting of similarities may indeed be explanatory. A term such as
"life" or "relationship" is obviously complex, and for most of us is

represented in many patterns in many parts of the net. If even a portion of the patterns representing life or a relationship corresponds closely with the network representing something simpler like a car trip, the dream may picture it. It will be explanatory metaphor based on a noting of similarities between the pattern representing something relatively simple and picturable, and a portion of the pattern representing something relatively complex.

As I see it, this noting of similarities is not an active process that requires a little man inside the head (a homunculus) making decisions to bring these two items together or throwing switches to allow excitation to move to a new subnet. Rather, I see it as a description of what happens as excitation plays across the nets of the mind, more loosely or broadly in dreaming, guided by the dominant emotion or emotional concern. If the person has just been traumatized and the dominant emotions are fear and terror, the flow of excitation will be to portions of the net representing images of terror, such as tidal waves, onrushing trains, or being chased by a monster. If the guiding emotional concern involves worries about a relationship—"this could be dangerous," or "this is getting out of control"—the excited regions will include the notion of going downhill, going faster, spinning out of control, failing brakes. Such excitation leads to and *is* in fact the picturing of a car going downhill out of control. Of course, this is not the only sort of image activated by such a concern about a relationship. The concern may also activate images of walking along dangerous paths, being caught in landslides, or houses falling apart and needing repair. This sort of emotional concern will be much less likely to lead to other regions involved in the storage of "relationship"—for instance, images of a wedding or images of two trees intertwined. Among the many potential images dealing with relationships that our nets have the ability to picture, the choice will be made according to what fits with the dreamer's emotional concern. No decisions have to be made or switches thrown. The propensity to produce an image of a car going rapidly downhill is simply what is there—what is stored in that pattern in the net.

Of course the specific image that comes up will be determined by various other factors, including cultural ones. For instance, in a culture that has no experience with wolves and where people do not read stories about wolves, the image of a wolf as something dangerous and threatening is unlikely to come up. Rather, the patterns we talked about might lead to images of a locally dangerous animal such as a wildcat or a jaguar. And in areas where a car is rarely seen and is considered a luxury item owned only by foreigners, a car is unlikely to be the typical image chosen for concerns about a relationship; the dreamer may instead dream about a bicycle or a cart.

I believe that noting similarities and bringing subnets close together are basic to dreaming and probably occur in every dream, but this does not mean that the similarities are necessarily obvious to the more focused, thick-boundaried waking mind. Jim's girlfriend found the dream similarity to her father clear. She states, "Odd that I'd never noticed that before"; likewise, the dreamers of tidal wave dreams, if they think about it, usually say, "Yes, that expresses just the way I feel; totally overwhelmed." But often the meaning of the dream is not obvious to the waking mind. Someone who dreams of rolling downhill in a car with the brakes malfunctioning, and who is in fact in a difficult relationship that is getting out of control, will not necessarily make the connection. Depending on many factors, she may forget the dream entirely, or remember it briefly but pay no attention to it, brushing it off as nonsense, or may take it literally and decide to check the car's brakes. Or, she may see it as a sign that someone will have an accident. If for some reason this person becomes interested in understanding the dream and works on it alone or with a therapist or someone else, she may come to notice the similarity with the relationship she is in, and then is likely to say, "Oh sure, that's so obvious; why didn't I think of it sooner?"

Some people seem to be better dream interpreters than others, or at least better at interpreting their own dreams. Who are these people? Aristotle answered this question long ago, using approximately the terms we have been using: "A good dream interpreter is one who notices similarities."[17]

THE DREAM AS METAPHOR AND CONTINUITY

All of this discussion of powerful metaphors in dreams does not imply that every element of every dream is an explanatory metaphor or can be seen as an emotional concern pictured as an image in the dream. There is also an element of "continuity"—an ongoing background that takes the form of imagery very close to or identical to that of our usual world. In fact a large part of many dreams consists of such background imagery or background plot. Even the most powerful dreams of tidal waves or chases by gangs also have more ordinary portions that seem to serve as continuity: "I was walking along a beach that was a bit like a beach on Cape Cod when suddenly. . . ." The car going downhill out of control may pass some more or less familiar-looking sign posts, signs, lampposts, or buildings. The dream does not present a metaphoric image simply in a static form like a painting on a wall. As has often been noted, dream scenes are somewhat similar to the scenes of a movie.

My conclusion from the many dreams I have studied, especially after trauma and in stressful situations, is that often the metaphoric image—the image that appears to be contextualizing or picturing an emotional concern—somehow stands out and might be considered the clearest or most vivid or most important part of the dream, but it seldom stands alone. There is usually a background of other elements, which can be traced if the dreamer is willing to figure them out. Often these elements have some relationship to the important metaphoric portion, the contextualizing image. There may be material that is associated by time or place of occurrence with an important metaphoric element. These are what author Bert States refers to as the metonymic elements of dreams—the chains of more or less accidental associations that "pull in" a number of related elements in the wake of an important metaphor.[18]

In some dreams, especially when there is nothing awfully important happening emotionally in the person's life, the entire dream seems to be background imagery or plot without any clear-cut metaphor or contextualizing image; although with interpretation, such ordinary dreams can lead to something interesting and meaningful. In fact, a number of workers have commented on the ordinariness of most of the dreams collected from random samples of normal subjects. One study, for instance, has found the average dreams collected in the sleep laboratory to be surprisingly ordinary and mundane.[19] A detailed examination of children's dreams concluded, "The most striking observation about children's dreams . . . lay in the surprising degree of mundane realism in the baseline content of children's dreams."[20] Another study, examining the photographic quality of dreams, asked a number of subjects to compare their dream images with photographs that had been altered along a number of dimensions. Generally they chose the unaltered, most realistic, ordinary photographs.[21] Thus the picture quality of the dream, as well as much of the content, may be quite ordinary.

It is worth remembering that the basic perceptual world of dreams is very much like our waking perceptual imagery as we move through the world; it often consists of quite ordinary pictures in motion. The metaphoric material is central and it sometimes stands out from the rest and appears unusually powerful, vivid, or bizarre; but then the dreamer or other characters react to it in fairly predictable ways.[22]

Overall, we have explored in this chapter how dreaming deals with our emotional concerns, specifically by portraying them in the form of picture metaphor. Metaphor is found everywhere in our mental processes, but especially when we get away from calculating or typing and move to the right on our continuum toward dreaming.

Our consideration of metaphor joins the two major strands developed earlier in our views of dreaming: (1) dreaming makes connections more broadly than waking, and (2) dreaming is guided by the dominant emotion—dreaming contextualizes emotion. The broad connection-making leads to bringing together subnets in the mind, finding overlaps between patterns, and thus noting and picturing similarities ("Jim is like my father"). But there are so many overlaps between patterns, so many possible similarities. Which will be chosen? The one that is consistent with the dreamer's dominant emotion or emotional concern. The one that allows not just a similarity (yes, relationships are sort of like a car trip) but an explanation of the dreamer's emotional state of mind—an explanatory metaphor. A car going downhill with poor brakes explains metaphorically this particular dreamer's emotional concern about this specific relationship.

Chapter Seven

THE FUNCTIONS
OF DREAMING

DOES DREAMING HAVE A FUNCTION?

In the previous chapters I outlined my views about the basic nature of dreaming and how dreaming differs from waking. Dreams make connections more broadly than waking in the nets of the mind—not randomly, but guided by the dominant emotion or emotional concern. Dreams contextualize emotion. Dreams notice similarities and produce explanatory metaphor. But is this simply the way things are, or does it all have one or more functions? Is making broad connections useful in some way? Is picturing or contextualizing an emotional concern in pictured metaphor of use to us in some way? Perhaps not. Many researchers, including myself, have suggested that the biological state of REM sleep has a definite biological function for the body—namely, restoration or regulation of some kind (see later)—and that perhaps that's all there is. Perhaps REM sleep plays its biological role in the body and dreaming is an epiphenomenon—it tags along without any importance of its own. In this view, dreaming is simply what we experience consciously while REM sleep is doing its thing. At one time I took this position and suggested that dreaming was useful as a window to let us see what was going on in REM sleep but did not necessarily have an additional function of its own.[1]

However, at this point I think we can go further. Based on the studies and clinical material surveyed in the last chapters, we can make at least a guess as to one or more possible functions of dreaming. Although it is very difficult to prove ideas about function, there is research that is at least compatible with these views. Since the proposed functions deal with the integration of trauma and new experience, we must first discuss the nature of trauma and its effect on the mind.

TRAUMA AND TRAUMATIC MEMORY

Trauma is generally defined as a wound or a shock, or more specifically, a startling, disturbing experience that has a profound effect on mental life. Thus by its very definition, trauma is something that can produce longlasting effects.

The nature of these effects has been the subject of great interest and great debate for at least the past 100 years. Pierre Janet, a French psychiatrist, wrote several major works exploring the psychological effects of trauma, and in fact a great deal of what he says is very consistent with modern research and thinking. Janet suggested that under ordinary circumstances, the thoughts, sensations, and emotions derived from any new experience are united in what he calls a single consciousness. This successful uniting, which he also calls integration, depends on fitting new experiences into existing cognitive schemata or frameworks. Sometimes, however, events do not fit into the cognitive schemata. Janet refers to these as events accompanied by "vehement emotion" and a "destruction of the psychological system." He then goes on to discuss how severe trauma produces many longlasting psychological problems.[2]

Sigmund Freud was also struck by the importance of trauma, and for a time he theorized that the neuroses he dealt with were to a great extent caused by childhood sexual trauma. He later changed his mind and suggested that in most cases childhood sexual wishes and fantasies rather than actual events were involved.[3]

In recent years the importance of trauma in producing a variety of psychological effects and psychiatric conditions has been reemphasized. Though psychiatric terminology is not fixed and has been changing somewhat every few years, it is worth noting that the current psychiatric classification, DSM-IV, recognizes a number of different conditions that can be caused by or at least partially caused by severe trauma.[4] There is Posttraumatic Stress Disorder involving nightmares and other intrusions such as flashbacks, as well as avoidance of whatever reminds one of trauma. We have discussed this in Chapter 2. There are also Dissociative Disorders characterized by strange lapses, losses of time, and disorientation; the most extreme type is called Dissociative Identity Disorder, formerly Multiple Personality Disorder. Also influenced by trauma, though sometimes not as obviously, are Anxiety Disorders, Somatization Disorders (in which a patient has a number of bodily symptoms without a clear-cut cause), and sometimes Depressive Disorders. In any case there is little question that trauma can have profound and long-lasting effects.[5]

It has been recognized since Janet that traumatic memories are somehow different from ordinary memories. Traumatic memory is a kind of intrusion in which the normal process of making and developing connections, producing ordinary memories and categories, is disrupted. It is recognized that one of the basic tasks of human development is gradually making sense of the world—not only integrating new material into existing schemata but developing new schemata, so that the world gradually becomes labeled, understandable, and safe. Therefore, unintegrated traumatic memories can obviously be disruptive, especially if they occur in childhood.

It is generally accepted that traumatic memory is not processed as other memories are. Something is stuck. For instance, author Doris Lessing wrote of her father:

> His childhood and his young man's memories, kept fluid, were added to, grew, as living memories do. But his war memories were congealed, stories that he told again and again, with the same words and gestures, in stereotyped phrases. [In this region of his mind] nothing is true but horror, expressed inarticulately, in brief, bitter exclamations of rage, incredulity, betrayal.[6]

Over and over, authors describing traumatic memories speak of lack of integration, of the traumatic memory being kept apart like a painful abscess, disconnected from the remainder of life. And it is generally suggested that the healing process after trauma involves integration or reintegration or reconnecting of these walled-off areas.

There is a considerable literature on the ways such healing and recon-nection can occur in a safe relationship provided by psychotherapy.[7] We will discuss this later on. I suggest that the process of dreaming may play a role in this integration or connection making as well.

DREAMING AND RECOVERY FROM TRAUMA

If we recall our discussion about the dreams of people who have experienced a severe trauma, we can glimpse at least the outlines of something functional happening. We have seen that their dreams pull together or make connections between the traumatic event and other kinds of traumas, stresses, and events in their lives, guided by the dominant emotions, first usually fear and terror, and later also involve guilt, shame, grief, and others. This may be a useful process, since obviously the posttraumatic state is a very disturbing one for the person, and perhaps the process of connection-making and pic-turing images during dreaming may reduce this disturbance by increasing interconnections and thus spreading out excitation.

This may not be immediately obvious, so let's look at it in terms of the various incomplete but nonetheless useful metaphors we have employed. If we think of the mind as a net in the concrete sense of a fishnet or a piece of woven cloth, we can think of trauma as a kind of tear in the net and the process of making connections as a reweaving. If we think of the situation after trauma as a storm-tossed sea with mountainous waves rearing up, then dreaming may be something that smooths out the water, disperses the storm's energy, and gradu-ally calms the seas. Or if we think of a kind of electrical grid with excessive excitation in one area and lack of excitation in others, dreaming may be "calming," by spreading out the excitation. None of these are full pictures of course, but they begin to give us an idea of what could be going on.

In terms of the actual but insufficiently understood neural nets in our minds, there mathematical models are being developed to describe various states of a complex net system. A net can be in a number of more or less unstable states; unstable states are characterized by higher "computational energy."[8] The net tries in various ways to settle into a state of greater equilibrium or lower computational energy. We can think of the terrified posttraumatic state as a time when the net remains in an unstable state with high computational energy. Then various processes that allow interconnecting or rechannelling, including perhaps dreaming, will gradually produce a lowering of this computational energy and an increase in mathematical "harmony."[9]

What emerges from these various attempts at picturing the situation after trauma is two closely linked functions of dreaming, which may be two parts of the same function. First, dreams reduce the disturbance or calm the storm, not randomly but by an emotion-guided increase in connections; second, this increase of connections can be adaptive for the future. I am speaking not of a consolidation of memory[10] but rather a broadening of memory through cross-connections, which may be useful in increasing adaptation for future functioning. Thus, a new trauma or stress will be less "singular," less catastrophic, more familiar, and more assimilable since broader connections are already available. In other words, we could say dreaming calms by cross-connecting.

In the anthropomorphic terms we have used previously, the original severe trauma may appear to produce a reaction that is somewhat like, "Help! I am absolutely terrified! I am helpless! This is the most horrible thing that has ever happened to anyone. I cannot survive this." But a future disturbance, after dreaming and other adaptive processes have occurred, will produce relatively less of this reaction and more of "Yes, this feels terrible but it's a bit like . . . ," "I've experienced something like this, others have too . . . and we've survived," or "I've worked on these feelings . . . they're scary but I have a context for them. . . . I can connect them with the rest of my world."

Another way of thinking about this is that dreaming can be therapeutic. In Chapter 8 I will consider many similarities between dreaming and dynamic psychotherapy; I believe that both can be thought of as making connections in a safe place.

A Contemporary Theory of Dream Function

What I am proposing in terms of the therapeutic, calming-by-cross-connecting function of dreaming is, I believe, considerably different from the views of Sigmund Freud, though there are certain similarities that we will discuss. It is also very different from the views of those who believe dreaming to be pure noise or junk to be discarded. However, the view I am suggesting is compatible with a number of recent theories of dreaming developed by authors starting from very different data bases but all concluding that there is some sort of adaptive, therapeutic, or problem-solving function of dreaming.

The psychoanalysts Thomas French and Erich Fromm wrote a detailed clinical work on dream interpretation in 1964 based on material from their clinical practices. Although these authors remain in agreement with Freud that the basic nature of dreaming is wish fulfillment and that a function of dreaming is to preserve sleep, they nonetheless add that dreaming has a function in solving or attempting to solve emotional problems.[11] They speak of "empathic groping" in dreams and provide a number of examples in which the dream appears to be grappling with and attempting to solve a current emotional problem. They emphasize that each current problem is a derivative of one or more nuclear conflicts from the dreamer's past. Such emotional problem solving is certainly related to what I have outlined here.

More recently, Ramon Greenberg and Chester Pearlman in Boston have continued clinical explorations along the lines initiated by French and Fromm and have added research work on REM sleep as well. Concerning function they suggest, "The dream represents the dreamer's effort to cope with a currently meaningful issue," and they emphasize especially that it is an "attempt to solve a current problem." Also, their studies "suggest a role in adaptation to emotionally important situations."[12]

Psychologist Louis Breger and his associates performed excellent studies on dreaming in several well-defined stressful situations, which we reviewed in Chapter 3. Their studies were designed to investigate the hypothesis that "dreams may serve a unique function in the integration or assimilation of affectively aroused information into these solutions embodied in existing memory systems." After presenting their studies, however, they modify this: "Something more must be done with dreams if they are to have an effect on a person's life." In other words, "One must work hard at making individual sense of one's dreams if they are to be more than fleeting, uninformative glimpses of what is within."[13]

Psychologist and sleep researcher Rosalind Cartwright suggests, based on her studies of men and women going through a divorce, that dreams have a role in adaptation to stressful situations.[14] She also provides the beginnings of some "outcome data" (see below).

Psychologist Harry Fiss has performed a number of studies involving subliminal perception and dreaming, on the basis of which he has suggested a "signal detection" function of dreaming.[15] This is related to what we have spoken about in a previous chapter about the dream somehow picking up body stimuli before they are accessible to waking consciousness. He also speaks more generally of the dream as a facilitator of self-understanding, and he comes up with a broad view of dreams as "facilitating the development, maintenance, and restoration of the self."[16] Another psychologist, Richard Jones, also suggests that the dream may perform "ego synthetic as well as ego defensive" functions—a slightly different way of describing the adaptive function of dreams.[17]

Several sleep laboratory studies also lend support to some kind of adaptive function. For instance, a group of psychologists including Goodenough and others and more recently David Koulack analyzed a group of studies involving the effects of pre-sleep films on dream content.[18] Based on these studies Koulack devised a complex adaptive theory in which dreams play a role in mastering stress, in several distinct stages.[19]

An intriguing model of dreaming has been developed by psychoanalyst Stanley Palombo. He calls it a "memory-cycle model." According to this model, a dream compares the memory of a significant past event with an emotionally significant part of the previous day's experience. The dream functions to match past and present experience to determine the proper memory location of the new experience.[20]

Psychiatrist Milton Kramer and his group have performed a number of studies on mood and dreams, leading to a "mood regulatory" function of dreaming, which is very compatible with what I have spoken of as "calming a storm." We discuss these studies below.

Thus many researchers, starting with different dream material, have suggested similar or at least compatible versions of an adaptive theory of dreaming. Perhaps we could jointly call this the "Contemporary Theory of the Functions of Dreaming," to which I hope I have made a contribution by adding the essential posttrauma dream series (the clearest case), and by clarifying the basic nature of dreaming, as noted in previous chapters. Of course, the fact that authors starting in very different places have reached similar conclusions, though encouraging, certainly does not prove the conclusions.

RESEARCH RELATING TO THE FUNCTIONS OF DREAMING

Let me state first of all that there is absolutely no research proving any particular theory of the functions of dreaming. This should hardly come as a surprise. Function is notoriously difficult to prove; in fact, a problem that ought to be simpler—the functions of sleep—has still not been resolved. I wrote an entire book in 1973 summarizing work on the functions of sleep in which I proposed distinct functions for REM and non-REM sleep.[21] There is now general agreement that sleep has a function and in fact that REM and non-REM sleep have separate functions, but there is still disagreement on the exact nature of these functions.

Although much research may be relevant in various ways, it does not establish a given view of function. For instance, supposing that all my studies and investigations on dreams after trauma, in stress, etc., were clearly confirmed by many others and my quantitative results on contextualizing images were similarly confirmed, this would certainly not prove, or even strongly support, my suggestion that the process is functional in terms of weaving in and adaptation. To demonstrate an adaptive function, I would have to show for instance some clear differences indicating better adaptation in persons who had dreamt and made connections following trauma as opposed to persons who had not. This is very hard to do, especially since we do not know of a situation where persons do not do any dreaming.[22]

There is one research project that at least approaches such a design and tries to measure adaptation. Rosalind Cartwright, whose work I have referred to before, has for some years been studying men and women undergoing the very stressful situation of divorce. Her group collected dreams from these people and also assessed their status using interviews and questionnaires, which led to a number of interesting findings. The finding of direct relevance here is that those who in the early days of the divorce reported more dreams about their spouses were coping better one year later on some measures (for instance, less depressed on one standard measure of depression) than were those who did not have such dreams.[23] This is a preliminary finding and can be interpreted in several ways, but it fits with the view that dreaming has an adaptive function.

Milton Kramer has gathered some relevant data on large groups of normal subjects. He has found that on a number of mood scales, a subject's mood reliably scores better in the morning than in the evening (a lower score on the "unhappiness" scale of the Clyde Mood Scales). A relationship was found between the change in unhappiness and certain aspects of dream content—most consistently, the number of characters in the dream: Subjects whose dreams contained more characters had greater improvement on morning mood on this scale. The results lend support to what Kramer calls a mood-regulating function of dreaming, similar to what we have spoken of as "calming a storm."[24]

Though the research data are certainly not conclusive, there appears to be a growing consensus, or at least overlap, among these various theories of function. And I believe all these views are very consistent with what I have proposed above.

I have spoken quite little so far about REM sleep, but we will discuss this more in Chapter 11 when we consider studies of REM deprivation. Dreaming should not be confused with the biological state of REM sleep. Nonetheless, most of our memorable dreams come from REM sleep, which is the biological place best suited for dreaming activity to occur; thus, a theory of the functions of dreaming should at least be compatible with the functions of REM sleep. The function of dreaming proposed here in terms of making connections and cross-connections certainly can be related to the well-known theory that REM sleep, especially in young organisms, helps to develop the nervous system[25]—presumably by making or organizing new connections. It is also compatible with the view that REM sleep functions in the "repair, reorganization, and formation of new connections in amine-dependent forebrain systems" (the cerebral cortex), summarized by the author in Shakespeare's phrase, "knitting up the raveled sleeve of care."[26]

Critics skeptical about any function of dreaming often question how dreams can be important if most of them are forgotten. I suggest that remembering an individual dream is not what is essential, though sometimes, as we shall see later, a remembered dream image can be extremely important in learning about oneself or even in producing a work of science or art. What is most important is probably the making of cross-connections in the mind nets, the broader redistribution of connection weights, etc., all of which can occur whether or not the actual dream content is remembered. Of course, it must be admitted that all our thoughts and theories about dreaming— including the present one—are necessarily based on examination of the subset of dreams that have been remembered.

*   *   *

In summary, what I have done here is suggest one group of functions for dreaming, namely, that dreaming interconnects or cross-connects, and calms the mind by cross-connecting. I have pointed out that this function agrees with a number of functions suggested by others during the past decades, and thus we might call it a contemporary theory of dreaming. I have also pointed out that this function is compatible with some of the functions suggested for REM sleep—the state underlying most dreaming. Overall, however, I must admit that this view of dream function, although consistent with a great deal of data, has certainly not been proven. This should hardly surprise us. First, as we have noted, we are still ignorant of the functions of sleep, which ought to be easier to pin down and understand. Secondly, we should recall that despite our occasional discussion of dreaming as though it were an isolated state, we actually consider it one end of a continuum, not totally separable from day-dreaming, reverie, and the remainder of the continuum. In these terms we might say that having the entire wake–dream continuum available is useful to us, but we would hardly expect to find a totally unique and distinct function for dreaming.

In this sense the functions proposed are not totally restricted to dreaming. Dreaming, at the right-hand end of the continuum, may simply be the best place (though not the only place) for reweaving and cross-connecting. There are other settings for "making connections in a safe place," as we shall see in the next chapter.

Chapter Eight

THE USES OF DREAMS

Self-Knowledge, Dreamworking, and Psychotherapy

In the last chapter we examined some possible basic functions of dreaming in terms of calming a storm by interconnecting or cross-connecting material in the mind. In this chapter I will discuss some further functions and uses of dreaming in terms of possible relationships among dreaming, psychotherapy, and more informal forms of dream understanding known as dreamworking. I will first consider whether dreaming itself can be considered in some ways a form of psychotherapy. Is dreaming itself therapeutic? We will then consider different ways in which remembered dreams can be used in psychotherapy and dreamworking.

Is DREAMING PSYCHOTHERAPY?[1]

I would like to suggest not only that dreams can be useful in therapy in many ways, as I discuss later, but also that dreaming bears similarities to psychotherapy, and that dreaming itself can be considered a form of therapy.

Definitions: Similarities between Dreaming and Psychotherapy

To argue that dreaming is psychotherapy or at least that there are significant similarities, it would be desirable to have precise and universally accepted definitions of dreaming and psychotherapy. However, although we appear to know what we mean by dreaming and by psychotherapy, we do not have a very clean, precise definition of either term.

For now I will be satisfied with a very broad, practical definition of dreaming. We all more or less accept Aristotle's original definition of dreaming as "mental activity during sleep." Research over the past decades makes it clear that we are talking about mental activity that occurs primarily or most readily in REM sleep, although similar dream reports can at times be obtained from non-REM sleep and especially from periods of sleep onset as well.[2] Dreaming activity has some obvious differences from focused waking activity in that it is more perceptual, is less verbal, and has a less intentional quality.[3] Dreaming can be thought of as a language in which we express ourselves at certain times, and which is considerably different from the thinking and verbal language we generally employ during waking. Some specific differences are important to our argument below.

Psychotherapy, again, is not easy to define, though we all more or less know what it is. Psychotherapy consists of two people (or more, in family and group therapy), occupying appropriate furniture, talking together, and attempting to help one of them (the patient, or client) feel better and solve his or her problems. However, there is imperfect agreement as to what is central to the process. For Freud psychoanalysis was defined as "making the unconscious conscious" or "where id was, ego shall be."[4] This describes the end result of what goes on in dynamic psychotherapy or psychoanalysis. But what allows this to happen? Various authors have emphasized in their descriptions aspects such as the setting, the trust between patient and therapist, the therapeutic alliance or bond that must occur to allow the uncovering work to proceed, the clarification and interpretation provided by the analyst, and the emotional "working through" by the patient. There is a broad definition attributed to Jung (though neither I nor a number of Jungian analysts have been able to find an exact quote) calling therapy a well-sealed vessel or container within which psychological work can be done. A sealed vessel is a useful concept and refers to a good therapeutic relationship or alliance and its various elements.

In therapy it is often emphasized that one must first establish an alliance—a relationship between therapist and patient in which the patient feels safe and trusting—and then start to do psychological work. Writings by a number of authors on the treatment of traumatized patients place a special emphasis on the container or safe place.[5] After a safe environment has been established, the patient can begin to tell her or his story and try to integrate the trauma.

Overall, I believe a useful attempt at a definition would be to say that psychotherapy involves *making connections in a safe place*.[6] I would argue that dreaming can be considered in the same way: making connections in a safe place. A safe place is provided by the bed, by the state of sleep, and especially by REM sleep, during which there is profound muscular paralysis that effectively prevents the dreamer from acting out the dream.[7] REM sleep is ideal from this point of view, but the other circumstances in which dreams or dreamlike activity occur are somewhat similar, though they involve muscle relaxation rather than true muscular paralysis. These include lying in bed during non-REM sleep, hypnagogic states, half-dozing or reverie, and daydreaming. We do not engage in dreaming while involved in active waking activities, especially not while involved in dangerous activities in "unsafe places." Dreaming involves the making of broad connections, as we have seen in previous chapters. We have examined how dreaming makes connections more broadly than waking by using pictured metaphor and have followed the connection making from immediately posttraumatic to various less dramatic situations. Connections are made between the trauma, the stressful events, the current problem, leftover daytime material (called day residues), and other material in the dreamer's mind, guided by the dominant emotion or concern.

Although a great deal more happens in psychotherapy, establishing a safe place and making connections are two of the most important elements. Connections in therapy can be of many kinds: Sometimes it is important simply to see anew, to remove from repression, something important that can then be integrated into one's life.

Sometimes seeing connections among different figures in one's present and past life is significant. Often the therapeutic process involves investigating and clarifying the connections between aspects of a current relationship and similar aspects of past relationships.

Other Similarities between Dreaming and Therapy

One important element of therapy is that the patient is asked, explicitly or implicitly, to try to substitute verbal activity—talking and trying to understand things in therapy—for "acting out." Rather than repeatedly getting into fights, or repetitively entering into inappropriate relationships, the patient is asked to try to stay put, to free-associate, to experience the relevant feelings and work on them in the therapeutic session.

It is worth noting that this injunction—"work on your problems here but don't act out"—occurs in dreaming as well. The well-established muscle paralysis of REM sleep ensures that the dreamer will be lying quietly in bed, experiencing a dream rather than acting out the dream.[8]

Another similarity is that some sort of free association occurs in both therapy and dreaming. Free association is an important technique of psychoanalysis and psychotherapy, and in fact it was called by Freud the primary rule of psychoanalysis. It involves asking the patient to say whatever comes to mind, regardless of how silly, disconnected, or embarrassing it may be. In dreaming, the same thing happens automatically. Dreaming, as we have discussed, is a spontaneous state of extremely free association in which our associations are not bound by the usual waking rules, and self-criticism is greatly reduced. One of the most salient characteristics of ordinary (nonlucid) dreaming[9] is our lack of surprise at and criticism of the dream content. Strange, frightening, and bizarre events emerge without our saying within the dream: "Hey, this is crazy. This is impossible."

There are also notable similarities in terms of affect or emotion. Emotion plays many roles in therapy. There are ups and downs in mood. Anxiety, anger, or sadness emerges as meaningful material is uncovered. But in a global sense, what happens in successful therapy is that as new connections are made, as difficult material is examined and integrated, painful emotions such as anxiety are reduced and give way to more positive emotions. There is evidence that the same thing happens in dreaming. The change in mood is most visible when examining a series of dreams after trauma, as discussed above, in which early dreams are fraught with overwhelming terror and later ones involve less extreme and more varied emotions. However, the same process can be seen in the course of a night, in examining evening and morning mood in self-report ratings. Mood is slightly more positive, with less variability in the morning. Dreaming seems to have a "mood-stabilizing" effect, as we have seen.

Some Differences between Dreaming and Therapy (which may also reveal similarities)

I have discussed certain important similarities between dreaming and psychotherapy. But of course it would be totally ridiculous to state that the two are identical. There are some clear differences, a brief examination of which may prove instructive.

First, there is an obvious difference in personnel. The dreamer dreams alone while the patient in therapy has another person present, variously used as ally, monitor, guide, teacher, identification figure, and transference figure. The real relationship with the therapist, and consequently the possibility of comparing and contrasting real and fantasized relationships, is a province of therapy that cannot be approached in dreaming. This is one extremely important advantage of therapy, and I in no way argue that dreaming can replace therapy here. A person who has been traumatized, especially one who has suffered trauma such as physical or sexual abuse by another person, often suffers more than anything else from disruption of personal relationships. Everyone, or at least everyone in authority, seems dangerous or threatening. Here the interpersonal relationship of therapy can be tremendously healing; a two-person relationship is absolutely essential in the healing process.

Second, the modality or language is clearly different. Therapy uses verbal and to a lesser extent nonverbal communication (such as body language and tone of voice) between patient and therapist. Dreaming makes connections using an entire language of its own, involving picture metaphor and a movielike recreation of reality that appears considerably different from the mode used in most therapy. This is a clear difference, but I believe it applies most to the "ordinary" or "preparatory" work of therapy and applies least to the important moments of therapy involving a new insight, or an "aha experience." These emotional moments when important connections are made often involve visual or other perceptual modalities:

> I suddenly saw it. It came to me in a flash. I saw my mother criticizing me, and turning away from me. And I realize that's just what I have been doing to my children. . . . I feel like screaming.

The experience is definitely not verbal; the patient may describe it verbally, but there is often a sense of an inadequate, incomplete portrayal, as in using words to describe a powerful dream.

A third apparent difference relates to remembering versus forgetting. Dreams are frequently forgotten; many people never or hardly ever recall a dream. Thus, if dreaming has a useful role or function, it probably performs this function even when dreams are not recalled. On the other hand, one assumes that therapy occurs in a normal waking state and that its interactions should be remembered as are other daily activities. Yet this is often not true; it has been noted by a number of analysts that, surprisingly, even in treatment considered successful by patient and therapist, the patient is unable to remember in much detail what actually happens during analysis and is unable to describe what appears to be important in the successful result. Apparently important connections may be made but not consciously remembered in therapy as well as in dreaming.

Fourth, place or setting is manifestly different in dreaming versus therapy. Psychotherapy (unlike most dreaming) takes place in an office or consulting room. However, it should be noted that the therapist and patient do not run around the office, play Ping-Pong, debate politics, or indulge in other activities of waking life. Rather, the emphasis is on peace, quiet, and relaxation. It has often been emphasized that certain aspects of the setting are especially helpful to psychoanalysis or psychotherapy, including quiet, lack of inter-ruption, use of a couch or comfortable chair, and dim lighting. All of these aspects of the setting help the patient free-associate and "re-gress" (get in touch with feelings and experiences from an earlier time). To put it differently, these aspects of the setting let the patient enter a dreamlike or at least daydreamlike state in which free associa-tion and making connections are easier. Thus, the "place" of therapy is arranged to be somewhat similar to the relaxed "place" experi-enced every night in dreaming, and this apparent difference in set-ting is not in fact as drastic as it seems at first glance.

Finally, time or scheduling also appears to be considerably dif-ferent. Therapy is a solidly scheduled activity, usually occurring one to five times per week for sessions of close to 50 minutes (occa-sionally as short as 30 or as long as 90 minutes). It is accepted that some such length of time is required; therapeutic work can very rarely be done in a session of one minute or five minutes.[10] Inter-estingly, the time devoted to REM sleep, the best time for dreaming, is not radically different. REM sleep averages 60 to 150 minutes per night, and an individual REM period late during the night, when the most dreamlike dreams occur, lasts 20 to 40 minutes. A comparison of dream reports from those later, long-REM periods with reports from early, much shorter-REM periods demonstrates that the later dreams are much richer and include more emotional material and more childhood material.[11] If indeed psychological "work" is being done in REM periods along the lines we have suggested, it is proba-bly done especially in the late 20- to 40-minute REM periods. Thus, the time periods required for adequate therapy and dreaming are not as different as they may first seem.

This consideration of obvious differences between dreaming and therapy has revealed that some of these differences are not as absolute as they first appear, and may actually reveal some important underlying similarities.

The Functions of Dreaming and Therapy

I have discussed some intriguing similarities between dreaming and therapy not simply to make an amusing analogy but also because I believe there may be a deeper underlying connection—a functional connection. I am suggesting that dreaming and therapy fulfill somewhat similar functions, and that we can learn about each by examining these similarities. In other words, "making connections in a safe place" may be an important and useful process. Indeed, the progression we have examined in dreaming as well as in therapy after trauma suggests a functional role in the integration of traumatic material.

First, let us look at therapy and see whether the suggested similarities to dreaming can help us understand its uses. Even though, historically, dynamic psychotherapy derives from psychoanalysis, which was "invented" more or less singlehandedly by Freud in an attempt to cure his neurotic patients, it may nonetheless be useful for us to think of psychotherapy not as a totally new "invention"—a scalpel devised for removing a tumor—but rather as an attempt to heal and integrate, which may well turn out to be similar to a natural function of the body and brain, such as dreaming. This is not an exceptional situation. For example, in the healing of a skin wound, the body has a whole series of natural mechanisms: leukocytes to ingest foreign material, fibroblasts to bring together the open edges of the wound, dermal cells to generate new skin, and so on. Medicine, by adding antiseptics and antibiotics as well as stitches and staples to join the tissues, is simply assisting nature's processes. In fact, Freud compared psychoanalysis to the cleaning and bandaging work of the surgeon who clears away obstacles and lets nature heal. He quotes the French surgeon Paré: "I bandaged; God healed."[12]

This view suggests also that sometimes nature needs only to take its course. A certain degree of psychological healing will occur simply with the passage of time, which among other things allows dreaming to occur. Sometimes psychotherapy can facilitate the healing process. Of course when psychotherapy is used, it is not a substitute for dreaming but an addition to it. The two processes can work together. Dreaming, as we have seen, makes connections in its own style, which may be useful in integrating or weaving in new material. This process can occur in the absence of therapy, and even without dream recall. However, recall of dreams and working on them in therapy adds to and facilitates the process. One can, in fact, imagine three processes that work together when all are available: First, at the most basic level, dreaming makes certain connections guided by emotion, probably important in the integration of new experience as we have seen. This occurs whether or not there is dream recall or ongoing therapy. Second, when dreams *are* recalled, the dreamer can consciously reflect on the dream material and sometimes make further useful connections, gain insight, and occasionally even solve important problems (see Chap. 9). Third, when in addition the dreamer is in therapy, the connections and insights obtained from the dream, as well as other material that comes up, can be explored and developed in the therapeutic relationship. When the three processes work together successfully, the dreamer feels not only that she has understood a particular dream, but that she can see a relationship, or an important part of her life, in new ways. There are now fewer loose ends; bits and pieces that made no sense now fall into place. There is a sense of togetherness and thus of feeling better because she knows what is going on and is more in charge of her life. All of this can result from successfully "making connections in a safe place."

This argument further suggests that the situations in which therapy is likely to be most useful are those in which dreaming appears to be helpful as well—specifically in the resolution and integration of trauma, in adaptation to stressful situations, and in dealing with stressful problems of everyday life. Conversely, there are situations in which neither type of "making connections" appears to help—for instance, illnesses such as severe depression (known as Major Affective Disorder) in which dream recall is poor and where I can find little evidence in my patients' records of progress in making useful connections in dreams. Similarly, there is a consensus among clinicians that dynamic psychotherapy (without medication) is seldom or never the treatment of choice in this type of depression.

Second, I believe that we can learn something about the functions of dreaming by examining its relationship to therapy. Usually we clarify or explain an entity by comparing it to something better understood; we explain one concept in terms of a simpler one. In this sense it may seem strange to suggest that we can be helped in understanding a relatively simple one-person activity such as dreaming—

usually occurring during a relatively well-defined biological state—
by comparing it to a large, ill-defined, two-person social interaction
such as therapy. In many ways, it is true that therapy is complex and
poorly understood; however, in at least one way we know more
about therapy. Since it has been designed as a medical or quasi-
medical treatment for certain problems or disorders, we at least
know what its function is, or is intended to be. This function is
obviously to treat, to help the patient deal with trauma and stress,
find new solutions for life's problems, examine and ameliorate his
relationships, and deal with disturbing emotions. Therefore, if we
take the many similarities between dreaming and therapy seriously, I
would suggest that a function of dreaming is to help us in all the
above situations. In other words, I believe that making connections in
a safe place is not only something basic that occurs during dreaming,
but that it is a basic function of dreaming. I suggest that dreaming
has a quasi-therapeutic role in resolving trauma, in facilitating
adap tation to stress, and in dealing with painful or difficult new
material.

In terms of the nets we have discussed previously, the suggestion is that dreaming and therapy function by increasing connections, cross-weaving and cross-connecting, thus integrating new material into the nets of the mind. Dreaming itself, dreamworking
(making further use of one's own dreams in waking), and formal
psychotherapy all have a role in furthering this sort of broad inter-
connection or integration. When it works properly, this prevents
traumatic material or other new material from remaining in a separate or "encapsulated" state and integrates it into the ongoing flow of
the mind, so that one can better cope with it and with similar problems in the future.

THE USES OF DREAMS: SELF-KNOWLEDGE

We now turn to a different question—the uses of remembered
dreams, which we'll consider here and in the next chapters. We'll
start with what is probably the most important—making use of

remembered dreams to increase our self-knowledge. This includes, but is not limited to, the use of dreams in therapy or psychoanalysis. It also includes all the many ways we can make use of our dreams by ourselves or in a group, in the interests of self-exploration—getting to know oneself. If one accepts that dreaming makes connections in the nets of the mind more widely and broadly than does waking, then clearly those who remember dreams are in a position to make use of this broad yet very personal material in examining themselves and getting to know themselves better. No one technique is necessary or is exclusively important, and the technique one uses will depend on whether one is working alone or with a therapist or a group.

I am merely suggesting that our dreams, representing one end of our mental processing continuum, are a part of us. Why not make use of this at times? Am I saying that everyone should become a dream specialist or devote his life to dreams? No, not at all. In fact, I think it is obvious that most of our lives are lived in the waking state. Our waking thoughts, plans, and processes can take us a long way in whatever we are doing, but once in a while it may be useful to take a fresh look to get to know oneself in a different perspective, to see things a bit more broadly. If we are walking down a street or out in the woods, we usually know enough to get where we are going even if we cannot see very far. However, once in a while it may be useful to climb a tree (climb a "dreamtree") to see a bit more. I think this can help even if the tree is high and sways a bit up top, or perhaps reaches up into a cloud, so that the climber cannot see very clearly. Occasionally one does see something new or catch a glimpse of something unexpected—one makes a new connection, as we have discussed.

How to Start Looking at Your Dreams

First of all, if you want to make use of your dreams, it is important to be able to remember at least some dreams and to write them down or record them. Some people do this anyway and have been doing it for years. If you are someone who is developing an interest in dreams but find you seldom remember dreams or hardly remember anything worthwhile, I can give you a few suggestions for increasing dream recall based on my sleep laboratory work as well as my clinical experience. First, a conscious interest in dreams will usually increase dream recall. You are more likely to remember a dream tonight, compared to an average night, simply because you have been reading about dreams today. And the more you become interested in dreams, the more you are likely to remember. Next, make sure that any dream you do recall upon awakening does not slip away. You can do this by always having pen and paper or a cassette recorder handy, or, if you have one, perhaps a laptop or notebook computer. Anyway, you want something on hand so that you can record a dream or perhaps record a few words that will help you recall the dream later.

What you do before you go to sleep can make a big difference in what you can recall. Usually you cannot simply remember dreams by telling yourself to remember, but what some people have found useful is to review at bedtime a major problem or emotional concern. Whatever your most important problem may be—something personal or interpersonal or perhaps work-related, but in any case something in which you are emotionally involved—think about it before you go to bed and try to formulate your problem as clearly as possible. However, don't try to come up with an immediate answer. Simply lay out the problem and then give your dreaming mind a chance to make connections or perhaps put things together for you. In my experience simply laying out a problem in this manner, which is very close to various "incubation techniques," actually makes you more likely to remember a dream, and it may well produce a dream that gives you some insight into the problem.

Most people will find themselves recalling some dreams and often helpful dreams by following the procedures above, but this is not always the case. Sometimes there are aspects of your actual sleep behavior that make it hard for you to remember many dreams. For instance, I found in a study years ago that people who sleep less than six hours are much less likely to recall dreams.[13] This is in part related to the fact that REM sleep tends to concentrate more in the late hours of the night so that "short sleepers" have relatively little of it. If your sleep time is very short and you do not insist on keeping it short, you can try to rearrange your schedule so that at least on some nights you will have eight or nine hours available to sleep. It is more likely that you will recall a dream on one of these long nights. In fact, good dream recallers frequently find that their longest and most complex dreams seem to occur on awakening from an unusually long night of sleep.

If all of this still has not produced satisfactory dream recall, you can take more drastic steps that I hesitate to recommend since they may be somewhat uncomfortable or painful. You can set an alarm to wake you repeatedly throughout the night, making it likely that you will awaken from a REM period. You might begin with one-hour intervals starting three or four hours after bedtime. Thus if you go to bed at 11 PM, set your alarm to wake you at 3, 4, 5, 6, and 7 AM. If this still does not work after several nights (and you're still willing to try), shorten the intervals to 45 minutes and set the alarm for 3:00, 3:45, 4:30, etc. Of course this technique only works for people who sleep very deeply and can get back to sleep easily. If you're a serious insomniac, don't try it.

Finally, if you have a very devoted bed partner or friend who is willing to help you in your quest for the elusive dream, you can ask him or her to watch you while you sleep and especially to watch your eyes. Usually, rapid eye movements are easily visible through your eyelids, so you can ask your friend to wake you when your eyes have been moving rapidly (intermittently, not constantly) for at least five or ten minutes. If you are one of the rare people who still can't recall anything after all these attempts, you might consider working with daydreams or reveries, since in many ways these are quite closely related to dreams.

Once you have begun to recall some dreams, I would recommend recording all of your dreams for awhile insofar as it is possible. Don't worry about immediately making sense of them or finding a clear-cut meaning for each. Keep doing this for awhile even if the dreams seem senseless at first. Often a series of dreams leads to something meaningful when a single dream does not. Then if you're still interested, you can work on your dreams by yourself, or with a helper, therapist, or dream group, as we will outline below.

Approaches to Working with Your Dreams

Now that you have some dreams written down or recorded, what should you do? Well, first of all, you don't have to do anything in a big hurry. It may be very helpful, especially if you're a champion "doer" who has to fill every minute with accomplishment, simply to sit back and look over your series of dreams peacefully and without haste. You might try just appreciating them as a somewhat different part of yourself, perhaps a part you don't know very well. Are there artistic, creative bits in you that you hadn't known about? Look for some major themes or concerns in your dream series. Or look for hints about solutions to problems (we'll discuss this in the next chapter). Then it's up to you. You can work on your dreams more formally by yourself, with a helper, with your therapist if you have one, or in a group.

Many find it easier or more comfortable to work on dreams themselves either because they have faith in their own powers or because they are worried about privacy—about letting others know their innermost thoughts—or for other reasons. There is nothing wrong with this, but the lone dreamer should note that on occasion another person, another viewpoint, can be most helpful. One is sometimes blind to one's own problems, and someone else can help one see something more quickly. Basically, the technique of working with one's own dreams involves laying out the dream and carefully considering each portion of it, each character, setting, action, and so on, asking oneself questions about it. I often tend to start with the most striking or intense image, which is most likely to be contextualizing an emotion, but there are any number of ways of starting. Some excellent nontechnical guides to working with one's dreams have been published.[14] These can be extremely useful, not by imposing a meaning on your dream—telling you that dreaming of x means y—but rather by providing a series of questions you can ask yourself to gain more understanding. These guides are all quite consistent with the view we have examined above that dreams provide metaphoric pictures of your emotional concerns. One final word: Don't give up too quickly. If there is an important underlying problem, it will affect dreams over and over again. So if you don't see anything obvious in one dream, simply keep trying in subsequent dreams. And remember, there is not necessarily one absolute meaning to a dream. The dream may simply show you some connections you may not have appreciated and allow you to make more connections upon waking.

Sometimes it is much easier to understand dreams with the help of another person—traditionally an analyst or therapist. There are a number of techniques for understanding dreams, starting with Freud and practiced in different ways by therapists of various persuasions.

The schools of therapy generally agree that the dream images are significant for the dreamer and that these are important ways for the dreamer to gain additional self-knowledge. The differences relate to technique. The classic psychoanalytic technique relies on free association regarding dream elements. The dreamer is asked what comes to mind about each element of the dream in turn, and is urged to speak of absolutely anything, no matter how trivial, nonsensical, or embarrassing. The dreamer and analyst then follow the chains of association wherever they may lead (see also Chap. 10).

Jungian analysts often start with a powerful, significant-seeming image and ask the dreamer to amplify this image or stay with the image and see what other images or what elaborations come to mind. This is called "amplification" and is sometimes combined with the technique of "active imagination," which involves beginning with an important dream image or dream character and then allowing the mind, in a relaxed state, to invent an imaginative story about it, in a sense continuing the dream while in a relaxed, daydreaming form of waking.[15]

Gestalt techniques ask the dreamer to enter into important elements of the dream. Often by play-acting, the dreamer is asked to "become the characters" and even to become the objects in a dream, experiencing what it might be like to be this character or that object. The belief is that this will lead to a feeling of powerful opposing forces in the dream and that resolution of these oppositions will often lead to some new insight for the dreamer.[16]

Approaches to the dream by Eugene Gendlin[17] and Robert Bosnak[18] emphasize the body feelings. The body feeling in either the dreamer or the interpreter, when the dream is told out loud, is used as a guide to what portions of the dream or what aspects of the meaning or "interpretation" are especially important or meaningful for the dreamer.

I will not discuss in great detail the many ways in which dreaming can be useful in therapy since this is a subject of any number of books and articles in the Freudian, Jungian, and other traditions. It may be much easier for a therapist or another person to see connections or concerns in our dreams, since we often employ various defenses to avoid seeing painful material. Along the same lines, a dream group can add a number of other people's views of our dreams. Montague Ullman, who is considered the "father" of group dreamwork, has provided a very useful outline for groups or people who want to share and help each other understand their dreams.[19] Such groups can be run with or without a professional "leader." The groups work on the principle that four (or six or more) heads are better than one and that we can gain from mutual support as well as insight from others by working on a dream with a group. Ullman emphasizes that the groups above all need to respect the dreamer's own viewpoint and not try to impose their views on him or her. He suggests that rather than telling the dreamer, "Obviously your dream means such and such," dreamgroup members use an approach such as, "Well, if it were my dream I would think along the lines of . . ." I have had experience with several such dream groups myself and find they can be wonderfully helpful as long as the feelings of the dreamer are properly respected. It is essential that the dreamgroup members keep in mind that no matter how convinced they may be of a particular meaning or concern, it is helpful only if the dreamer can see it and use it. It may often be harmful to push an interpretation on an unwilling dreamer, even if the interpretation has some truth to it (this is, of course, a well-recognized principle of therapy as well). The dreamer's associations and insights must always play the primary role, and the dreamer, whether in therapy or in a group, must be allowed to develop her own insights and interpretations.

DREAMWORKING

The "dreamworking movement"—learning about oneself through one's dreams, usually with informal help from others—is very modern and yet very ancient as well. It is a widespread grass-roots sort of movement; there may be several hundred thousand Americans participating in some form of dreamworking with partners or, most commonly, in groups—yet it has had to make its way against two different sorts of powerful cultural opposition. First of all, the Western scientific establishment in past centuries has tended to place a very low value on dreams, from the "träume sind schäume" (dreams are froth) of the 19th-century German scientific establishment to some modern views that dreams represent random activation of the forebrain, which "tries to make the best of a bad job." Second, the "psychotherapy establishment," which by now consists of many thousands of psychoanalysts, psychiatrists, clinical psychologists, and clinical social workers, is also rather hostile to the idea of "dreamworking," although they do grant that the dream has some value when examined in proper (therapeutic) hands and situations.

Thus, one powerful group insists that dreams are pretty much worthless and another powerful group says that dreams may play a part in carefully structured therapy but should not be handled by laypeople. However, there is a revolution in progress against these dominant forces. The people are on the march! As I see it, the people have always loved dreams, and the people in one fashion or another generally get their way. There are now thousands of small dream groups or dream workshops springing up with a variety of backgrounds and viewpoints, but all sharing a fascination with dreams.[20] And indeed, how can we not be fascinated by our dreams? They are so much a part of us and yet they include something different, something strange, something perhaps we had not known was there. We are looking into a mirror, perhaps a distorting mirror, but something much more interesting than the simple, two-dimensional distorting mirrors at the fair. We are looking at ourselves in a multidimensional, many-sensed, emotionally guided mirror. For those who want to know themselves from as many viewpoints as possible, how can this fail to be fascinating? This is one revolution I completely favor. Vive la révolution, vive le rêve!

Does Our New Theory of Dreaming Help in Working with One's Dreams?

I believe the techniques of working with dreams introduced by Freud, Jung, Ullman, and a number of others have a great deal to recommend them, and I have used them all. I am not attempting to substitute an entirely new method. However, what we have said in previous chapters on the nature of dreaming leads to at least two useful points in working with dreams in both therapeutic and nontherapeutic settings.

The first comes from our emphasis on the powerful dream image contextualizing an emotion. This leads to the suggestion that when time and energy are limited (as is usually the case), it is probably worth starting with the most striking image or images in the dream—the places that are most likely to contain a "contextualizing image" in the sense we have discussed. In my experience, starting at this point is likely to lead fairly quickly to something emotionally important for the dreamer, but of course the dreamer and the therapist together must then decide to what extent they wish to elaborate on it and whether to analyze the rest of the dream content as well. I do not by any means want to imply that the remainder of the dream—the story line—is unimportant or not analyzable. In fact, the dream story, too, may contextualize an emotional concern. Everything in the dream will turn out to have some significance; the problem is that except perhaps in long-term, five-times-per-week psychoanalysis, there is rarely time to explore all the ramifications. In general, with limited time available, one allows the patient to decide what if anything in the dream to investigate. Often what is chosen is indeed the central metaphor or contextualizing image, but sometimes the patient will be interested in a small detail, and this can frequently be significant as well. At times the patient will simply present the dream and have no idea where to go; in such cases my experience is that the most striking image is a logical place to start. However, everything is relative; in some cases, a sensitive therapist will intuitively feel that attacking the central and obviously important image could be dangerous or threatening, and may prefer to begin with something else and leave this central issue for another time.

The second point comes from our overall view that dreaming can be seen as one end of a continuum—the opposite end from focused waking. Dreaming is a broader way of dealing with or combining material in our minds. In examining or working with our dreams we are simply making use of the broad connective powers of dreams (climbing our dreamtrees) and perhaps seeing a little bit of something new about ourselves. I believe this is all we should ask of dreams—a little broader insight, a little help—though the help can sometimes be very important or even earthshaking (see following chapters). We need not consider each dream a puzzle that needs to have a perfect solution, or a strange text that needs a definitive interpretation (I realize that I am in disagreement with Freud and a number of others here) (see Chap. 10). I agree that in principle every detail of every dream is determined in some way and that if one spends enough time one can sometimes reach what appears to be a complete understanding of all the details in our dreams. However, we are usually deceiving ourselves. Even in Freud's best-studied dreams, later authors have found a great deal more than Freud found in his initial interpretation. Since we are speaking in practical terms in this chapter, I believe that the practical course is to assume modestly that the dream may help us in understanding ourselves. This is quite likely to happen if we simply allow the new connections in dreams to emerge, whether or not we completely "solve" the puzzle or understand every detail of the dream's meaning or meanings.

Summary

In this long chapter I first argued that the dream itself may be a form of psychotherapy, useful to us whether or not we remember our dreams. When we do remember dreams, we can use them in many ways to increase our self-knowledge. Overall, I emphasized that dreams can make new connections and may often lead us to further connections and insights when we are awake. They may also lead us to further questions. I do not believe it is generally useful to look for the single "solution" to the puzzle of a dream.

My main point is that dreams can be immensely helpful in increasing our self-knowledge, and this can be done by oneself, with others in a dreamworking setting, in a formal dream group, or through formal psychotherapy. I have suggested a few hints based on our previous discussions as to ways of looking at dreams, but my main message is that there is no one way to do it and there is no one guru we must consult or one school of therapy we absolutely need to follow. The dream has already made connections, often more broadly than we can do in wakefulness. If we wish, we can now examine the products of these broad connections and make use of them, relate them to the rest of our lives, etc.—in other words, make further connections in our waking lives. Self-knowledge is making connections.

I have insisted essentially on the overall importance of using the dream in getting to know oneself. But there are many ways to do this, and I have discussed a number of them. I've found much that is useful, but let me end with a few flat disagreements. From what I have said I hope it is clear that I *disagree* with all the following statements one finds implicitly or explicitly in many treatises on dreams: (1) You must work to understand your dreams completely; a dream can do nothing for you unless you analyze it completely. (2) You must work on your dreams with a well-trained psychoanalysist or therapist; everything else is useless. (3) You must work on dreams in this particular way (whatever it is); only this way leads to the truth. (4) It is dangerous for laypeople to work on their own dreams. (5) Every dream is a puzzle that needs to be solved; once you have solved the puzzle and achieved its real meaning, you are done and the dream is of no further importance.

None of these statements is true, in my opinion. There are many paths to self-knowledge and many ways dreams can help us on the journey.

DREAMS, PROBLEM SOLVING, SCIENCE, AND ART

DREAMS AND PROBLEM SOLVING IN ORDINARY SITUATIONS

It is not unusual to feel that one has solved a problem while asleep. At times it appears to be just plain sleep that does the job. Many people report going to bed with an unsolved problem and waking up with a solution or a path to a solution; and often there is no indication that a dream was necessarily involved.

Sometimes dreaming does seem in a general way to be related to finding a solution. One wakes up with a feeling that one's dreams have been playing with a problem, trying to find solutions, or there are bits of dreams dealing with the problem, picturing parts of it over and over; and then one finds a solution in the morning but without recollection of a specific dream that solved the problem. Finally, there are occasions when a solution really appears to come in a dream, or the dream at least produces something definite that suggests a solution, which is then easily arrived at in the morning. Several researchers have attempted to study problem solving in dreams more directly. For instance, in 1974, sleep researcher William Dement gave 500 undergraduate students three different "brain teasers" to read over before going to sleep. For example, "What does the following series represent: H I J K L M N O?" The answer is in the footnote at the bottom of the next page. If you wish you can try solving the problem yourself while you sleep. The study found that seven of the 500 students reported dreams that solved the puzzle and a few others

151

came close. Most of the students recalled no dreams or dreamt about totally different subjects.[1] The study does demonstrate an occasional dream solution to such puzzles, though most students apparently were just not interested.

Morton Schatzman, a psychiatrist working in London, published a series of similar "brain-twister" puzzles in a popular magazine in England. He asked readers to see if they could solve the puzzles in their dreams. One of his problems was, "Can you arrange six identical matchsticks to form four equilateral (equal-sided) triangles?"* Schatzman reports that 11 people appeared to solve the problems in their dreams; however, it is unclear how many of the 50,000 readers of the magazine actually tried to solve the problem.[2]

Such cases, though they are apparently not common, are intriguing. The dream definitely pictures a solution and it appears plausible that a solution was found in the dream, although one cannot rule out the possibility that the solution came to the sleeper outside of the dream and was then "pictured" in the dream. In both of these experiments the majority of subjects did not come up with a solution and did not even dream about the problem. Thus the occasional solutions, though suggestive, can hardly be considered strong evidence for problem solving in dreams.[3]

My impression after having tried a few small experiments of this kind is that upon reading such a puzzle one usually either works on it and solves it while awake or dismisses it as silly or unimportant. It seldom truly becomes an "emotional concern," as we have discussed in previous chapters, that would have the force to produce dream images, though occasionally this may be the case. I asked Morton Schatzman whether he could characterize in any way the people who had solved his puzzles (most of whom he knew only through their

---

*The solution to Dement's problem is "water" (H to O or H_2O). The solution to Schatzman's matchstick problem is to use three of the matchsticks to form a triangle on a flat surface and then pick up the remaining three matchsticks and use them above the surface to form a pyramid, starting with each point of the triangle and meeting above the center of the triangle. This produces a four-sided pyramid, each side of which is a perfect equilateral triangle. These problems are of a kind that have a single solution which appears "obviously right." They were chosen as problems whose solution is visual and thus could presumably be pictured in a dream. The few people who solved the puzzles did see water or a pyramid in their dream.

correspondence). Though he could not be certain, he said these appeared to be people who had taken the problem seriously and had followed his instructions to "take the problem to bed" with them and "incubate" it. In these people the puzzle may indeed have become, at least temporarily, a significant emotional concern.

A recent research study found evidence of problem solving in students asked to incubate a "problem of personal relevance" and work on it in their dreams.[4] Independent judges scored all dreams as to (1) whether the dreams were about the problem, and (2) whether the dreams contained a satisfactory solution to the problem. Overall, 51% of dreams were scored as being about the problem, and 25% as containing a solution. The perceived solutions involved connections between the incubated problems and related material in the students' lives. For instance, in one case the incubated problem was:

> I have applied to two clinical psychology programs and two in industrial psychology because I just can't decide which field I want to go into.

The resulting dream was:

> A map of the United States. I am in a plane flying over this map. The pilot says we are having engine trouble and need to land and we look for a safe place on the map indicated by a light. I ask about "MA," which we seem to be over right then and he says all of MA is very dangerous. The lights seem to be farther west.

The student continues:

> I wake up and realize that my two clinical schools are both in Massachusetts (MA), where I have spent my whole life and where my parents live. Both industrial programs are far away, in Texas and California. That was because I was originally looking to stay close to home and there were no good industrial programs nearby. I realize that there is a lot wrong with staying at home and that, funny as it sounds, getting away is probably more important than which kind of program I go to.

This dream looks at the problem in a new way. It restates the problem, which leads toward finding a new solution in waking life. The phrase "MA is very dangerous" further suggests that getting away from home, and perhaps especially from mother, is probably an important emotional concern.

In these students the incubated problem was almost always a personal or interpersonal problem that was already important to the dreamer. The conditions of the experiment suggesting "incubation" of the problem before going to bed assured that at least to some extent this problem would be a kind of emotional concern that night.

My overall impression is that the problems solved or partially solved in dreams are far more often interpersonal problems or personal problems dealing with one's health, or perhaps major problems in one's work, than brain twisters, crossword puzzles, or arithmetic problems. The former category, of course, is where we place most of our emotional energy, so these are the problems that are likely to produce emotional concerns capable of influencing and being pictured in our dreams. Our discussion of the nets of the mind with more tightly and more loosely woven portions and, related to this, our data on how seldom we dream of the 3 R's, also strongly suggest that it would be very unlikely that we would solve verbal or arithmetic brain twisters in our dreams. When such "abstract" problems have been apparently solved in dreams, the dreamer was intensely involved with a particular problem—as in the scientific discoveries below—so that it was no longer an amusing puzzle but had become an intense emotional concern.

In other cultures and traditions, too, dreams are often called upon for problem solving, but again it is the major problems of life that are brought up—problems that involve truly emotional concerns. Thus the young man in various Native American cultures who goes on a dream quest is usually instructed to spend several days fasting or preparing himself in ways that allow him to rid his mind of small details and focus instead on some major questions—usually the question of what his role in life will be (we will discuss this in Chap. 14).

Overall, it does appear that solutions or at least hints about solutions to problems occur in dreams even to ordinary people (see below for some extraordinary cases in artists and scientists). One point that comes through clearly is that the mind of the dreamer must be prepared. A person with no interest in math will not suddenly wake up one morning with a dream solving a mathematical problem that has been worrying mathematicians for hundreds of years. A solution comes to a prepared mind, and the "solution" is most often simply making a new connection—something that had not previously been realized. Further work is required of the waking mind to make full use of this new connection. In this light, the problem solving that occurs in dreams is not really different from the connection making we have examined in other situations. For instance, the cases we have mentioned previously in which a woman dreamt "my boyfriend turned into my father" or "Joe turned into a wolf" might be considered to be problem-solving dreams as well. The new connection in the dream provided an insight that allowed the dreamer to come to a new decision, or simply to reevaluate whether this boyfriend was the right one for her.

DREAMS AND SCIENTIFIC PROBLEM SOLVING

It is well known that scientists sometimes report that solutions to their scientific problems have come to them in their dreams. I find this is especially the case with problems so important that they have become a primary emotional concern for the scientist. In the realm of practical science one of the best known examples involves Elias Howe, who was trying for a long period (1840–1845) to invent a machine that would rapidly and efficiently do the work of a seamstress—in other words, a sewing machine. He already had in mind the rough idea of a machine that would repeatedly jab a needle through a piece of cloth pulled across the workspace. But he couldn't get any further than that. He could not figure out how to make the machine catch and tie the thread. While working on this problem, he had a dream of being a missionary somewhere and being caught by natives (a common picture he might well have seen often in a magazine of his time). But as the natives danced around him waving their spears, he noticed something unusual. The spears all had holes through their tips! On waking he realized that this was the solution he had been waiting for. If he placed a hole through the tip of his needle, the thread could be then caught after it went through the cloth and his sewing machine could be perfected. And it worked![5]

Chemistry gives us another well-known example. The famous French chemist August Kekulé had been trying for some time to describe the structure of the benzene molecule. He knew it had to contain six carbon atoms, but neither a straight row of six nor a branching chain—the usual molecular structures being considered— would give it all the chemical properties he knew characterized benzene. While worrying about this problem he reports dozing in front of the fire:

> I turned my chair to the fire and dozed. Again the atoms were gamboling before my eyes. This time the smaller groups kept modestly in the background. My mental eye, rendered more acute by repeated visions of the kind, could now distinguish larger structures of manifold conformation: long rows, some- times more closely fitted together all twining and twisting in snake-like motion. But look! What was that? One of the snakes had seized hold of its own tail, and the form whirled mockingly before my eyes. As if by a flash of lightning I awoke; and this time also I spent the rest of the night in working out the conse- quences of the hypothesis.[6]

Based on this image he realized that a ring structure for the six carbon atoms was the solution he had been looking for. It is interesting that as Kekulé described this scene he was unlikely to have been in REM sleep and possibly he was not fully asleep at all but rather just falling asleep or in a state of reverie or daydream; but for our purposes this doesn't matter much. Very dreamlike dreams can occur at dream onset: Reverie and similar states are close to dreaming on our continuum, and as we have noted they are good states for making connections.

Apparently, at least some discoveries occur or come together in dreams. However, we must be cautious since we have only the word of the dreamer for the report, and it has sometimes been pointed out that this person may have reasons for overemphasizing the role of the dream. For instance, in Kekulé's case, arguments have been made that he may have emphasized the dream origin of his benzene ring theory in order to avoid giving credit to other scientists whose work helped lead him to his discovery.[7]

Despite this caveat, there is little question that important scientific problems can sometimes be solved in dreams, at least as reported by the solvers. And this is not a rare occurrence. Over 50% of mathematicians responding to a questionnaire reported that they had at least once solved a problem in their dreams.[8]

I am a scientist myself, among other things. I have occasionally had images in my dreams that at least gave me hints as to fruitful directions in my scientific work. For instance, while beginning to think about dreaming and connections for my present work, I was not sure how to visualize the ensemble of units we have been discussing. I thought of a net or a web, and of course the surface appearance of the brain. During this time I had a dream of a whole pile of Persian carpets loosely tied together. Though I have not started speaking of "the Persian carpets of the mind," this image does have something attractive and perhaps useful in it. It could be translated as a layering of nets. It includes the idea that there are tightly woven areas (individual carpets) with looser connections— some rough cord tying the carpets together, perhaps. The image is also consistent with much of what we know of the cortex, which is kind of like a thick rug (or a pile of thinner rugs?). The cortex has been said to have "two and one-half dimensions," implying that there is much more length and width than depth. And it appears that the basic "weave" representing the length and breadth of the carpets is somehow qualitatively different from the "vertical" connections going from the surface of the cortex to the depths.[9] So this may be an important image, although I have not yet made full use of it.

Many scientists state that they get their best ideas not necessarily dreaming, but daydreaming and in reverie, and that the ideas come to them in pictures. An inventor I know describes his creative process in this way:

> Often my best ideas come to me in the middle of the night. I'm not sure whether it is a dream or just fuzzy thinking when I'm half asleep. It's usually a problem I have been thinking about for a long time. I have it all solved except for one thing and suddenly I see a picture, and it all makes sense when I work it out the next day.

In these various, disparate examples it is worth nothing that all the dreamers' minds were well-prepared to solve the problem. Then what seems to happen is that a single new connection in the form of a new image shows up in the dream, finally provides the long-sought solution or a step toward the solution. Again it is not always clear that this necessarily occurs in a dream; it can sometimes occur in a dreamlike reverie or in a fuzzy, half-asleep state, when the mind is functioning toward the dreaming end of the continuum.

DREAMS AND ARTISTIC PROBLEM SOLVING

Numerous artists have acknowledged help from their dreams in producing their works of art. Some of the most famous include Mozart, Wagner, Coleridge, and Robert Louis Stevenson. Some even insist that the entire work came to them during a dream and all that they had to do was paint it, sculpt it, or write it down. Because of the visual-spatial nature of typical dreams, the most numerous examples are from the visual arts. For instance, among painters there are a number of well-known examples listed in Table 1.[10] In fact, so many artists are currently doing paintings based on dreams that the Association for the Study of Dreams has been able to mount an exhibit each year of at least 30 to 40 new dream-inspired paintings.

Sculpture and architecture can similarly make use of dreams. In a recent example, the sculptor Penelope Jencks received a commission a few years ago to sculpt a large, bronze statue of Eleanor Roosevelt for a park in Manhattan. Jencks described some difficulty in her work with the sculpture. She collected numerous pictures of Eleanor Roosevelt and at one point even asked Phoebe Roosevelt, one of Eleanor's great-granddaughters, who bears some resemblance to her, to sit as a live model. Jencks was still not convinced that she was getting Eleanor's face and head just right. Jencks reports:

> A strange dream helped me immensely. I was working away in the studio, in the dream, kneeling and sculpting, when I heard someone say, "Oh, here comes Mrs. Roosevelt." I instantly thought, "What a relief, I will never have to search for a model again." She walked right in that door. She was 20 feet tall. I thought, "I will never be able to sculpt this heroic figure." Without saying a word, she smiled at me with such a benevolent

Table I. Classic Works of Art Based on a Dream

Works for which the artist recorded a dream account:

A. Durer	*Vision of a Cloudburst in a Dream* (1525)
F. Goya	*The Sleep of Reason Begets Monsters* and most
	other sketches in Los Caprichios (1810–1815)
W. Blake	*Young Night's Thoughts* (c. 1818)
E. Burne-Jones	*The Rose Bower* (1870–1890)
F. Kahlo	*The Dream* (1940)
P. Birkhauser	*In the Night of 13 October 1942* (1975)
	The World's Wound (1953)
	Having Speech (1975)
	At the Door (1965)
	With Child (1966)
	The Women with the Cup (1971)
	Spiritua Naturae (1976)
	Lynx (1976)

Other works known to be based at least partially on a dream:

H. Fuseli	*The Nightmare* (1781 and 1790 versions)
P. de Chevannes	*The Dream* (1883)
J. A. Fitzgerald	*The Dream* (19th cen.)
B. Dossi	*La Notte* (19th cen.)
A. Kubin	*Each Night a Dream Visits Us* (c. 1900)
	Man (c. 1900)
	The Dancer (c. 1900)
	Dream of a Serpent (c. 1905)
Henri Rousseau	*The Dream* (1910)
Odilon Redon	*The Dream* (1904)
Salvador Dali	*Dream Caused by a Bee* (c. 1930)
	The Dream (1931)
	The Dream Approaches (1933)
	The Broken Bridge and the Dream (1945)
René Magritte	*Le Rêve d'Androgyne*
Paul Nash	*Landscape from a Dream* (1938)
W. Paalen	*Rêve de Glaçons* (1938)
Max Beckman	*Dream of a Young Girl* (1946)
Jim Dine	*Walking Dream with a Four Foot Clamp* (1965)

Table reprinted with permission from Barrett D. Dreams and Creative Problem-Solving. Presidential address, Association for the Study of Dreams, Berkeley, CA, July 1966.

smile, not a touch of grandiosity, that my fears melted away. Then she disappeared. But I am secure in the knowledge that I found Eleanor Roosevelt in my dream.[11]

Film is another art form that obviously can be, and often is, derived from dreams. Perhaps the best known example is the classic film *Un Chien Andalou*, by Louis Buñuel and Salvador Dali. It was based almost entirely on two dream images. One image was from a dream of Dali's in which he saw a whole mob of ants coming out of his hands. And the other came from a Buñuel dream in which he saw a knife cutting an eye. Among other well-known films, Ingmar Bergman's *Hour of the Wolf*, Robert Altman's *Free Women*, and Akira Kurosawa's *Dreams* were all based on dreams of the directors. There is an especially close relationship between film and dreams; in fact, dreams are often called movies we show ourselves at night, or movies of the mind.

Dreams are much less frequently auditory, although some composers do describe creative dreams in the auditory mode. The best-known example comes from the composer Giuseppe Tartini. He reports that in his dream the devil came to him with a violin and played a difficult piece of music including a prolonged trill. Tartini says he simply set this down in musical notation upon awakening and it became his well-known "Devil's Trill Sonata."[12]

Mozart claimed that some of his music came to him in dreams, but he did not provide any details. Recently singer and songwriter Billy Joel attributed a central role to dreams in helping him create music. He states, "I always dream music. I know all the music I have composed has come from a dream."[13]

Such examples are not common, however. There appears to be less influence of dreams on auditory than on visual art. Even among musicians the visual-spatial portions of the dream are often especially important. For instance, Vladimir Horowitz had a discussion about piano fingering with a less-known pianist, Leonid Hambro, in which they shared the fact that both of them sometimes dreamt the exact fingering for a portion of a piece they were preparing for a concert performance. They both experienced seeing and feeling their hands playing difficult passages in their dreams, and when they tried these out in the daytime, they found that the dream had shown them the best way to do it.[14]

Some poets and other writers have attributed their work to dreams. I have no reason to question that dreams play a part. However, I am a little skeptical about a complete written work appearing in dreams, especially since I have found that we seldom read and write in dreams.[15] A well-known example is Samuel Taylor Coleridge's poem "Kubla Khan," which he claims came to him complete in a dream and he simply wrote down 40 lines or so, as much as he could remember, until he was interrupted by a "person from Porlock," and thus had to leave the poem incomplete. However, Coleridge scholars have found several different versions of "Kubla Khan," so some believe Coleridge was using a literary frame device in claiming that the poem had come to him in a dream and that his claim was not to be taken literally.[16]

Robert Louis Stevenson claimed that his stories often came to him in complete form in his dreams.[17] Biographers are not certain exactly what he meant, and some have assumed that he saw the stories written down. I consider it much more likely that what Stevenson saw was one or two dramatic images rather a written story. For instance, when he claims that Dr. Jeckyll and Mr. Hyde came to him in a dream, I can easily imagine that the image of a respectable doctor turning into a monster came in a dream; it is in fact a very common sort of dream image. But then I suspect that his agile writing skills took over and completed the story.

ARTISTIC THINKING, SCIENTIFIC THINKING, AND DREAMS

We have discussed in the previous pages ways in which making a new connection in dreams can play a role in scientific, as well as artistic, problem solving or creation. But I think we can go further than that. Despite society's view that science and art are somehow opposites, or at least totally different forms of activity, I think it is clear there are certain commonalities, and these can be related to our view of dreaming. The common element in scientific and artistic discovery is seeing something in a new way, or making a new connection, and of course we have explored here the ways in which dreaming is especially good in making new connections.

Making a new connection can be thought of as a sort of basis or lowest common denominator of ordinary problem solving, artistic creation, and scientific discovery. In fact, this same making of new connections is the basis of learning about oneself (self-knowledge), whether practiced in isolation, in the normal course of life's interactions, or with the help of a therapist. "Know thyself," meaning know thyself as much as possible and in new ways if possible, lies at the basis of all these human disciplines.

A tradition certainly exists that seeks a commonality between science and art and similar human activities. For instance, Arthur Koestler in his well-known essays on creativity tries to relate three different human experiences: the essence of humor, which he calls (the "haha" experience); scientific discovery (the "aha" experience); and artistic creativity (the "ah" experience). Koestler finds the commonality between art and science (as well as humor) in what he calls "bisociation." He speaks of this as the bisection of one framework of experience by another, which leads to something new and unexpected.[18]

I was always impressed by Koestler's analysis, and I believe it contains a great deal of truth. But is bisociation very different from what we have been talking about as making metaphor or making a new connection? Bisociation does provide a clear visual framework for making connections: two "planes" of intellectual activity that intersect to produce a "line" of new possibilities.

Perhaps bisociation is the most complex or elaborated form of a process that in its simplest form is metaphor formation or the making of new connections. The phrase, "Man is a wolf" captures a certain aspect of humanity by juxtaposing it with another, perhaps better-known or simpler entity—wolf. The first person who said, "Man is a wolf" had a real "aha" experience: He had made a discovery! But this is not so different from the dream, "Joe turned into a wolf," or for that matter, "My boyfriend turned into my father." The dream-inspired connection is a new insight, too.

This metaphoric structure is probably most easily seen in poetry but can be examined in visual art as well. For example, many of George Moore's beautiful sculptures are simultaneously women's bodies and rock formations. His sculptures represent a form of bisociation. If it occurred in a dream, we would call such an image a condensation of a woman and a rock formation, or the visual statement of a metaphor: This rocky landscape is (like) a woman. Cubist painting can be seen as an attempt to explore the hidden two-dimensional and three-dimensional solids hidden in our faces and elsewhere in the world. The cubist is saying something like: "This is a body but it is also an interesting collection of simple shapes."

We can visualize all this in terms of the nets of the mind, discussed in previous chapters. What we are talking about is simply overlap in the complex, distributed pattern of connections making up each concept. Thus, at the simplest level there is some overlap between the representation of Jim and the representation of Father. Dreaming makes it easier to accept or notice this overlap. There is an overlap between part of the representation of "man" and the somewhat simpler representation most of us have for wolf. A certain portion of "man" overlaps with "wolf," and again we can notice this more easily in dreams. Stevenson probably had at the back of his mind the notion that respectable-appearing people are sometimes monsters. His dream noticed and dramatically pictured this overlap, perhaps instigated by a particular situation he was experiencing at the time—an emotional concern.

Certain rock formations do indeed bear a slight resemblance to the human body, but it takes Moore to point this out to us and use it. Moore was somehow more aware of this overlap than others, and he had the talent to express it. Possibly the first image of a woman/ rockscape came to him in a dream; it is certainly a plausible dream image. But in any case the point is that artistic creativity uses the same mechanisms in terms of the nets of the mind, and it is very similar to the overlap mechanism we have already discussed that allows our dreaming mind, more readily than our waking mind, to portray a relationship as a car in motion. This basic noticing and picturing of overlap is a net-based description of our earlier formulation that "making connections more broadly" or "making new connections" lies at the heart of artistic and scientific creativity and of the dream.

Thus, I would say that the basic mechanism we have discussed in dreams, the making of new connections, thereby producing new metaphors, also lies at the heart of scientific and artistic creativity. We might even say that science and art are in this sense based on the dream—or at least on the basic mechanism of dreaming.

THE DREAM AS A WORK OF ART

The romantic poet Paul Richter said, "Dreaming is involuntary poetry."[19] Several recent articles have made the same point—that the dream can be considered in some ways a work of art.[20] Although the reader may have noticed that I am a bit prejudiced in favor of dreams—I do tend to value them highly—nonetheless, I am forced to admit that most dreams are certainly not satisfactory works of art. An ordinary dream may sometimes look like a pile of interesting stuff picked up on a beach, or perhaps a brief attempt at some kind of work, rather than a successful work of art.

I have no particular interest in supporting the extreme thesis that a dream is a work of art. Nonetheless, I think it may be useful to notice some important similarities. First of all, as we have just reviewed, there is a common mechanism—the making of new connections— that occurs in dreaming as well as in artistic and scientific creativity. If we consider the artist as someone who can see things a bit more broadly or can make connections a bit more easily than most, we can see this as a developed form of an ability we all possess in dreams.

Secondly, our formulation that the dream contextualizes the emotion of the dreamer and provides a metaphor explaining the emotional state of the dreamer may be applied to works of art as well. Artists in many fields and of various persuasions have often stated that what they are doing is expressing their important emotions in a particular form, namely, their artistic medium. For instance, in an essay on poetry, T. S. Eliot introduced his famous phrase "objective correlative"—the poem or poetic image is an objective correlative of an emotion.[21] Thus Eliot's own poetic image, "Would I were a pair of ragged claws scuttling across the floors of silent seas" is often cited as an objective correlative for the feeling of awkward social embarrassment and shyness felt by Prufrock, the protagonist of the poem. And, in fact, this is a very dreamlike image.

Finally, a dream can often have a powerful impact on the dreamer, not unlike the impact of a work of art. Many of us have had "impactful dreams" that have a lasting effect on us, either an emotional effect or an effect on our lives. Most of us remember at least a few instances of a dream that produced a strong emotional state that "stayed with us" for a time after we awoke. The majority of recalled dreams are perhaps remembered briefly at awakening and then forgotten, and do not seem to have a great effect on the emotional state of the dreamer after awakening. Psychologist Don Kuiken calls these "mundane dreams" to differentiate them from the "impactful dreams" that do have an emotional effect, which he has investigated in detail.[22] Among impactful dreams he differentiates between nightmares (which we have already discussed in detail), existential dreams, and transcendent dreams.

Existential dreams are described as having "intense emotion at the end of the dream," usually a group of distinctive "distressing feelings including discouragement, agony, guilt, anger and sadness." The dreamer is left troubled or confused. This can sometimes be important and useful to the dreamer. For instance, my friend and colleague William Dement, a well-known sleep researcher, used to smoke quite heavily. He had a dream in which he saw an X-ray of his chest showing advanced lung cancer. Still in the dream, he discussed it with his doctors and with his family and realized that there was no hope for him. He woke up with a terrified and poignant feeling that he would never live to see his children grow up, and then later a marvelous feeling of relief that this was after all a dream rather than reality, and that he could change things in his waking life. Indeed, he immediately stopped smoking and has never gone back to the habit in the 30 years since the dream.

Transcendent dreams are powerful dreams that end with a feeling of ecstasy and awe. For example, "Everything was very bright, the woods were very lush and green." This dreamer was in the process of winning a bicycle race even though she had an old three-speed bike and everyone else had fancier equipment. She realizes that this is the end of the race, and she has won. She opens a soda pop, and is aware of "fatigue and perspiration, which feels really good."[23]

These powerful emotional reactions to dreams are quite similar to reactions at having a new insight in psychotherapy, and frequently outside therapy, too. These are also the reactions to a meaningful work of art.[22]

Overall, there is little doubt that dreams can be impactful in this emotional sense and can even change our lives considerably. Kathleen Sullivan, who runs a talk show on dreams in California, reports a powerful dream that changed her life[24]:

> The dream was a simple one. I'm on a field trip with my class when the children see something exciting and call me to them. "Hurry, Ms. Sully! Come and see!" I run to them and find the most enormous spider's web—it is about 18 feet in diameter. At first I am thrilled by its beauty but then I see an eagle splayed out, wing to wing, inexorably caught in and filling the web, her head bent to the left. I feel a level of grief and horror never before experienced. I fall to my knees, sobbing hysterically, and awaken unable to catch my breath as the hysteria fills my awake world with anguish. The need to understand that experience became the focus of my life.

This existential dream carries no single message. Rather, the dreamer used the powerful, emotion-filled dream image to lead her to examine herself and consider making changes in her life. Indeed, she changed her life considerably; now, rather than teaching school, she devotes much of her time and energy to exploring her dreams and those of others.

In these cases, meaningful feelings and actions develop directly from the dream. Dreaming plays a powerful emotional role—"you must change your life!"—a role attributed by the great German poet Rilke to a powerful work of art:

TORSO OF AN ARCHAIC APOLLO[25]

Never will we know his fabulous head
where the eyes' apples slowly ripened. Yet
his torso glows: a candelabrum set
before his gaze which is pushed back and hid,
restrained and shining. Else the curving breast
could not thus blind you, nor through the soft turn
of the loins could this smile easily have passed
into the bright groins where the genitals burned.

Else stood this stone a fragment and defaced,
with lucent body from the shoulders falling,
too short, not gleaming like a lion's fell;
nor would this star have shaken the shackles off,
bursting with light, until there is no place
that does not see you. You must change your life.

We have seen here that the making of new connections in dreams can at times help solve problems and can lead to scientific and artistic creation. In fact, a basic ingredient of creativity is the making of a new connection. Although I do not consider a dream, in general, to be a work of art, I have pointed out several intriguing similarities. Making new connections is basic to dreams and to art. Contextualizing or picturing an emotional state is basic to both. And the two can (not frequently, but importantly) have the same powerful impact. A dream can change our lives.

Chapter Ten

THIS VIEW AND
FREUD'S VIEW

Any number of scientists, clinicians, and others writing about the mind or the brain have had something to say about the dream. In some works this has been expressed as fascination, even adoration, and in others more as annoyance. However, I believe there are two broad views of dreaming that have essentially dominated the discussion for the past decades. One view, especially dominant among biological and neurological scientists, is that dreams are in one way or another fairly meaningless junk. The second view, dominant among psychoanalysts and other therapists, is that dreams are meaningful and interpretable in ways originally derived from the writings of Sigmund Freud.

I will not say much about the biologists' views of dreams here. These are of some interest though they are by no means all similar. For instance, one group of authors proposes that dream material is more or less random; both important and unimportant material will thus enter dreams.[1] Another group proposes that dreams include specifically what is *not important*, what is being discarded by the brain.[2] I think it must be clear from my discussion in previous chapters that I do not agree with these views of dreaming. I completely agree, of course, that there is a biology of dreaming. In fact, I have spent years of my life studying the biology of sleep, especially REM sleep, which underlies dreaming.[3] However, our gradual understanding of the biology underlying dreaming does not make dreams unimportant or meaningless any more than our developing knowledge of the biology of waking thought makes thought unimportant or meaningless.

The other broad view of dreams derives basically from the work of Sigmund Freud. Some will argue that the work of Carl Gustav Jung or the existentialists[4] or Gestalt therapists[5] is so different from Freud's that they cannot be considered in the same breath. There are in fact some vast differences, although Jung, the best known of these theorists, often acknowledges his great debt to Sigmund Freud and then talks about certain differences in viewpoint. In this work I could try to contrast my views with those of Jung and many others, but this would take us far afield. For instance, I am a great admirer of Jung's work and frequently make use of some of his insights about the relationship of dreams to myths and legends. But Jung has never systematized his entire thinking on dreams, so it would be an arduous task to try to compare the present views with Jung's views in detail.

Freud, on the other hand, was very systematic in laying out his theory of dreams. His work was not only the first but in many ways the clearest, so I think it will be fruitful to examine the views I have proposed and contrast them with those of Sigmund Freud, the great explorer in the wilderness of dreams. I can easily find areas of clear agreement and disagreement with Freud's work.

SIGMUND FREUD

It is not easy for me to speak critically of Sigmund Freud. He is one of the towering figures of our age. He was, as he liked to say himself, a conquistador—a conqueror of new territory. He explored and opened up entire realms of ourselves of which we had not been aware and of which we often still prefer not to be aware. Freud is one of the pillars of 20th century intellectual thought. It is impossible to imagine what that edifice would look like without him.

I personally knew Sigmund Freud. Well, "knew" is an exaggeration. I met him once; however, since I was 2 at the time and he was 80, it was not a great meeting of the minds. Yet early influences are important (no disagreement there!), so who knows? Perhaps the reverberations of that meeting are active still. But my meeting him brings up another reason why criticism is difficult for me. I met him because my father was one of Freud's best-known pupils and followers. He was not one of those who had a great split with Freud, but one who remained a solid Freudian to the end of his life; indeed, most of his writings were developments of Freud's thoughts and attempts to integrate Freud's thinking with academic psychology, in order to make psychoanalysis the basis of a general psychology.[6] Because of this, my father, Heinz Hartmann, was often referred to in psychoanalytic circles as "Freud's son." This of course would make me Freud's grandson, an intriguing position that I do not find entirely comfortable.

Freud was an incisive genius. He made us all interested in dreams and he made the study of dreams, to a certain degree, respectable to the skeptical Western mind. His view that dreams are the "royal road to the unconscious" is in my opinion still a useful summary 100 years later. His method of working on dreams by simply asking for free associations to each element of the dream has a clarity and elegance that can hardly be denied even if it is not the only way of working with dreams. And in my opinion, all therapists working today, at least all therapists making use of psychodynamic principles, must, if they are honest, consider themselves Freudians, or at least Freudians with variations.

But of course Freud was human, and he made mistakes. Some of his mistakes were in fact related to his powerful drive to find a simple, satisfying answer to complex problems. He obviously desired, and felt he had achieved, a simple solution when he came up with "every dream, when the work of analysis is complete, turns out to be the fulfillment of a wish."[7] I believe, as I will discuss below, that he went too far on this issue, but the motivation in terms of a love of simplicity is understandable. I share it myself and have tried to achieve simplicity in a somewhat different way, for instance, in my overall statements that "Dreaming makes connections more broadly than waking," and "Dreaming contextualizes emotion."

I think Freud made a brilliant contribution to our overall knowledge by emphasizing the central place of dreaming in our understanding of the human mind. As he puts it, "Every dream reveals itself as a psychical structure which has a meaning which can be inserted at an assignable point in the mental activities of waking life."[8] In other words, the dream is a meaningful mental product. This strikes me as clearly true and this will stand even if some of what Freud said needs to be modified.

I realize that I cannot engage here in a full discussion of all Freud's work on dreams or do justice to the complexities of his thought. What I will do is consider in turn Freud's major theses about dreams and discuss how each of these appears in the light of the "contemporary theory of dreams" developed in the previous chapters. I will highlight agreements and disagreements, and discuss what parts of Freud's dream theory I can keep and what parts I must drop or alter in order to follow the proposed "contemporary theory." We will consider the following of Freud's theses:

The dream is the royal road to the unconscious.

Every dream is the fulfillment of a wish.

There is a latent dream underlying each "manifest dream" (and the job of the analyst is to translate the manifest dream into the latent dream).

The dream work involves at least four basic mechanisms that turn the latent dream into the manifest dream. The process is controlled by dream censorship.

Free association is the principal and best way to deal with dreams and other such material.

Sexual symbolism. When personal associations are lacking, we can sometimes translate dream images directly into roughly corresponding sexual organs and sexual activity (a cigar or a dagger equals a penis).

The function of dreaming is to preserve sleep.

I realize that splitting Freud's thoughts up into separate theses in this way runs a risk of losing the wholeness and interconnectedness of his work, but I believe it is the best way to highlight the places where my current thinking is compatible or not compatible with his work.

THE ROYAL ROAD TO THE UNCONSCIOUS

First, let me review one of Freud's statements with which I agree completely. I am perfectly content with Freud's general formulation that dreams are the royal road to the unconscious (as it is usually stated). Freud's exact statement is, "The interpretation of dreams is the royal road to a knowledge of the unconscious activities of the mind."[9] Freud is speaking about patients he is treating in analysis; he finds that almost anything that comes to the patient's mind is useful and can lead eventually to important unconscious material, but that when a dream comes up, it is an unusually good and a direct road. As Freud puts it, our usual repressions are at least partially lifted when we dream and so the dream gives us more rapid access to usually unconscious material.

This can easily be related to our discussion of making connections in the nets of the mind. We have seen repeatedly that at the right end of our continuum—and especially in dreaming—we can make connections and thus become conscious of material, especially emotional material, that we were not aware of in our conscious, focused waking thoughts.[10] Because dreams make connections more broadly and more loosely than waking thoughts, and since our emotional concerns guide these connections, dream material often leads quickly to emotional concerns that had been neglected or perhaps pushed away (repressed) in waking.

We have discussed in previous chapters how our emotions influence all our cognitive processing, awake and asleep. However, this influence is least marked when we are engaged in a sensory input-to-motor output task such as typing, or trying to judge where a fly ball is going to land; there is clearer emotional influence at the right end of the continuum. Thus if our task is to start with a report of mental activity and derive the person's emotional concern, this will be easier with a piece of dream material than with a piece of focused waking thought of equal length. In other words, an analyst and a patient should be able to get into emotionally important material more readily starting with a two-minute dream than a two-minute report of the patient's work activity (although I have no quarrel with the view that everything, including work activities, will eventually lead to underlying emotional concerns). In fact, this process is not limited to the deeply repressed conflicts prominently discussed in Freud's work. On a very ordinary level I often have had dreams such as the following:

> I am walking along when I see a group of people in discussion. I am not sure who they are, but they include my colleague, Dr. Jones, wearing some odd-looking old clothing.

I first tend to dismiss such a dream as dull and apparently unimportant, but then I think "Why Dr. Jones? I haven't seen him in six months." I think about it and then remember I have a meeting coming up soon: I am supposed to give a talk to Dr. Jones' group, but I have completely forgotten about it. Often it turns out there is an important reason for my forgetting it; usually it's a talk I had not especially wanted to give, and/or I am annoyed at Dr. Jones for some reason. My focused waking thoughts had avoided or pushed away these concerns. My dream quickly brought them back.

DREAMS AS WISH FULFILLMENT

There are several major theses of Freud's with which I do not agree. First, and obviously requiring pride of place, is Freud's thesis about wish fulfillment. He felt this was his most important contribution, and he fantasized that it would be inscribed in stone at Bellevue, the place where he originally had the dream (the "Irma dream") that led to his formulation about wish fulfillment. In 1900 Freud wrote a letter to his friend Fliess:

> Do you suppose that someday a marble tablet will be placed on this house, inscribed with the words "In this house on July 24,

1895, the secret of dreams was revealed to Dr. Sigmund Freud?"
At the moment there seems to be little prospect of it.[11]

In fact, a number of years later, after Freud's death, the city of Vienna did inscribe exactly those words at the house in Bellevue where he had the dream, posthumously fulfilling Freud's wish. Freud's actual words were, "When the work of analysis has been completed, we perceive that a dream is the fulfillment of a wish."[12] He used "A dream is the fulfillment of a wish" as a title of one of his central chapters, making it clear that it represented a major discovery. Later, in view of some objections, he tentatively amended this to the "fulfillment or attempted fulfillment of a (disguised) wish."

I can explain my disagreement with Freud in several ways. First, I do not find Freud's arguments for wish fulfillment entirely convincing. For instance, in his "dream of Irma's injection" (see Chap. 3), Freud's most densely analyzed dream, there is no question that Freud is concerned about the health of his patients and about his reputation as a clinician. These are clear emotional concerns. And a concern such as "Am I responsible for this patient's problem?" can certainly be pictured in terms of a wish: "I am not responsible. . . . Someone else is; Dr. X is responsible." Freud makes a fairly convincing case that such a wish (in fact several such wishes) that someone else be responsible, can be found in the dream. Though all these wishful thoughts may be present, I am not convinced by Freud's statement at the end of his analysis: "The dream represented a particular state of affairs as I should have wished it to be. Thus its content was the fulfillment of a wish and its motive was a wish."[13] Yes, the wishes can be found in the dream, but surely looking at the Irma dream as a whole does not strike one as "presenting a state of affairs as I would have wished it to be." One is tempted to say that if fulfillment of that wish is the center of dream, couldn't the dream have pictured it a little more simply and clearly? Perhaps not. I am aware that Freud would answer in terms of the dream censorship and the need to preserve sleep, which do not allow for an entirely direct expression. These issues will be discussed further below. Freud does report a number of dreams that I agree portray fulfilled wishes, but I believe there may be a broader principle at work.

Portraying a wish as fulfilled may be one way to picture an emotional concern, but not the only way.

Sometimes Freud's arguments for finding a wish fulfillment in every dream are convoluted and again not very convincing. For instance, Freud writes that he had been explaining to a woman patient that dreams are wish fulfillments. The next day she brought in a dream in that she was traveling with her mother-in-law to a place in the country where they were to spend their holidays together. At first this seemed a complete contradiction of his wish fulfillment view since he and the patient both knew that she disliked her mother-in-law and would never have wanted to spend a vacation with her. But Freud says that when he and the patient analyzed the dream they found in it the wish that Freud might be wrong, and so this wish—that Freud might be wrong in his wish-fulfillment thesis—was fulfilled in her dream! He feels this interpretation is strengthened because he had recently made a painful interpretation to the patient that she had not wished to accept, so she had a strong underlying wish that Freud be wrong in general.[14] Freud believed this demonstrated his wish-fulfillment view of dreams. I am not as convinced as he is; I see it more as evidence of Freud's ingenuity and his rhetorical skills.

The place in which I find Freud's view least successful is exactly in the large groups of dreams we have discussed previously as paradigmatic: dreams after trauma as the trauma resolves, and dreams in stressful situations. I am not speaking particularly of the repetitive posttraumatic dreams of PTSD.[15] I am, rather, referring to the far more frequent dreams after trauma or in a stressful situation, which we have spoken of as contextualizing the emotion or emotional concerns of the dreamer—for instance, the frequent dreams of being engulfed by a tidal wave or being in the path of an onrushing train dreamt by a person who has experienced a severe trauma and is gradually recovering. In such dreams, which I have studied for many years, free association led the dreamer unerringly back to the traumatic situation and especially to his feelings of absolute terror and fear, sometimes tinged with guilt and other emotions. In some cases the dreamer was led to other, earlier traumas and related material, and following the chains of association did lead to therapeutic progress. However, working with these dreams did not lead to anything like latent dream thoughts that could be construed as wishes fulfilled in the dream. There was absolutely no way in which "the dream represented a particular state of affairs as the dreamer would have wished it to be."[16]

Since I believe that such dreams are very important and that they lead directly to an understanding of other dreams in less traumatic situations, I cannot accept the idea that every dream represents the fulfillment of a wish. I think that our previous formulation about dreams making connections broadly and contextualizing the emotional concerns of the dreamer has greater generalizability. Not that wish fulfillment is a useless notion. In fact, I would certainly accept that there are times when one dreams about a concern by picturing a distressful situation as resolved, or a wish as fulfilled.

I have no problem with Freud's wish-fulfillment explanation of some young children's dreams, for instance his daughter's dream, "Stwawbewwies, pudden, omblet," and young Hermann's dream, "Hermann has eaten all the cherries."[17] Both children were apparently hungry and really desired the food they dreamt about. If we can assume that little Anna's life was fairly peaceful and at that moment her chief emotional concern was her desire for more strawberries, then we could ask how a dream would picture, or contextualize, this emotional concern. In fact, there are not many ways of doing it; her dream, and Hermann's, chose a fairly obvious way to picture this wish or concern.

Likewise, when experimental subjects were asked to sleep in a thirsty state, they had significantly more dreams with thirst-related content than when not thirsty. This included drinking water or other liquids; again, drinking water is one obvious way to portray the concern of thirst, and I have no objection to calling this particular contextualization of an emotional concern the fulfillment of a wish. But the thirst-related content also included seeing a glass of water in the distance, walking around looking for a drink, and simply feeling thirsty and scratchy.[18] Such dreams or dream elements can easily be included in our view of dreams picturing an emotional concern, but it is difficult to think of them as wish fulfillments.

Overall, my impression is that Freud's thesis of wish fulfillment, now almost 100 years old, has received little support in the research literature,[19] and in addition it is not followed closely by clinicians. In

terms of research, the carefully controlled study of subjects artificially made thirsty, mentioned above, is often considered to solidly
support Freud's thesis. However, as I have mentioned, I believe it
better supports a broad view of contextualizing emotional concerns
either by portraying the wish to drink as fulfilled or by portraying
the thirsty sensations without wish fulfillment.

Finally, Freud's "Every dream is the fulfillment of a wish" is
seldom used clinically by therapists and analysts today. Many therapists working in a variety of frameworks do not acknowledge any
debt to Freud at all, but there is a trend even among Freudian
analysts and therapists to pay increasing attention to the manifest
content of the dream and not to hunt down all details of the latent
dream thoughts to find a wish. I have recently asked four different
colleagues whom I consider very solid and orthodox Freudians their
views about "Every dream is the fulfillment of a wish." Not one of
them said, "Yes, I agree with that fully." Their answers were more
along the lines of "Well, Freud was very smart and I don't want to
disagree with him too much. However, in my own work I have to
admit that I do not always find a wish in the dream. Of course with
enough free association the patient and I can often come up with a
wish, but even then the wish is not always central to the dream."

MANIFEST AND LATENT DREAM: THE DREAMWORK

Freud uses the term dreamwork to describe the process by
which the dream is constructed from underlying thoughts. I consider
some of Freud's discussion of the dreamwork, especially his discussion of condensation—bringing several settings, characters, or thoughts
together to form one dream image—to be excellent. There is no
question that condensation plays a part in construction of dreams,
and we have spoken of this as one way that dreams make connections.

Freud gives various examples of how a number of dream
thoughts are involved in producing one dream image or element. He
describes a criss-crossing of paths; "associative paths that lead from
one element of the dream to several dream thoughts and from one
dream thought to several elements of the dream." He concludes, "In

the case of every dream which I have submitted to an analysis of this kind I have invariably found these same fundamental principles confirmed: the elements of the dream are constructed out of the whole mass of dream-thoughts and each one of those elements is shown to have been determined many times over in relation to the dream thoughts."[20]

Condensation is a good description of the way dreams throw together material from different places in our lives to form a single dream element. For example, a setting in my dreams might be a place somewhat like the house I live in now but also contain elements of one or more previous homes. Likewise, a person in a dream often looks in some way different from how he really does, or has features belonging to someone else; here, the dreamwork has condensed these two people. As a very simple example, the image "Jim turned into my father," or "I dreamt of Jim but he looked different, a bit like my father" involves the condensation of a great many thoughts about Jim and thoughts or memory elements of Father.

This also brings up another small disagreement with Freud. By dreamwork Freud means the series of steps taken in the mind to transform the "latent dream" into the manifest dream. I do not believe that the term latent dream is useful. It has led some analysts to consider the actual dream—the manifest dream—as merely an unimportant screen and the latent dream as the "solid gold." Freud's position may sometimes be useful in a practical sense when one is trying to understand unconscious material in a patient or in oneself, but it obviously loses something when one tries to explore the dream in its own right. The dream *is* the manifest dream. The latent dream is not a dream but a group of underlying thoughts, concerns, and wishes.

Freud in fact sometimes used the term "latent dream thoughts," which seems much more reasonable since the material does consist of thoughts in the broad sense. I disagree with the term "latent dream" not only because we are speaking of thoughts and concerns and not a dream, but because "the latent dream" suggests a one-to-one translation or substitution. It suggests—and this is an analogy that Freud himself uses—that the dream (manifest dream) is a text written in a kind of foreign language, and that with a proper "key" we can then translate it into a text in our own (waking) language. I do not believe this is the case. In fact in most dreams I have worked with or analyzed and, in my opinion, most of those Freud himself worked on, what emerges from analyzing a dream is not a single latent dream but rather one or more emotional concerns and a whole array of related memory material—a whole web, if you will, in the nets of the mind.[21]

DREAM CENSORSHIP

Freud spends a great deal of time discussing censorship, in both the formation of dreams and elsewhere. Censorship refers to an agency or force in the mind that prevents certain material, especially disturbing material such as sexual wishes, from reaching consciousness. It is not easy to discuss dream censorship in isolation, as Freud later makes it part of his broader account of repression. Censorship keeps unconscious material from becoming conscious, or in Freud's later terms, censorship, and more broadly repression, are the ego's mechanisms for fending off disturbing material coming from the id. Freud states that repression is greatest in our normal waking condition. Dreaming involves the partial lifting of repression so that some material does get through. However, dream censorship—a force producing partial repression—keeps out or alters any material that would be too disturbing or would awaken the dreamer.

Overall, I believe that Freud's discussion of repression is a valuable one and that its value is constantly evident in psychotherapy and in examining people's motivations and actions, including one's own. Certainly there are things we would like to keep out of awareness for a number of reasons, and repression is a good name for this. I do object, as many have, to Freud's notion of censorship insofar as it implies a homunculus—a little man in the head who decides what is rejected or accepted. But I believe we can keep and use repression if we see it as related to channels in the nets of the mind, and to the relative ease or difficulty in making connections among different regions.

Certainly, to use our several imperfect metaphors for the net, we could envisage a trauma producing a tear in the net, which would make communication difficult between adjacent areas, or we could visualize an emotion-generated storm in the sea, which would make it difficult to travel from one nearby region to another. In terms of the biology of the cortex, this might involve some form of inhibition of widely dispersed but potentially communicating subregions.

There are unquestionably times when something important is blocked off and cannot be accessed by waking thought. It makes perfect sense to look at dreaming as a "partial lifting of repression," and in fact this can be related to what we have called the broader making of connections in dreams. However, I have a problem with Freud's view that there is a basic need to censor or distort all material related to sexual wishes. In hindsight, at least, this seems to be more a characteristic of late 19th-century Victorian culture than a universal attribute of the human mind. We will discuss this again when we speak of sexual symbols below.

FREE ASSOCIATION

Another important aspect of Freud's work is his invention of the technique of free association, which is in use wherever psycho-analysis or dynamic psychotherapy is practiced. Broadly, free association means that the person undergoing analysis (or for that matter a person trying to understand a dream) is asked simply to say whatever comes to mind. The instructions are to keep nothing out because it sounds absurd or unrelated or embarrassing, but simply to bring up without reservation whatever thoughts come to mind. This is easy to say, but many find it very hard to do. Free association has proved to be an immensely useful technique not only in therapy but also in dream interpretation. Applied to dream interpretation, Freud's technique means reporting what comes to mind about each element of the dream in turn. The chains of association starting from each element in the dream, then, lead back to the material that, according to Freud, originally formed the dream. In Freud's terms, the associative chains reverse the path of dream formation, leading back from the manifest dream to the latent dream thoughts. The chains of association do not simply diverge, but often intersect in the sense that certain thoughts or wishes in the patient's past come up repeatedly in chains starting from different dream elements. These recurring elements are what Freud calls the latent dream. For instance, in Freud's dream of Irma's injection, he proceeds by starting with each phase of the dream, beginning with "a great hall," and continuing with various people and events that come up in the dream. The chains of associations lead him to concerns about several other patients and his worries that he may have mistreated a patient and is responsible for the ensuing problems. Several such chains then lead him to the wish that if there is anything wrong with his patients, it not be his responsibility but rather someone else's.

I use the technique of free association all the time and am grateful to Freud for inventing and introducing it. However, I have several concerns. First, on a theoretical level, it has often been pointed out that the thoughts arrived at by free association (the "latent dream thoughts") may not necessarily constitute the thoughts and material that originally formed the dream. In other words, something meaningful often emerges, but it is not necessarily something that led to the formation of the dream. For instance, a patient and I sometimes work on a dream that she dreamt some days or weeks before. Often among the material that comes up in the chains of association are daytime events that occurred *after* the time of the dream, and also sometimes daytime wishes and concerns that came up later and were not present at the time the dream occurred. Nonetheless, these elements are incorporated into the chains of free associations in a similar manner to other material, and sometimes they help form quite a coherent pattern of underlying thoughts and concerns. These can be meaningful and can be worked with therapeutically, but they could not have produced the dream originally. Thus, contrary to Freud, what was arrived at by the process of free association cannot be exactly what formed the dream in the first place. One cannot simply reverse the process of association to arrive at the process of dream formation.

On a more practical level, one major problem with free association is that it is more or less endless and that if one truly goes on associating to each element of the dream and says whatever comes to mind, one can easily fill up reams of paper and hours of time or weeks of therapy: The mass of material can easily become over-whelming. Sometimes the chains of association do converge on one prominent underlying wish, fear, or concern in such a striking fash-ion that the dreamer and therapist are both convinced that this is the principal meaning of the dream. Often, however, this is not the case, and it is much more difficult to be certain of what is going on. On the one hand, the mass of associations may lead the therapist or dreamer to abandon finding any meaning. On the other hand, it allows the therapist to impose his or her own preconceptions on the material, since almost any idea or hypothesis will find some resonance or some confirmation in all this material. This imposition of meaning is often not consciously planned by the therapist. It can happen without the therapist's being quite aware of what is happening, and it constitutes a major problem in doing therapy.[22]

Whether or not the amount of material is overwhelming, one must be very aware of the dangers of free association. It is by no means always a direct path leading back from a manifest dream to a single latent dream as its interpretation; rather, a number of delicate strands or threads can begin with the dream material but diverge in many directions. It is essential to keep in mind that the threads are under the influence not only of whatever thoughts or concerns origi-nally produced the dream, but of many later forces as well. Many thoughts and concerns may be in the air at the time the dream is being told and interpreted, including the dreamer's mood and state of mind on that particular day, feelings toward the therapist or listener, and many other factors. These threads are likewise influ-enced by the interests, thoughts, and theories of the therapist or other listener, who may often, without noticing it, alter the flow of associa-tion simply by asking or not asking certain questions, by pointing to one word or phrase rather than to another, or even by tone of voice.

Thus, there are problems with free association as a means of approaching dreams, and the technique must be used with delicacy and caution. But when handled carefully and if conducted by a therapist who is trained and adept at sticking with the dreamer's material without introducing his own preconceptions, there is no doubt that free association can be helpful in dealing with and understanding dreams. I would add that Freud's technique of free association to each element is by no means the only way to understand dreams. For instance, Jung and Jungian analysts use a technique called amplification.[23] In this technique an element or image in a dream is held in the mind and considered from all aspects, played with, fantasized about, connected to other images, stories, or myths, and perhaps drawn, painted, sculpted, or depicted in other ways, all of which can help the dreamer gain further insights. Jungians have also developed a technique called active imagination[24] in which one starts from the dream story, or a strong dream image, and then extends the story or makes up a new story, usually with oneself as a character. We have considered in Chapter 8 various other approaches to dreams, all of which have their functions.

Sexual Symbolism

Freud's view of sexual symbolism in dreams has certainly caught the public imagination. Many who have not read Freud or have read only bits and pieces appear to believe that using sexual symbols was Freud's main technique of dream interpretation. This is unfair to Freud since he emphasizes that dreams should be interpreted using the free associations of the dreamer whenever possible, and that referring to "standard sexual symbols" is only a secondary method, useful when there are no free associations or when they do not lead to a satisfactory interpretation.

Freud does spend many pages of his work on dreams discussing sexual symbolism. Some of his best known comments are:

> All elongated objects, such as sticks, tree trunks and umbrellas
> . . . may stand for the male organ—as well as all long sharp
> weapons such as knives, daggers and pikes. Boxes, cases, chests,
> cupboards and ovens represent the uterus, and also hollow
> objects, ships and vessels of all kinds. Rooms in dreams are
> usually women. If the various ways in and out of them are
> represented, this interpretation is scarcely open to doubt. Steps,
> ladders or staircases, or, as the case may be, walking up or down
> them, are representations of the sexual act. . . . It is highly

probable that all complicated machinery and apparatus in the dream stands for the genitals (and as a rule the male ones)."[25]

These constitute many of the well-known "Freudian symbols." Another early analyst, William Stekel, gives hundreds of additional examples of sexual symbols.[26] But after discussing all of these symbols, Freud also states:

> At the same time however, I should like to utter an express warning of overestimating the importance of symbols in dream interpretation, against restricting the work of translating in dreams merely to translating symbols and against abandoning the technique of making use of the dreamer's associations.[27]

What can we do with all this sexual symbolism? Can we relate it to our contemporary theory of dreaming? To a limited extent I agree with Freud. There is certainly overlap in the nets of our minds between the patterns representing penis and patterns representing other long, thin objects, which can show up in a number of different ways in jokes, stories, and cartoons as well as in dreams. Along the lines previously discussed, the dream is especially good at making such connections.

But Freud would say it was much more specific than that: The latent thoughts often involve sexual organs, or sexual intercourse, and these are almost invariably translated into the symbolic objects of the dream. Indeed, the dreams Freud discusses from his patients and others appear to be full of sexual symbols including brooms, cigars, daggers, bushy entrance paths, and so on. Apparently, Freud's patients and friends dreamt of those symbols and very seldom dreamt openly of actual bodies, penises, or sexual intercourse. However, things appear to have changed to a certain extent. My patients and the many persons from whom I have collected dreams frequently dream of sexual intercourse and sexual organs directly. I cannot help thinking that social climate plays a role. In Vienna of the 1890s, the use of sexual symbols representing or disguising the sexual organs was extremely common in speech, writing, jokes, and no doubt also in dreams, whereas now the climate does not require the hiding of direct sexual material to such an extent.

I have a number of long series of dreams in my files from young men who obviously wanted sex but for one reason or another were deprived of it. Their dreams often appeared to relate to this sex-deprived state. I have not done a careful quantitative study, but these dreams can be roughly divided into three groups. The first large group consisted of fairly straightforward dreams dealing with women in various states of undress, with foreplay, and with sexual inter-course, without disguise or symbolic representation of organs or intercourse. There was a second smaller but sizable group of dreams very similar to those Freud analyzed; these involved excitedly run-ning up stairs, bursting into rooms through narrow passages, or engaging in fencing matches. These dreams do appear to depict sexual organs symbolically in Freud's sense. One of the men repeat-edly had dreams of a child in a the bow of a little boat or canoe; on waking, he immediately associated this image with the appearance of the clitoris in the vaginal opening. Third, there was a smaller group of dreams whose relationship with sex was less direct; these involved long romantic stories, sometimes taking the form of medieval quests searching for a rose, or a hidden treasure in the mountains, battles over the reputation of a lady, and so on. These were similar to myths; Jung would have been very familiar with dreams of this kind.

Apparently, sexual organs and sexual intercourse can appear in dreams in a number of different forms, and there is certainly no universal rule against picturing them directly. One recent study com-pared the percentage of students who reported dreaming of sexual activity in 1958 and in 1996; the same questionnaire was used. Whereas only 36% of women students described dreaming directly of sexual activity in 1958, 72% did so in 1996.[28]

These findings lead to the question of who, under what condi-tions, dreams of sex directly, who dreams of knives or other symbols, and who dreams of mythical stories. Presumably the social climate, as suggested above, makes a difference, and of course the personality of the dreamers plays a role, too, but we will not pursue this in detail here.

In this context it may be of interest to examine some writings of ancient dream interpreters. For instance, a famous Greek Byzantine dream expert, writing in around the 10th century AD under the Arab name Achmet, summarizes his dream interpretations and those of the other dream interpreters he respects. Among the men who came to him for help, dreaming openly of the penis was apparently quiet common. Achmet wrote:

> The penis is judged as a man's reputation, power, and children. If someone dreams that his penis is large and erect, his reputation will be widespread and he will beget sons. . . . If the dreamer is a king, he will be long-lived and then he may see his son succeed him. . . . If the dreamer is a commoner he will grow in his way of life. . . . If a woman dreams she has a penis she will have a son who will honor his family.[29]

Here the situation is quite different from 19th-century Vienna. The penis is dreamt of openly and the dream interpreter tries to relate it to what he guesses or knows are the main concerns of his clients—his kingdom, his power, his children.

Overall, I agree with Freud to a limited extent: There may well be connections in the mind between the penis and various elongated objects, and these may show up in dreams. However, the connection is not the simple organ-to-symbol translation that Freud describes. If we think of representation in the nets of the mind along the lines discussed in previous chapters, we might first say that the penis is represented in a pattern that overlaps somewhat the pattern for cigar or dagger, so a general activation of the patterns representing penis might sometimes lead to cigar or dagger or mixtures of the two. But remember that in my model I do not speak of a direct substitution, where one object represents another. Rather, we have considered in detail the pictorial representation (contextualization) of an emotional concern. Thus, in my series, a man whose main concern at a particular time is sexual deprivation may portray his emotional concern directly in dreams of sexual organs, naked women, or sexual intercourse, but he may also picture these concerns in other ways. If he lives in a time and place where sexual organs are mentioned only indirectly and this is consistent with his personality, he may picture his concerns by the use of sexual symbols and come up with a dream that includes "Freudian symbols." Or if he is a young writer in love with romantic poetry and literature, developing his writing skills, attending a boys-only boarding school (an actual case), he may dream of the same emotional concern in a more storylike or mythlike way and produce what looks like a very "Jungian" dream.

Thus, I am not disagreeing totally with the existence of sexual symbols; I believe there are connections of this kind in the mind. However, I believe dreaming does not involve a one-way translation of a sexual organ, for instance, into a sexual symbol. Rather, the dream will find one of a number of ways of picturing the emotional concern of the dreamer.

THE FUNCTION OF DREAMING IS TO PRESERVE SLEEP

I am not happy with Freud's formulation that the basic function of dreaming is to preserve sleep, though I have to admit there could be a kernel of truth in it. I have outlined at length my views on the functions of dreaming in terms of handling trauma or new material, weaving, and cross-connecting. These proposed functions could be compatible with preserving sleep as well. For instance, calming an emotional storm can, among other things, preserve sleep, so perhaps sleep preservation could be a function, though not *the* function, of dreaming and still be consistent with my views.

Is there any research to support Freud's view? The most direct attempts have involved Freud's own paradigm—examining what happens when a stimulus is introduced during sleep. Will it, as Freud predicts, produce a dream rather than an awakening? I would say that at least in its strongest form this view is currently untenable. The view that dreaming preserves sleep might predict that an external stimulus such as the ringing of a bell, if it occurred during non-REM sleep (which constitutes 75% of the night), would induce REM sleep and thus produce dreaming. Research into this possibility has shown this not to be the case.[30] Alternatively, one might predict that such external stimuli might induce a dream from non-REM sleep incorporating the stimulus—a non-REM dream. Again this has not been found in any studies.[31] However, it might be possible to keep Freud's thesis in some form. Data partially consistent with Freud's formulation involve the effects of a stimulus presented during the 15–25% of the night that constitutes REM sleep. Introduced at this time, a stimulus is indeed incorporated into the dream at least some of the time (data vary from 9% to 75%).[32] In these situations sleep, or at least REM sleep, may be said to be preserved, although no studies show that sleep was actually lengthened or deepened by such incorporation. These findings have led some to modify Freud's view to "perhaps the dream functions only to preserve *REM sleep*."[33] Though I believe that Freud's formulation as it stands is untenable, I could accept a broader reading of Freud implying that the dream functions to handle disturbance (internal or external). What I have spoken of as the calming of a stormy sea and the weaving in of new material is consistent with Freud's formulation in this more generic form.

Dreaming versus the Dream

Finally, I have a disagreement with Freud about his overall emphasis on the *dream*, where I would focus on the *process of dreaming*. Freud's emphasis, repeated in numerous places, is that a dream is a strange, irrational, apparently meaningless mental production somewhat like a slip of the tongue or a neurotic symptom. A dream seems totally meaningless until it is subjected to interpretation that establishes that the dream (or slip of the tongue or symptom) derives from entirely rational underlying wishes and dream thoughts distorted by intrapsychic forces. At this point, after interpretation, Freud suggests that we can let the manifest dream go since we have now arrived at valuable underlying material that can be used in the analysis.

I do not see dreams in this way, and I prefer to examine the entire process of dreaming rather than a single dream. I consider dreaming a form of mental functioning that, as we recall, falls at one end of a continuum with focused waking thought at the other end. A dream is a piece of this process; it is not a quirk or an irrational mental product at all, and it is certainly not a husk that can be discarded after the underlying dream thoughts have been discovered.

First of all, and this is a minor point, a dream is not a well-delimited event. I often wake in the morning remembering a lot of dream material but being quite unsure whether I had three dreams or one long dream in three scenes. Even awakenings from REM sleep in the laboratory produce material that is unclear in this way. We do not know what "a dream" is unless we wish arbitrarily to call whatever is remembered after one REM awakening "one" dream.

Mainly, I think we need to focus on the entire process of dreaming and to learn its laws as we have been doing in this book and as was done by Freud in his discussion of the dreamwork. The dream then can then be considered a somewhat arbitrarily defined segment of this process of dreaming.

A Possible Synthesis

I have summarized above my agreements and disagreements with some of Freud's major theses on dreams. Despite disagreements on some principal points, I also see similarities between Freud's views and those I have outlined here, and ways in which Freud's thinking could be placed in the context I have been developing. I will outline this in a very sketchy fashion.

First, I believe it is not too difficult to map some of Freud's major thinking about the mind onto the neural nets we have been discussing. Most of the workings of the mind—our thoughts, memories, dreams, and so on—are functions of patterns of activation and connection in the neural nets based in the cerebral cortex. Freud's concept of the ego, especially the part of it functioning in a relatively untroubled manner (conflict-free ego sphere)[34] corresponds to the smooth functioning of the neural nets of the cortex. This functioning is often influenced massively by what is going on emotionally— which I have called in very general terms emotional concerns. This for Freud involves derivatives of the id consisting of various wishes, fears, and emotions, all deriving from basic, unavoidable childhood conflicts. In anatomical terms this implicates, roughly speaking, the influence on the cortex of subcortical structures, especially the amygdala and other parts of the limbic system dealing with emotion.

Using this rough view of the neural net and its anatomy, Freud and I could then agree that the dream is instigated by an emotional concern within the mind, though this might be a major disturbance triggered by external trauma, or a minor concern caused by a blood pressure cuff. This emotional concern or internal disturbance, which Freud would describe in his own terms, then guides (in my terms) the making of connections in the neural nets. Freud would certainly agree on the emotional instigation, and he might agree in a general sense that this guides the formation of connections. In fact, his discussion of condensation and the other mechanisms of the dream-work can be considered a description of how such connections are made and put together to form a dream. Freud would insist on the primacy of a wish rather than other concerns, and would also insist on a relationship to childhood wishes and conflicts. Though I do not think that a wish is always involved, I certainly agree that it is possible and often useful to find relationships between current emotional concerns and childhood events or conflicts.[35]

Thus, in this broad sense, the connecting process of dreaming is guided by an underlying concern, and this broad making of connections produces a cross connection or calming (calms a stormy sea), which is perhaps not far from Freud's view of the dream handling drives and wishes by forming a compromise that preserves sleep. There are some similarities after all, though perhaps I've pushed a bit hard in trying to produce a synthesis.

An Apology to Jung

There is likewise much in the current theory of dreaming that can be considered consistent with Jung's view of dreams. I am a great admirer of Jung's work, and if I were writing a general survey of work on dreams I would devote a lot of space to him. However, I have not discussed Jung in detail here since he did not write out systematic theses about dreaming with which I can agree or disagree. Therefore I apologize to Jung for my neglect.

There is one relevant topic I can discuss briefly which comes up repeatedly in Jung's work: the idea of "compensation" in dreams.[36] Compensation is usually contrasted with "continuity," and there is a great deal of debate as to whether dreams are continuous with waking life or compensatory.[37] Continuity implies that the thoughts, feelings, and imagery of dreaming are continuous with the waking thoughts of the dreamer, while by compensation Jung meant that dreams deal with the material neglected or avoided by waking consciousness. Jung puts it in his own way, stating that dreams reflect the neglected "inferior functions of the psyche." Jung is quite emphatic: "The relation between the conscious and unconscious is compensatory. This is one of the best-proven rules of dream interpretation. When we set out to interpret a dream, it is always helpful to ask: What conscious attitude does it compensate?"[38]

There is a great deal of research evidence relating the content of dreams waking thoughts or waking activity, which is usually

Table 2. Major Propositions about Dreaming

Proposition	Freud's View	Biologists	This View
1. Dreams are irrational or psychotic mental products	Yes	Yes	No
2. Every dream is a fulfillment of a wish	Yes	No	No
3. Dreams are "the royal road" or at least a good road to the unconscious	Yes	No	Yes
4. Dreams are disguised—the product of "censorship"	Yes	No	No
5. Dreams are essentially a random pattern of activity	No	Yes	No
6. The dream (manifest dream) is important without interpretation or translation	No	No	Yes
7. Dreams are useful (functional) even if forgotten	No	No	Yes
8. Dreaming is on a continuum with waking, reverie, daydreaming	No	No	Yes
9. In dreams begin responsiblities	No	No	Yes

taken as supporting the continuity between dreaming and waking.[39] I would claim that our present theory is quite consistent with the occurrence of both continuity and compensation in dreams. Most of what we have summarized in previous chapters suggests continuity. The emotional concerns we have found guiding the formation of dreams are the emotional concerns of the dreamer awake as well as asleep. However, when I spoke of *unresolved* emotional concerns influencing dreams more than other concerns, this is a way of describing compensation. In fact, Freud's view of repressed material surfacing or returning in dreams is also consistent with Jung's view of compensation.

I have reviewed in this chapter Freud's theses on dreams and some major areas of agreement and disagreement. To a lesser extent I have also discussed the views of Jung and the modern biologists. Table 2 summarizes Freud's views, the biologists' views, and my views on the principal points.[40] The last item, "In dreams begin responsibilities," has not been discussed and will be taken up in Chapter 14. I believe the theory I have been developing here is more consistent than Freud's with the research and clinical material we have reviewed, and I also believe it is more consistent with what those of us who love dreams and/or work with dreams in therapy are already doing and feel that we already know.

In the next chapter we will relate this view of dreaming to what we know of the biology of sleep and dreaming.

Chapter Eleven

THE BIOLOGY OF DREAMING

I have spoken relatively little so far of the biology of sleep and REM sleep. Yet, any believable view of the nature and functions of dreaming must at least be compatible with relevant biological occurrences during sleep, especially the biology of REM sleep, which is the usual and best-suited biological place for dreaming to occur.

REM AND NON-REM SLEEP

The discovery of REM sleep produced an outburst of important exploratory research starting in the 1950s and blossoming in the 1960s. It was an exciting time to be involved in sleep research, and I well remember the sense that important questions were being answered about the biology and basic nature of dreaming, and that these insights would help us to understand the biology of mental illness and the biology of the mind. I optimistically called my attempt to synthesize the work of my laboratory and others in this field the Biology of Dreaming.[1] We were, of course, studying the biology of REM sleep. The most important features of REM sleep (see below)—the EEG desynchronization, eye movements, changes in the peripheral autonomic nervous system, etc.—were intriguing in themselves and appeared to us to be leading straight to a complete understanding of dreaming.

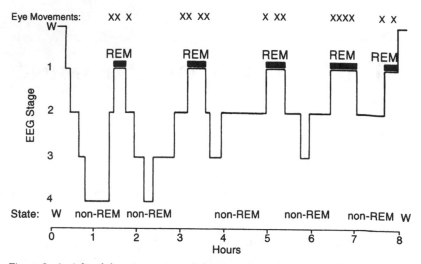

Figure 8. A night of sleep in a young adult. We go through four or five cycles of sleep, each cycle consisting of a period of non-REM sleep (subdivided into stages 1–4) and a period of REM sleep.

The basic findings, in brief summary, suggest a picture of human sleep somewhat as follows (see Fig. 8).[2] As sleep begins, the brain waves and other measures show the onset of sleep and a deepening over 30–60 minutes. However, a night of sleep does not consist merely of gradual deepening, followed by lightening. Rather, every 90–120 minutes, sleep seems to change dramatically. A totally different state of sleep emerges, characterized by rapid eye movements (REMs), by brain waves that appear activated, resembling very light sleep or even waking, but accompanied by profound relaxation of most muscles (similar to very deep sleep). This surprising new state of sleep, which can be called neither light nor deep, but only different, has been given many names, but is now generally known as REM sleep. There are typically three to five REM sleep periods in a night of human sleep, taking up 20–25% of sleep. The remaining 75–80% of sleep is referred to as non-REM sleep. So different is REM sleep from the rest of sleep on almost all biological measures that some researchers have suggested that we pass our lives in three states of existence: waking, non-REM sleep, and REM sleep.[3]

These two basic states of sleep, REM and non-REM sleep, are found throughout life, though the amounts differ at different ages. These two states of REM and non-REM sleep have been found in almost all mammals that have undergone study.[4] Recordings from the brains of animals have demonstrated a number of centers and pathways involved in REM and non-REM sleep. It has been shown for instance that the alternation between REM and non-REM sleep depends on the reciprocal activation and inhibition of several centers in the brainstem; these centers send neurons up to the forebrain and down to the spinal cord to produce the changes that differentiate REM from non-REM sleep.[5]

What made this complex biological state of REM sleep so exciting from a psychological point of view was the early discovery that people who were awakened from REM sleep usually reported dreams while non-REM awakenings produced few or no dream reports.[6] Though this is still the basic finding, life turns out to be not quite so simple. A large number of studies have shown that while most REM sleep awakenings do indeed produce reports of dreaming, it is not the case that awakenings at other times produce no dreams. Very dreamlike dream reports, though seldom as long, can sometimes be obtained from awakenings just at or after sleep onset and sometimes from ordinary-looking non-REM sleep as well.[7]

Therefore, it now appears clear that the well-studied biology of REM sleep can more accurately be considered a biology that supports and facilitates dreaming rather than biology absolutely necessary for the occurrence of dreaming. There is no question that REM sleep is a good setting for dreaming, but it is not the only one. What we know as dreaming can be and most often is initiated by the activation of the forebrain, including the cortex, by the brainstem, but dreaming can also be initiated by limbic seizures that do not involve the brainstem, and it can be activated by the anatomically less-defined changes that occur at dream onset. Thus the true biology of dreaming we are seeking cannot be a biology of the body as a whole or the brainstem, but must be basically the biology of the cortex and some underlying subcortical structures.

DREAMING AND THE BIOLOGY OF THE CEREBRAL CORTEX

Evidently, the physiology defining REM sleep above is important, but it is a physiology that facilitates dreaming. It is not yet the exact biology of dreaming. The biology most relevant to understanding dreaming as opposed to focused waking must be at the level of the detailed biology of the cerebral cortex and its neural nets, which are extremely difficult to study directly. There must be a complex pattern of excitation and inhibition in the neurons making up the nets of the mind for each particular dream image and dream. There must also be a style or general pattern of such activation and inhibition of the cortex that underlies the experience of dreaming in general as opposed to waking thought in general.[8]

The biological pattern we are seeking that underlies dreaming must be one that is regularly induced in the cortex by the conditions of REM sleep, but which can also occur at times in other states. For instance, it can occur briefly at the onset of sleep and perhaps at certain very relaxed times (reverie) during waking, when we know dreams or dreamlike experiences are found. So far, we are incapable of studying directly the huge number of individual neurons and individual neuronal connections in the cortex, but we can at least approach this presumed cortical pattern in several ways.

Neurology of Dreaming

First we can examine the neurology and neuropsychology of dreaming and perhaps determine what sort of brain damage can eliminate or alter dreaming in predictable ways, which should give us an idea of what portions of the brain, especially the cortex, are involved. There are older surveys of brain damage and their effect on dreaming, and also a detailed series of studies recently published by Mark Solms.[9] One of his chief conclusions is that the experiencing of dreams depends on cortical, not brainstem, mechanisms. Only certain cortical and subcortical lesions produce total cessation of dreaming, while other cortical lesions produce specifically cessation of visual dreaming. Solms concludes from all his studies of brain damage that certain cortical and subcortical areas are especially important in the normal dream process.[10]

Brain Imaging Studies

Secondly, we are able to use various new recording and imaging techniques to look at the overall activity produced by firings of large numbers of neurons. For example, brain electrical activity mapping (BEAM) studies have recently been able to demonstrate certain definite similarities between the patterns of cortical activation during sleep onset and the patterns during REM sleep.[11] The similarity of patterns is consistent with the fact that dreamlike mental content often occurs at sleep onset.

Studies using the very powerful techniques termed positron emission tomography (PET) as well as functional magnetic resonance imaging (fMRI) have also demonstrated many similarities between brain activation during REM sleep and during waking but with certain clear differences.[12] For instance, carefully controlled PET studies show REM sleep to be characterized by a decrease in activity in the frontal areas of the cortex but increased activity in posterior areas, consistent with the highly visual nature of dreaming. These studies also show powerful activation of some subcortical regions during REM sleep, especially the amygdala, a center known to take part in emotion. This finding is consistent with the powerful influence of underlying emotion we have discussed. These techniques are still being perfected, but the results mostly agree with, and help to refine, the lesion studies above.

Pharmacology of Dreaming

The administration of drugs or chemicals can certainly influence dreaming. There are large numbers of small clinical studies on drugs and dreaming, but the results are not easy to summarize. Many different drugs tend to reduce REM sleep and reported dreaming,[13] so it may be more important to look at a few situations that involve an increase in or intensification of dreaming. Cholinergic drugs—those

that increase the effect in the brain of the transmitter acetylcholine—
very definitely increase both REM sleep and reported dreaming.[14]
This is consistent with the known role of acetylcholine in the mechanisms of REM sleep. Dopaminergic drugs, which increase effects of
dopamine, increase reported dreaming without increasing REM
sleep.[15] One controlled study showed that small doses of l-DOPA, a
precursor of dopamine, increased the vividness, "dreamlikeness,"
and detail of dreams without increasing REM sleep.[16] Such studies
provide at least a hint that brain dopamine plays a role in the intensity of reported dreams.[17]

Neurochemistry of Dreaming

Another approach involves studying neurochemistry, the natural chemical milieu, and examining in detail the chemicals (neuro-
humors) that flood the cortex during REM sleep as opposed to those
present during waking. In fact, this approach has led to the discovery
of some clear differences between REM sleep and waking. REM is
characterized by the almost total absence of released norepinephrine
at the cortex.[18] In fact, as early as 1973, I spoke of dreaming as "the
activity of the cortex without the influence of norepinephrine and the
related amines."[19] I believe that the lack of norepinephrine at the
cortex during REM sleep is an important determinant of the characteristics of dreaming we have discussed, including the making of
broad connections.

All these approaches provide not definitive answers but con-
verging hints about the biology of dreaming, which clearly involves
the detailed biology of the cerebral cortex.

BIOLOGY OF THE CORTEX, AND NETS OF THE MIND

In rough terms, following our discussion of "nets of the mind" in
previous chapters, I would first reiterate that there appear to be
broader connections and thus less sharp focus in dreaming than in
waking. Focus can perhaps be put in terms of "increased signal-to-
noise ratio" or "inhibitory sharpening"—the presence of areas of

strong excitation in a central area, clearly separated from surrounding areas of inhibition. Such inhibitory sharpening would be found most clearly in active focused waking, and least in dreaming. This is consistent with the biology of REM sleep, since norepinephrine has frequently been described as producing inhibitory sharpening,[20] and release of norepinephrine almost entirely stops at the cortex during REM sleep.

Perhaps this is also relevant to the biology underlying the entire continuum we have discussed previously. I suggest that there is a high level of norepinephrine and related amines released at the cortex during active, focused waking activity and somewhat less when the person is drowsy, in reverie, or falling asleep, and least of all during REM sleep. There is not yet much evidence for this, though studies do suggest a reduced firing of neurons that release norepinephrine at the cortex as an animal becomes drowsy and falls asleep—times when in humans there appears to be more dreamlike activity.[21]

We can think of the relationship between waking and dreaming in terms of signal-to-noise ratio, highest in waking, and lowest in dreaming. Again, increasing the signal-to-noise ratio is one way in which the functions of norepinephrine have been described. Signal-to-noise ratio is not a perfect description of what happens at the cortex, since under many conditions we cannot specify a priori what is signal and what is noise. However, the clearest case would be focused waking activity, such as an outfielder chasing a fly ball in which "signal" consists of the sensory input, such as seeing the ball and the terrain plus associated processing, leading to the appropriate required motor output—running to catch the ball. In this case there is one clear signal; activity in the surrounding cortex would be considered "noise." In more relaxed states or in reverie, when one is playing with ideas or seeking something new, what was previously "noise" may be very important. The extreme of this condition occurs in dreaming, when there is no "signal," when the sense organs and the highly specialized signal-processing regions of the nets are relatively inactive. Now the nets are dominated by "noise" in this sense. But as we know, noise need not be random or unpleasant. It may on occasion be beautiful, emotion-guided music.

Thinking less chemically now but simply in terms of pathways being used in the cortex, I would suggest that focused waking thought involves the repeated use of certain well-worn pathways with relatively little straying off the path; dreaming would be the opposite, with a great deal of wandering (Fig. 1, page 81). Thinking of excitation flowing along in a single channel or rut (A-B-C-D) is, of course, a great oversimplification. "A" in Figure 1 is a whole state at a given moment, involving distributed activation in many different cortical areas. "A" then leads to a second, third, and fourth state in fairly regular and predictable sequence in the active waking state. Thus, during active focused waking functioning, pattern A would almost always lead to pattern B, followed by C and D, whereas during dreaming the patterns would be more diffuse and much less predictable.

This sort of picture is of course very compatible with our two previous descriptions. The "rut" pattern we discussed above can also be characterized as inhibitory sharpening and a high signal-to-noise ratio (corresponding to A-B-C-D processing). This view of waking versus dreaming is also consistent with a number of biological studies. First, many studies of REM sleep have demonstrated the irregularity and less-controlled character of various physiological measures. As early as 1967, summarizing the characteristics of waking and REM sleep, I pointed out that activity level in the brain was high in both waking and REM, but they were different in that waking was characterized by fine adjustment, or good feedback, whereas REM was associated with rough adjustment or poor feedback.[22] Among the best-studied examples of this is the finding that temperature adjustment in mammals (homeothermic animals) works very well during waking and during non-REM sleep, whereas the adjustment is almost completely lost during REM sleep. We are "poikilothermic" (cold-blooded) animals during REM sleep.[23] The present view simply extends the same principle to the spread of excitation in the cortex. There is a great deal of control or negative feedback during focused waking, and this is not present during REM sleep.

FUNCTIONS OF DREAMING AND FUNCTIONS OF REM SLEEP

We have discussed a possible function of dreams involving the making of connections in a broad manner, "weaving in" trauma and other new material. Because most dreaming occurs during REM sleep, any suggested function of dreaming should be at least compatible with the functions of REM sleep, the biological state underlying most dreams. Ideally, functions of dreaming, representing the cortical or "highest level" aspect of REM sleep, should have a function consistent with the other, "lower-level" functions.

Unfortunately, there is not complete agreement on the functions of REM sleep, though many intriguing lines of research suggest that it must have some function. I believe there are at least three broad areas of research on the functions of REM sleep that could be relevant to the functions of dreaming we have discussed earlier.

One large area of research deals with the possible role of REM sleep in learning and memory formation. A number of studies have used the approach of REM deprivation in humans and animals. Although the results do not agree perfectly, there is some consensus that REM deprivation interferes with learning, especially on relatively complex tasks. In numerous animal studies REM deprivation has been shown to interfere not with the very simplest forms of stimulus-response learning but with complex learning that involves integrative skills. These studies are not always easy to interpret since REM deprivation involves some form of mechanical stimulation or device that forcibly keeps the animal from entering REM sleep, and this is inevitably a stressful procedure. Thus various ways have to be devised to control for this stress, and the control measures have introduced other problems of their own. Regardless, there is at least agreement that REM deprivation interferes with some forms of learning.[24]

More striking findings have come from a different approach to the same problem, studying the effects of learning upon subsequent sleep. Such studies in animals have demonstrated increases in REM sleep following certain kinds of learning. For example, a whole series of animal studies has shown clearly that REM sleep is remarkably increased after learning—usually for a number of hours after an emotionally important learning task. Several studies have even shown that rats that are learning a task properly have definite increases of REM sleep whereas rats that seem unable to learn the task do not show this increase.[25] Some studies find an effect of the same kind in humans, but only when the learning is very intense. One study has demonstrated increases in REM sleep in a few subjects after very intense language-learning that lasted several weeks and that was emotionally quite important to the students.[26] Another study demonstrated an increased REM sleep tendency in subjects who had gone through an emotional "marathon group" weekend that involved a great deal of emotional upset and learning.[27] Studies of sleep following simple learning tasks—learning lists of nonsense syllables or associations—have not shown changes in REM sleep.[28]

Thus both of these research approaches lead to the conclusion that REM sleep is necessary or at least useful for some kinds of learning to occur. And the human studies suggest that it is not little puzzles or word lists, but rather, complex, intense, or emotionally important learning that is involved. Since learning almost certainly involves formation of new connections in the brain, this function of REM sleep is certainly consistent with the connection-making function of dreaming I have suggested earlier.

There is a second body of research showing that all mammalian species with one or two probable exceptions have REM sleep and that REM sleep is always especially prominent in very young animals.[29] Levels are especially high at birth; some animals studied in utero have shown similarly high or higher levels of REM sleep. Obviously this is a time when the nervous system, especially the brain, is developing rapidly. These data have led researchers to propose that REM sleep "functions to develop the nervous system" in the immature animal.[30] Looking across species it is also noteworthy that mammalian species, which are born relatively immature and thus need to have more brain development after birth are those species that show more REM time in both young and mature animals. Perhaps these are the species that need and use more connection-making (see next chapter). Development of the nervous system must involve making new connections and altering connections among neurons, so this is clearly related to what we have discussed about making connections in dreams.

A third body of research—chiefly pharmacological and neurochemical studies—led me to suggest that a function of REM sleep is the restoration or resensitization of norepinephrine-dependent systems in the forebrain. The idea was that these systems at the cortex and elsewhere somehow wore out or became less sensitive during the day or during waking activity, and that one of the functions of sleep—and especially of REM sleep—was to restore or resensitize these systems.[31] The role of these norepinephrine receptors and norepinephrine-dependent systems is not certain, but it appears to involve regulation at a number of levels.

At the most basic level such regulation involves the body's homeostatic mechanism, including homeothermy, the ability to maintain relatively constant body temperature despite variations of outside temperature; this is an essential attribute of the mammalian (and avian) body. In fact, carefully controlled studies on long-term REM deprivation show that this lack of heat control (thermoregulation) is what kills rats after several weeks of REM deprivation.[32] I think it likely that a whole series of such control mechanisms may be similarly affected, but since the lack of heat regulation has the largest effect, it kills the animals before the other disturbances are very noticeable. At a behavioral level, studies in animals and humans suggest that REM deprivation produces a disregulation of emotional behaviors, leading to impulsivity and/or poorly regulated social behavior.[33] As we have noted, these regulatory systems are probably not functioning well during REM sleep. We can think of the systems as somehow "off-line" or "being restored" during REM sleep.

Thus, speculatively, I see REM sleep as restoring especially those regulatory systems—including thermal regulation—that are not functioning well (out being restored?) during REM sleep. At the cortical level during REM sleep, the cortical activity (dreaming) makes new connections, "ties up loose ends," producing better cortical functioning during waking the next day. In other words, much as relatively unregulated (poikilothermic) REM sleep is necessary for later homeothermy, so perhaps is the broad cortical connection-making of dreaming necessary for better focused thought the next day, or in future days.

The three research-based views of the functions of REM sleep we have reviewed are not at all mutually exclusive. They are quite consistent with each other, and all are related to making connections in the central nervous system at various times and at various levels. First, at the earliest or most basic level, a newborn or very young animal needs to develop its nervous system, by making and regulating connections between neurons. Presumably this happens all day and all night, but quite likely the connections relating to specific skills and abilities (tightly woven areas) are best made in waking, while broader weaving-in occurs especially in REM sleep.

This has already taken us to the second function. The role of REM sleep in learning. Learning is especially prominent in young animals but obviously continues into later life. REM appears to play some role in new learning, especially when it is complex and emotionally important (the animal and the human studies ensured that the learning was emotionally significant). Finally, on a subtler level, each day in the life of an adult as well as a child brings new material to be integrated, loose ends to be tied up, tears in the fabric to be rewoven. This could occur very widely in the cortex. (Research above pointed especially to areas receiving norepinephrine input from the brainstem, but this may include most of the small-neuron regions of the cortex.)

All these closely related functions of REM sleep are very consistent with our view of the functions of dreaming. We need to keep in mind, of course, that consistency, though an important virtue, does not guarantee truth.

As mentioned, I tried to summarize the characteristics of REM sleep back in 1967, referring to it as a state with a "high activity level" but "rough adjustment" (poor feedback). This was to distinguish REM sleep from waking characterized by a high activity level with a fine adjustment (good feedback), and from non-REM sleep, characterized by a low activity level. In some sense this overall description of REM sleep can also refer to what we have learned about dreaming—high-intensity activity with rough adjustment or poor feedback in the sense of not being constrained by the rapid input/ output processing mechanisms of waking.

SUMMARY

In this chapter we have explored the biology of dreaming in many ways, and concluded that it involves the biology of the connections among the neurons of the cortex. Overall, our views on the nature and functions of dreaming are related to, and consistent with, what we know of the nature and functions of REM sleep.

Chapter Twelve

THE EVOLUTION
OF DREAMING

Dreams of Our Ancestors; Dreams of Our Children; Dreams of Animals

YEARS AGO

Suppose we tentatively accept the notion proposed here that dreaming makes connections broadly, guided by emotion, and that this can be useful in integrating trauma and sometimes in problem solving. The question arises as to why all this has to be done at night in dreaming. Can't we do these things all the time, or during the day while awake?

Indeed at present many of us do have opportunities to do some of this connecting while awake. Some of us (certainly not all) have the luxury of a certain amount of leisure time. We can sit back, relax, work on problems, write poetry, paint, perhaps see a therapist or counselor at times—all of which in some sense involve "dreamlike states" that can be helpful in making connections (making connections in a safe place). However, our ancestors 20,000 or 100,000 years ago probably did not have much leisure time or time in a safe place:

> I am an early hunter/gatherer. I am an omnivore; I am perfectly willing to eat fruit, nuts, and berries though there is not much fruit where I live and there are no planted crops as yet. I subsist on the food I can find, and whatever meat or fish I can occasionally catch. I live in a group. We move around quite a lot following game or trying to find other sources of food. I spend my time hunting, gathering berries, sometimes organizing others to hunt and gather. Sometimes I meet with others and we try to

decide where our group should move next. We are concerned
because neither the game nor the berries are as plentiful as they
were a few years ago, and we do not know in what direction
things might be better. I have a mate and two children and I
spend time with them whenever possible, especially at night
when it is too dark to hunt or find food. But even then we are
busy. There is some time for making love in the evening, perhaps
time for hugging and playing with the children, but most of our
time is taken up cooking meat, cleaning up, sharpening tools, trying
to build ourselves a small private shelter within the larger cave.

There is a lot to do and there is a lot to worry about. Perhaps
there will not be enough food; perhaps that large bear will come
again and kill or hurt the children; perhaps the big ugly man
from that other group will come again to try to take my mate—
he was here making threats just a few days ago. I have little time
to daydream or relax, or to do nothing. There is certainly no
opportunity for dreamlike activity during the day, while awake;
I need to be alert and I have a lot of problems to solve. At night I
find myself as safe a place as I possibly can. My mate, my
children, and I are curled up behind our own semiprivate portion of the large cave. It's not perfect but it is as safe as it gets.
There I curl up, fall asleep, and have all kinds of weird dreams. I
like my dreams when I remember them. A lot of them are
strange dreams, but sometimes they are fun. Once in a while
they give me new ideas, though most of the time I forget them
pretty quickly. That's too bad, but maybe that's all right, too. I
remember one time a bunch of us were running through the
woods hunting and I was trying to remember the details of this
long crazy dream I had. I guess I didn't pay attention to where I
was going; I tripped over a root and went splat. Thinking about
dreams can be dangerous sometimes.

After the bear attack I dreamt about huge bears and other
large animals and about scary monster-creatures chasing me,
and I had a dream about a whole roof of a cave falling in on me. It
was frightening. I had dreams, too, about old times, about other
animal attacks. It wasn't all from one time though; I seemed to
plunk together different animals and different times, and I had a
dream where we all got together with big sticks and chased the
bear away—sort of like what happened last year but a little
different; the dream-bear was really huge. I seem to dream a lot;
all sorts of strange dreams. Sometimes they are interesting and
they get me thinking. Sometimes I think they might even be
helpful—like the time we were hungry and could not find any

berries. I slept and saw a little furry animal with seeds stuck in its mouth; the seeds dropped and somehow in my dream those little seeds fell into the earth and turned into new plants. Maybe I actually saw something like that once; I'm not sure. But it's something to think about. Perhaps we could gather the seeds of the plants and put them in a new place and see if they would grow and help feed us. I think we should try this.

In other words, the functions of dreaming we have discussed previously may have been especially important for us at earlier times in our species' development. We had not much time and perhaps not much inclination to sit down and daydream, to integrate our traumas, or to think up crazy new ideas. Only our dreams gave us a chance to do this—to make broader and wider connections, to integrate trauma or other new material, and also to bring material together in new ways that occasionally may have been useful to us in our waking lives.

REM Sleep in Mammals

Can we be certain that human beings had dreams 100,000 years ago, or even that they had REM sleep? Can we go back further than this, before we were human beings? Do monkeys dream? Do other mammals dream?

Almost all mammals do have REM sleep. There is a great deal of literature that I will briefly review on the distribution of REM sleep throughout the animal kingdom. However, there is little information on dreaming, since we cannot ask the animals whether they experience dreams as we do.

Some form of sleep is widespread in the animal kingdom, but researchers have found it hard to reach a consensus on exactly how far back in phylogeny sleep can be said to exist. Periods of relative immobility (which might be called protosleep) can be found even in some very primitive invertebrate creatures. Sleep itself is usually defined by both behavioral and physiological (electrical) criteria. Behavioral sleep involves (1) quiescence, (2) a stereotyped species-specific posture, (3) elevated arousal threshold, and (4) reversibility with stimulation. Defined in such behavioral terms, sleep is definitely present in all mammals, birds, reptiles, and probably amphibians and fish, although there are a few disagreements here. There is also some evidence that insects have behavioral sleep.[1]

The electrophysiological criteria of sleep involve some form of the brain waves found in non-REM and REM sleep, which we have reviewed in the last chapter. Using such criteria, mammals, birds, and reptiles have been shown to have distinctive sleep patterns in almost all studies, but there is no clear evidence of sleep in fish or amphibians.[2]

REM sleep seems to have been a later acquisition. Although a few studies in reptiles find spike activities suggestive of REM sleep, most do not find signs of two different states of sleep. However, there is good agreement that REM and non-REM sleep occur in birds and mammals.[3] As in mammals, young birds have greater quantities of REM sleep than adult birds. For instance, in chickens, perhaps the best-studied species, it is very easy to find REM sleep at around the time of hatching, but as they grow older they have only momentary episodes of REM activity. One study showed an increase of REM sleep after imprinting (an early form of learning) in chicks, supporting the idea of a role for REM sleep in learning and making connections.[4]

When we get to mammals, which have been studied in great numbers and great detail, there is agreement that the two states of sleep are present in all mammals with one or two small exceptions—the very primitive mammals known as monotremes (a group that includes the spiny anteater), which appear to have no REM sleep.[5]

Furthermore, REM and non-REM sleep show regular and predictable features across species. For instance, the length of the REM/non-REM cycle, sometimes called the sleep–dream cycle, which is about 90 minutes in humans (see last chapter), is closely related to the size, metabolic rate, and brain weight of the species. Thus mice have a cycle length of 11 minutes while elephants have a cycle length of over 120 minutes.[6] The total amount of REM sleep also varies considerably among species, but this variable is not related to size or brain weight. The closest relationship, as we have mentioned, seems to be with altriciality—a measure of how immature the animal is at birth.[7]

In any case the modern mammals we are most familiar with all have REM and non-REM sleep, and all have more of both when they are young. Furthermore their REM sleep has characteristics very much like human REM sleep, including for instance rapid movement of the eyes and activation of the brain, especially prominent in the occipital areas related to vision. Thus mammals definitely have REM sleep, and it activates the visual parts of their brains. This is suggestive, certainly, but does it prove that animals dream?

David Foulkes, who has done excellent work on the development of dreaming in childhood, calls dreams complex, symbolic, visual-spatial constructions that he finds are only very gradually acquired during human childhood. Since he finds that young children are barely able to dream, he concludes that other species are therefore probably incapable of such visual-spatial construction.[8] I personally consider it more likely that other species experience some form of dreaming, though the structure may be different, for instance less complex and less metaphoric and involving a mix of sensory modalities different from ours.

DREAMS OF THE BLIND

In fact, in our own species dreams are not always visual-spatial constructions. There are studies that show that REM sleep and dreaming occur in the blind; however, in the congenitally blind, dreaming lacks visual-spatial structure. There is definite structure, but it is built upon other senses such as touch, quite similar to what the person experiences in waking life. Here is a powerful dream of a 10-year-old, congenitally blind girl:

> I was walking back to my house from the garden. It seemed to be very early morning. There was a heavy dew on the grass and moisture like before the sun rises. I was carrying things in my right arm, I think squash and tomatoes. Then I heard it coming toward me, a very large animal, its head waist-high to me. I dropped the vegetables and reached out slowly. It sniffed at my fingers and though I was terrified, I knew I shouldn't make any jerky motions. Its tongue, twice the width of my hand, licked my fingers curiously. My head slowly entered into its mouth, being pulled in by its raspy tongue. Its upper jaw had razorlike teeth, three or four rows deep. It was just inspecting me, tasting and

smelling my flesh. I felt its nose and lips and knew I could do nothing to defend myself if it decided to bite me. It purred more and more threateningly and was beginning to nudge me backwards when I woke up.[9]

Helen Keller, who was born blind and deaf, describes childhood dreams in her autobiography. She mentions several vivid dreams in which she seems to be a cat or something similar creeping through the tall, wet grass near her house. She powerfully describes the feeling of the wet grass against her skin, the feeling of her own movement, her hands and feet across the ground, the smell of the early-morning grass, and the warmth of the sun on her skin.[10]

It is interesting that in both these cases the dream world is built especially on the tactile senses though with a suggestion of taste and smell as well. Dreams obviously do not require vision specifically. Rather they recreate the perceptual world of the dreamer.

In persons who become blind after birth, if they became blind after the age of five or so, some clear visual imagery remains. Those whose blindness occurs after the age of 10 often continue to dream visually for their entire lives, though their visual sense sometimes deteriorates slightly with time.[11]

It is possible that in these blind people dreaming has an additional function in helping them practice and maintain their visual sense even though they are not taking in new visual information. I had a conversation some years ago with Father Thomas Carroll, the head of a famous school for the blind outside Boston. He was interested in my research on dreaming, and, based on his experience with persons who became blind in adolescence or young adulthood, he proposed that it might be useful for them to remember their dreams and rehearse their dreams in wakefulness to allow them to maintain their visual sense. I agreed with him that this was an excellent idea, and we decided that a research study should be done on whether this would produce improvements over years of life, but as far as I know, the study was never done. Another researcher, the blind psychologist Raymond Rainville, apparently had a similar idea. He suggests that the capacity to visualize is extremely important for those blinded during their lifetime, and that dreams may help them to realize that although they are blind they have not lost their "visual intelligence."[12]

The main reason I have discussed dreams of the blind is to make it clear that dreams do occur even without the visual sense so important in most of our dreams, and that they apparently involve spatial constructions built of whatever senses are available. Dreams of mentally retarded adults and adolescents have likewise been studied. These appear to be short and somewhat simplified—similar to the dreams reported by young children. They have structure, are usually visual-spatial, and definitely appear to be dreams.[13]

Do Animals Dream?

Arguing by analogy from these human situations, I would suggest that, most probably, animals (mammals) that have clear-cut REM sleep experience some form of dreaming. The form is unlikely to be exactly like ours, but it is quite likely that dreaming consciousness for these creatures has similar characteristics to their waking consciousness. For instance I would guess that mammals that depend heavily on their sense of smell in waking would also have smell-filled dreams.

There is one behavioral study that directly supports the idea that monkeys experience dreaming or at least see something during their sleep. The study involved training monkeys to respond by pressing a bar when they see any picture projected on a screen in front of them. These monkeys were then observed while they slept, and the author reports that the monkeys had definite periods when they started to press the bar in their sleep, suggesting that they were "seeing" something. This is certainly suggestive evidence, though the study can be criticized.[14]

There have also been several studies of sleeping cats that have had lesions placed in the portion of the brainstem responsible for muscle inhibition during REM sleep. These cats entered REM sleep, and rather than lying quietly with only their eyes moving, they stood up, walked around, and chased imaginary creatures, all without waking up. It appeared to the observers that the cats were "acting out their dreams."[15]

There is no doubt that there is great variation among species. I would consider it likely that any given mammal probably has something that can be called dreaming activity, but we cannot be sure about its exact nature. The best I can do is guess that its dream world is experienced very much like its waking world and that its dreams resemble human dreams as much as its conscious waking imagery resembles human conscious waking imagery.

ONTOGENY OF DREAMING: CHILDREN'S DREAMS

Regardless of the amount of time a given species spends in REM sleep, there appears to be a clear-cut development in terms of the amount of REM sleep. Well-studied species including humans, monkeys, cats, and rats, all have a high level of REM sleep at birth, which falls gradually to adult levels. For instance, in our own species a typical newborn child spends over 16 hours of the day asleep; 50% of this sleep is REM sleep, so the newborn obtains eight hours of REM sleep per 24 hours. This falls rapidly in the first years of life, so that by adolescence the amount is only slightly greater than the usual young adult total of about 100 minutes per night.[16] What is the newborn baby or the one-year-old child experiencing during REM sleep? We do not know for certain. I would not be surprised if it included some form of sensory experience, similar to waking experience, but without the complex spatial structure or the plot of later dreaming.

Dreaming of course is not identical to REM sleep. The ontogenetic development of dreaming has also been studied in the laboratory. It appears, according to careful research, that fully formed visual-spatial dreams as we know them in adults do not develop in children until the age of five to eight years.[17] Nonetheless, numerous anecdotal reports and clinical examples indicate that some form of dreaming, especially nightmares, occurs in children considerably younger than that. Nightmares of some kind are frequently reported at the age of two to four years such as "a monster was chasing me," though it may not be clear in detail exactly what was experienced by the child. There are in fact case reports suggesting that some early form of dream or nightmare occurs in the second year of life. These are often very brief fragments and of course are not carefully described since the child barely knows how to speak. One account goes simply, "Da thing on me"; another, from a girl just two years old, was a bit more specific: "pider on Sophia . . . off Sophia's leg . . . Dad no more pider please." Or a nightmare in a two-year-old, "Get me down!" which occurred the night after he had been held down on a table so that a doctor could examine his throat.[18] So at least fragmentary dreams and nightmares can occur by the age of two, but the development of full visual-spatial space takes considerably longer.

What about all the aspects of the nature and functions of dreaming we have discussed in past chapters? Can we find evidence in children's dreams of making connections more broadly, integrating trauma and stressful material, and contextualizing emotion in the form of explanatory metaphor? From some points of view, children's dreams might be an especially good place to look, but from other points of view, children's dreams present difficulties. They might be an ideal place to look since children are presumably less complicated than adults. (Although we keep finding that this must be taken with many grains of salt.) We could at least assume that a young child has fewer different emotional concerns at one time than does an adult, which might make the process easier to study. On the other hand, a child may have less developed and less structured dreams. If the child does have structured dreams, the child will have less verbal ability in describing the dream and probably more difficulty in distinguishing the dream from waking thoughts and fantasies.

I have not personally gathered any large quantity of material from children, though I have attempted to obtain dream series after trauma and stress in children as well as adults. In the example we discussed in Chapter 2, the 14-year-old boy, still technically a child, who was locked into a hotel room describes quite clearly the process of making connections and contextualizing emotion in his dreams and nightmares: "My dreams were playing with the theme of my being trapped . . . and bringing in all kinds of things from my life, from stories I have read, from my imaginings."

There are data on children's dreams collected from a number of sources. The most systematic collection is a series of sleep laboratory studies already mentioned.[19] The subjects were normal children, and no information was obtained about any trauma or emotional concerns they might have had. Generally, the dreams were quite short and one of the chief conclusions was how very banal and ordinary the dreams were. There are almost no nightmares in the series. These children's dreams are of great value in explaining the development of dream structure. But, since we have neither a clear-cut trauma nor any known emotional concern, nor any associations by the dreamers that might lead to their concerns, we cannot make use of these dreams in examining our views about dreams after trauma and contextualization of emotional concerns.

There are a number of less systematic studies of children's dreams, usually involving children seen in counseling or psychotherapy, and such series tend to involve more emotional and traumatic dreams. In general the authors conclude that these dreams usually deal in some way with the anxieties and conflicts present in the child's life, sometimes relating to external traumatic events but frequently combining these with the inevitable conflicts or characteristics of the child's developmental phase. In other words, when there is no specifiable external trauma, the dreams and nightmares usually deal with such things as the child's vulnerability and aggressive feelings toward recently born siblings. We discussed this in detail in Chapter 4.

Frederick Stoddard, a psychiatrist who works for a hospital specializing in burns in Boston, describes an eight-year-old boy who had serious burns after playing on a sidewalk with another boy who threw matches into a puddle of what turned out to be gasoline. He dreamt repeatedly that his house had blown up or his house had fallen down and his family was not there to help him.[20]

Psychiatrist Lenore Terr studied a group of children who had been kidnapped and buried underground in a bus. She does not report detailed dreams but says almost all the children reported nightmares and dreams about the incident or about similar imagined frightening events.[21] Both authors comment about the large numbers of nightmares and anxious dreams in these children, but they do not provide any long dream series that would help examine the development of dreams such as we have discussed after adult trauma.

Kathleen Nader, a therapist who practices in southern California, has worked clinically with children after trauma and provides a number of case studies summarizing her experience with preschool children.[22] She says:

> Young children (after trauma) often report monster dreams or
> dreams that symbolically represent their experiences, their fears,
> and their sense of vulnerability. Preschool children exposed to a
> hurricane dreamed of the hurricane, of being chased by a large
> eye (they had heard of the eye of the hurricane), and a variety of
> monsters. Head Start children exposed to the Los Angeles riots
> in 1992 dreamed of monsters, witches, fires, and guns. Preschool
> children undergoing bone marrow transplantation dreamed of
> ghosts coming to take them away, dragons coming to take them
> away, or being chased by mutilators.

It certainly appears that these children, like the adults we considered
earlier, may dream of the trauma directly but also have many dreams
that picture or contextualize their fear and vulnerability.

Nader describes a five-year-old boy with leukemia who had
relapsed after bone marrow transplantation and was clearly getting
worse. He "began to dream of spacemen coming to take him to their
planet. In his early dreams he was afraid of these spacemen. In later
dreams he found them friendly and decided it was safe to go with
them. He died a few months after befriending them." This young
boy's very powerful creative dreams were clearly picturing metaphorically his feelings about his approaching death.

We have briefly reviewed here material on children's dreams,
concentrating especially on nightmares and dreams after trauma.
The material from children's dreams certainly appears consistent
with the themes we have developed in examining dreams after
trauma and stress in adults. Though the material in young children is
often fragmentary and the language describing it is still not well
formed, there is little question that the dream and nightmare fragments portray the emotional state of the children. We have also
considered in a more speculative way the dreams of animals and the
dreams of our ancestors many thousands of years ago. In the next
chapter, we will return to adults and look at individual differences—
how much variation there is in the way people dream, and how
people lead their lives in a more or less dreamlike fashion.

Chapter Thirteen

DREAM PEOPLE AND
THOUGHT PEOPLE

Individual Differences

People are different. We are no more alike in our mental activities than we are in our height or our hair color. I suggest specifically that people differ greatly on how dreamlike their minds are, whether they are awake or asleep. This will lead us to some new general perspectives on how we dream and how we think.

We have spoken so far as if the same processes applied to all people, but obviously there are great differences among us with regard to most aspects of dreaming. For instance, some people remember one or more dreams every night, while others hardly ever remember a dream. Some have a lot of nightmares and some none at all. Some have vivid, exciting, beautiful, or memorable dreams while others seem to have relatively dull dreams. Some are very interested in their dreams and find them fascinating, whereas others could not care less about them.

I do not plan to discuss here in detail the many studies of individual differences related to dreaming, since this would take us far from our chief concerns.[1] However, I do want to discuss one important human characteristic—a dimension of personality that turns out to relate closely to the nature of dreaming as we have examined it. Specifically, I want to suggest that some people live their lives more "dreamily" than others. If we consider our diagram portraying the continuum from focused waking thought through dreaming (Fig. 5, page 90), I suggest that there are some people who live their lives much more at the left-hand end of our continuum (in focused waking thought), some of course are in between, and others live their lives more at the daydreaming and dreaming (right-hand) end of the continuum.

THICK AND THIN BOUNDARIES

My collaborators and I have studied in detail a personality measure known as thick versus thin boundaries.[2] Boundaries (boundaries in the mind) is a broad general psychological term: There are many types of boundaries (Table 3), but they are to some extent interrelated. Overall, what we mean by boundaries is this: We can speak of the contents of our minds in many different ways. Most of us speak of such things as thoughts, feelings, or memories. If we are psychoanalysts we speak of ego, id, superego, drives, and defenses. If we are cognitive scientists we may talk of perceptual processes, semantic processes (language meaning), memory processes. No matter what terms we use, we are speaking of regions, functions, or processes that are separate from one another and yet obviously connected with one another. The boundaries between them are not absolute separations. They can be relatively thick or solid divisions on the one hand, or relatively thin or permeable on the other.

Boundaries are more than a descriptive concept. I believe that the thickness of boundaries represents an important dimension of personality, one that can help us understand aspects of our lives that no other measure can explain. As a first approximation of what I mean, there are people who strike us as very solid and well-organized; they keep everything in its place. They are well-defended. They may seem rigid or even armored; we sometimes speak of them as "thick-skinned." Such people have very thick boundaries. At the other extreme are people who are especially sensitive, open, or vulnerable. In their minds, things are relatively fluid. They experience thoughts and feelings—often many different feelings—at the same time. Such people have particularly thin boundaries.

Thickness and thinness of boundaries refers to the degree of separateness (thickness) versus fluidity or merging (thinness) in all mental functions. Someone with very thick boundaries keeps perceptions, thoughts, and feelings distinct and separate. He will typ-

Table 3. Types of Boundaries

Perceptual boundaries
    Between sensory inputs
    Sensory focus or "bandwidth"
    Around perceptual entities

Boundaries related to thoughts and feelings
    Between two thoughts or two feelings
    Between thought and feeling
    Around thoughts and feelings (free association)

Boundaries related to states of awareness or states of consciousness

Sleep–dream–wake boundaries
    Between sleep and waking
    Between dreaming and waking
    In and around the dream
    Daydreaming

Boundaries related to play

Boundaries related to memory
    Early memories
    Recent memories and memory organization
    Personal past
    Future plans

Boundaries around oneself (body boundaries)
    Barriers against stimuli
    The skin as a boundary
    Posture and musculature as boundaries
    Personal space

Interpersonal boundaries

Boundaries between conscious and unconscious and between id, ego, and
  superego

Defense mechanisms as boundaries

Boundaries related to identity
    Sexual identity
    Age identity: Between adult and child
    Constancy of identity

Group boundaries

Boundaries in organizing one's life

Boundaries in environmental preferences

Boundaries in opinions and judgments

Boundaries in decision making and action

---

ically say something like, "Feelings are fine in their place, but I always keep them separate from my thoughts. I don't let my feelings influence my thoughts and actions." He, or she, also keeps time and space well-organized, tends to think in black and white, has a clear, demarcated sense of self, and is usually very solid, well-defended. We have found that salesmen, accountants, and lawyers on the average have quite thick boundaries.

Someone with very thin boundaries is the opposite. This person may experience synesthesia ("seeing a sound"—associating it with a particular color, for instance), often has vivid fantasies not always distinguishable from reality, and allows thoughts and feelings to merge. This person will say, "I never think without having associated feelings. I can't even imagine what a thought would be like without a feeling." He or she is also less well-defended, tends to think in shades of gray, has a less solid sense of self, and becomes over-involved in relationships. Artists often have very thin boundaries.

Thick and thin boundaries also extend outside of ourselves, involving the space around us, our feelings for groups, the differences between the sexes, and society in general. There is a whole continuum of course, but I am emphasizing people who have either very thick or very thin boundaries. Speaking of the two sexes, someone with very thick boundaries makes statements such as "I am a man, you are a woman. Vive la différence!" While someone with thin boundaries is more likely to say, "I am a man, but I can see a lot of feminine things about myself as well."

When involved in relationships a person with very thick boundaries will always maintain his own space: "This is my stuff, this is my space, this is my way of doing things. Those are yours." Whereas someone with thin boundaries will tend to emphasize "our" rather than mine or yours, and sometimes even may merge and feel "at one with the other" rather than remaining a distinct individual.

In dealings between groups and nations, someone with thick boundaries is likely to feel that things go best if each nation is absolutely clear about its own interests, its own position; then they can negotiate from there. An Israeli prime minister a few years ago stated, "You make peace with enemies, you don't make peace with friends." The thin-boundary position is very different. It emphasizes that "we are not necessarily enemies, we are not really so different when you come to think about it. We have a lot of common needs and goals."

I have used examples from people with very thick or very thin boundaries to emphasize the differences, though most of us are in between or may have thick boundaries in some ways and thin boundaries in others. We have developed a boundary questionnaire, which has been taken by over 2,000 people, to examine the quantitative aspects of boundaries. Most of our conclusions above and below stem from the use of this questionnaire[3] (see Table 4). Using this measure, the dimension of thick and thin boundaries represented by the score from the boundary questionnaire is not related to most well-known measures of personality, with one exception. Boundary thinness is highly correlated with another personality measure called "openness to experience." People who score thin on the boundary scale score unusually open on that measure.[4]

BOUNDARIES AND DREAMS

There are some clear-cut relationships between dreaming and thinness of boundaries measured on the boundary questionnaire. First of all, in almost 800 people tested, there was a highly significant correlation between thinness of boundaries and dream recall frequency. The correlations were even higher when only people especially interested in dreams were studied.[5] In other words, people who scored high, which means thin boundaries, recalled many more dreams. A subgroup of frequent dreamers (reporting seven or more dreams per week) had significantly thinner boundaries than nondreamers. In fact, the frequent dreamers had thinner scores in all 12 categories of the boundary questionnaire, covering everything from sensitivity to views about organizations and the world.[6] Finally, the dreams of people with very thin boundaries were rated by judges as significantly more vivid, emotional, dreamlike, and nightmare-like, and with more interaction between characters than the dreams of those with thick boundaries.[7]

To illustrate, here is the first dream report in our files from the

Table 4. Boundary Questionnaire: Examples of Questions

Category 1: Sleep/Dream/Waking
1. When I awake in the morning, I am not sure whether I am really awake for a few minutes.
37. I spend a lot of time daydreaming, fantasizing, or in reverie.

Category 2: Unusual Experiences
61. At times I have felt as if I were coming apart.
100. I have had déjà vu experiences.

Category 3: Thoughts/Feelings/Moods
15. Sometimes I don't know whether I am thinking or feeling.
74. I can easily imagine myself to be an animal or what it might be like to be an animal.

Category 4: Childhood/Adolescence/Adult
4. I am very close to my childhood feelings.
40. I have definite plans for my future. I can lay out pretty well what I expect year by year at least for the next few years.

Category 5: Interpersonal
53. When I get involved with someone, we sometimes get too close.
103. I am a very open person.

Category 6. Sensitivity
6. I am very sensitive to other people's feelings.
42. I am unusually sensitive to loud noises and bright lights.

Category 7: Neat/Exact/Precise
19. I keep my desk and work table neat and well organized.
43. I am good at keeping accounts and keeping track of my money.

Category 8: Edges/Lines/Clothing
32. I like heavy, solid clothing.
44. I like stories that have a definite beginning, middle, and end.

Category 9: Opinions re Children, etc.
33. Children and adults have a lot in common. They should give themselves a chance to be together without any strict roles.
56. I think a good teacher must remain in part a child.

Category 10: Organizations
10. In an organization, everyone should have a definite place and a specific role.
58. A good relationship is one in which everything is clearly defined and spelled out.

Category 11: Peoples/Nations/Groups
11. People of different nations are basically very much alike.
105. There are no sharp dividing lines between normal people, people with problems, and people who are considered psychotic or crazy.

Category 12: Beauty/Truth
36. Either you are telling the truth or you are lying; that's all there is to it.
76. When I am in a new situation, I try to find out precisely what is going on and what the rules are as soon as possible.

thick-boundary and thin-boundary groups. A dream of a "thick" male:

> I was in a room, squarish in shape, with concrete walls on three sides. The fourth side was all glass or unglazed and open. The view seemed to be from inside the bottom of a large concrete dam looking out at the spillway many feet below. There were three of us in the room; two were college friends. We were joined by a fourth person, whose name I don't now recall, who came toward us from what seemed like a long, small, square concrete tunnel.

A dream of a "thin" female:

> I was making a trip with my son. Our belongings were stacked high on a pickup truck type of vehicle. Our destination was blocked by a line of traffic which was bumper to bumper, lining both sides of a highway, both to and from our destination. The truck stalled in a railroad crossing, and my son and I pushed the vehicle over the crossing. The scene melted and transformed to a scene at the end of my destination where the president and his wife were seated at a set of tables, stacked haphazardly and covered with dust. I offered them coffee, and again the scene dissolved into the next room where my mother was emotionally tugging on me to meet her needs. I looked in the mirror, which was misted, and observed with horror that my eyes were injured with two fleshy pendants hanging from my irises. As I watched, the fleshy hangings increased in size and I awoke with my heart pounding from anxiety.

These two dreams are different in a number of ways typical of the two groups. The dream from the "thin" person is longer, more vivid, more emotional, more disturbing. These dreams even suggest that the "thick" person may dream literally of thick boundaries such as the solid concrete walls, whereas the thin person dreams of things changing their size and shape: ". . . the fleshy hangings increased in size."

Also, we found that certain definable groups who scored significantly "thicker" than average on the boundary questionnaire (naval officers, lawyers) tended to report very few dreams, much fewer than average. Conversely, groups that scored thin on the boundary questionnaire (several groups of art students and music students) reported more dreams than average.[8] Thus thin boundaries and dreaming are clearly related in many ways.

Further, in terms of their mental functioning, people with thick boundaries are described as more focused, thinking in a straight line, thinking from A to B to C to D with relatively few detours, whereas people with thin boundaries explore all kinds of side connections.[9] Their thinking is less straightforward but more flexible, more creative. In all these senses the usual mental processes of those with very thick boundaries resemble the processes of focused waking, whereas the usual mental processes of those with thin boundaries involve something more like daydreaming or dreaming.

In other words, different people tend to function at different places on the focused waking-to-dream continuum (Chap. 5). We examined this in one study, which involved asking each of a group of students to write down their most recent dream and their most recent daydream. The students also took the boundary questionnaire.[10] The dreams and daydreams were then rated on a blind basis by several judges on such measures as "bizarreness." Overall, as expected, dreams were rated much more bizarre than daydreams. However, the reports of thin-scoring students were rated more bizarre than those of thick-scorers, so much so that on the average, the *daydreams* of the "thin" students were rated just as bizarre as the *dreams* of the "thick" students.

To give a flavor of the reports, I will first contrast the most bizarre daydream reported by the two groups. The "thick" students' daydream rated as most bizarre was:

> As I was sitting in algebra class, my instructor was walking back and forth in front of the class talking. As he was talking one of the students stood up and started throwing eggs and tomatoes at him.

Here is the "thin" daydream scored most bizarre:

> I am seeing outlines of things. Then I see what appears as an eye. The eye winks and the surroundings jumble around and turn to mist. There seems to be a pit with levels of ledges. That is the only way to go, but I don't go down there. I stay my ground and wait and wait but nothing happens till I look up and try to reach

a light and then turn around and get comforted by the warm darkness that surrounds this place.

This student's daydream certainly sounds more bizarre and sounds quite dreamlike. In fact, it was rated just as bizarre as the most bizarre *dream* reported by the "thick" students:

I had a dream that I found to be very frightening. For some reason my girlfriend was in the guillotine and I was told that from a distance of 20 feet I had three seconds to save her. I dashed toward her and stopped the blade with my hands. I suffered severe cuts to my hands but I was able to save her life, which was all that really mattered to me.

This pales in comparison with the most bizarre dream of a "thin" student:

It was basically an unfurnished room, with white walls and floor, evenly lit. Someone was there, and I was watching him with disgust and some horror. I noticed he was naked and hairless, and pretty androgynous. He had a hungry smile and evil eyes. Between his legs was a vagina, and he was going through some kind of birthing, but he seemed unmoved by this. He was watching the top of a baby's head come out of him with some satisfaction, and I saw he had an ice cream scoop. I realized with quiet shrieking horror what he intended, and tried to go find someone to stop him, but the door led nowhere, and nobody could hear me, and I turned back to see that he had scooped out and eaten the baby's brains, and left its hollow-skulled body on the floor next to him as he smiled and smacked his lips. I woke up feeling very disturbed.

Obviously some dreams are extremely nightmarish, strange, and bizarre. This is much more frequent in people with thin boundaries.

Thought People and Dream People

People with thick boundaries, relatively speaking, are "thought people." People with thin boundaries are "dream people." What I am suggesting is that the continuum running from very thick boundaries to very thin boundaries bears a similarity to our familiar continuum from focused waking thought at one end to dreaming at the other end (Fig. 5, page 90).

In other words, the previously discussed "state" continuum running from focused waking at one end to dreaming at the other end is also the personality continuum ("trait" continuum), running from very thick boundaries to very thin boundaries. Focused waking activity can be thought of as a "thick-boundary state of mind," while dreaming with its broader connections can be thought of as a "thin-boundary state of mind."

How can we understand these relationships in terms of our mental processing in the nets of our minds? We can think of the networks as a number of relatively tightly organized regions or groupings, connected and surrounded by somewhat looser, less tightly woven pathways (see Fig. 2, page 83). The tightly woven or closely connected regions would represent something like the calculation of trajectories in hunting game, chasing a baseball, etc. Other tightly woven regions might be devoted to reading, to writing, to recognition of faces, and similar tasks. In this scheme, people with thick boundaries who function chiefly in a focused waking mode have excellent and well-functioning connections *within* regions but do relatively little connecting between or across regions. On the other hand, people with thin boundaries may not be as fast and efficient at some of the specific tasks: They have less efficient functioning within regions, but they have more connections between regions. They can shift back and forth easily.

I have been speaking of people with very thin or very thick boundaries, people who function at one end or the other of the continuum, to emphasize a point and for clarity. I hope it is understood that most of us function somewhere in between. We are not at one extreme or the other. We may have thick boundaries in some senses and thin boundaries in others.

Although having thin or thick boundaries appears in most ways to be a personality "trait"—a long-term characteristic—it is worth noting that we are not stuck in the same boundary state all the time. We all have dreams, though some of us have more than others, and we function in a "thinner boundary" way at that time. Similarly, daydreaming and the other states to the right on our continuum can be considered to be somewhat thinner boundary states than ordinary waking. Biological and chemical factors can play a role in shifting our boundaries, as well. Some people find that their boundaries are quite thin when they are very tired, and then they find their boundaries have thickened again the next morning after a good night's sleep. Those who have taken psychedelic drugs, such as LSD, report that under the drug's influence they have thinner boundaries in a number of senses. On the other hand, taking stimulants such as amphetamines, or for some people, antidepressants, definitely produces a thickening of boundaries.[11] In the most extreme case, people given large doses of amphetamines first became intensely focused; they are the opposite of distractable, keeping their thoughts entirely on one line of thought. Eventually, with more amphetamine, they insist on imposing their one line of thought even in a situation where others cannot see it. They become suspicious and eventually frankly paranoid, insisting against all the evidence that a certain pattern of thought or a certain idea is absolutely true. They are stuck in a rigid, one-dimensional line of thinking, which is characteristic of extremely thick boundaries.[12]

Summary

In this chapter we have considered how people differ from one another, which at first might seem to take us away from our principal focus on dreaming. However, I hope that our consideration of individual differences has reinforced one of the important notions advanced in this book concerning the continuum from focused waking to dreaming. It turns out that this "state" continuum is also reflected in an individual difference "trait" continuum, running from people with very thick boundaries to people with very thin boundaries. There are "thought people" who have thick boundaries and spend their lives more at the thinking end of the continuum, and there are "dream people" more toward the other end of the continuum. The mental processes of the thought people involve a great deal of activity within the tightly woven regions of the mind, whereas the processes of the dream people involve more activity across or between these regions.

Chapter Fourteen

DREAMS, MYTH, RELIGION, AND CULTURE

THE VALUE OF THE DREAM

It has frequently been noted that our modern Western culture values the dream less and pays far less attention to it than most other cultures in the past or present. Perhaps it's just that we're smarter and more advanced than anyone else? But perhaps not!

Many of our modern biologists—and for that matter 18th- and 19th-century biologists as well, with somewhat different concepts—dismiss dreaming as more or less random products of a poorly functioning brain. As we have seen, one group considers dreams "garbage," consisting of what the system wants to throw out,[1] while another group considers dreams to consist of the forebrain "making the best of a bad job" in dealing with random activation from the brain stem.[2] Freud appears to have had a mixed attitude toward the value of the dream. On the one hand he values dreams greatly for their role in analysis as "the royal road to the unconscious," but on the other hands he considers dreams to be in a category with slips of the tongue and neurotic symptoms: All are compromise formations among the forces of the psyche—irrational products that need to be understood in terms of the more important and meaningful underlying thoughts. For Freud, once these latent thoughts are arrived at, the dream can be more or less thrown away.

It is noteworthy that the Freudians and biologists, though they have reached far different conclusions, both pride themselves on having achieved a new "scientific" view of dreams, as opposed to the older views, which they feel can be discarded. For the biological theorists the old theories to be discarded include prominently the theories of Sigmund Freud, while for Freud the theories to be discarded were not only the religious and mythical views of dreams, but also the 19th-century biological view that dreaming is the product of a poorly functioning brain (a view very similar to that of recent biologists).[3]

My own belief is that any culture's long-lasting view of dreams (or of anything else) is of value. Anything that has persisted for a long time has presumably served some adaptive purpose and contains at least a kernel of human truth or usefulness. I don't say this as an article of faith or to establish my broad-mindedness, but more as a simple result of a belief in the widespread workings of natural selection.

I have proposed in this book a contemporary theory of dreams, but I do not thereby mean that we should throw out and disregard all previous theories. Rather, I believe that the dream theories and dream uses of other cultures, including those sometimes dismissed as primitive or superstitious, may contain important truths and may in fact be quite compatible with the way I now think about dreams. In this chapter we will first discuss some prominent ways of dealing with dreams in a number of nontechnological cultures and show that they fit surprisingly well with the view of dreams developed in this book. Prominent among these is the well-known "dream quest." I will also discuss dreams as a voyage of the soul and the belief that the soul of a dead person remains with us or remains above ground for a few years. We will discuss Western religions, and we will consider the way dreams lead us outward to something beyond us, as well as the relationship among dreaming, play, and art. Finally, I will take seriously the mysterious old quote: "In dreams begin responsibilities."

THE DREAM QUEST

As a starting point, let us look at the broad question faced by young people in all cultures: "What is my place in this world?"

(sometimes abbreviated inadequately to "career choice"). We often expect young people to explore a few possibilities, study, try a few jobs, and see what appeals to them. For most of us today there is no institutional method for making such a choice. We should be aware, however, that some cultures have established a methodology for career choice and, surprisingly, that dreams play a prominent role in it.

In a number of indigenous North and South American societies, a young man—in some cases a young woman, too—is traditionally sent out on a "dream quest" at some time around puberty.[4] The aim is for the young person to go off alone and—sometimes with the aid of food deprivation, sleep deprivation, or mild hallucinogens— experience an important dream that will show him a future path. It may also show him a guide or guardian spirit to help him. The dream—either directly in its manifest content, or with the help of interpretation after the youth's return—will help him decide on a career: whether to become a warrior, a farmer, or perhaps a shaman.

Irving Hallowell, an anthropologist who worked with the Ojibwa, who live in what is now Ontario and Manitoba, reports one example:

> Dream fasts generally served as initiation rituals for Ojibwa boys (although there are accounts of Ojibwa girls going on dream fasts as well). Before leaving for the fast, the boy was given carefully washed clothes and a specially dyed animal skin to sleep on. He would then head into the forest with his father, grandfather, or other male relative, who would help the boy find a suitable spot to build a wasizon (a sleeping platform up in the trees). The boy would spend up to 10 days and nights on the wasizon, alone and fasting, until he had a dream in which a pawagan (spirit being or other-than-human being) bestowed a blessing on him.

One particular boy's dream experience was described to Hallowell as follows:

> When I was a boy I went out to an island to fast. My father paddled me there. For several nights I dreamt of an ogima (chief or superior person). Finally he said to me, "Grandson, I think you are now ready to go with me." Then ogima began dancing

around me as I sat there on a rock and when I happened to glance down at my body I noticed that I had grown feathers. Soon I felt just like a bird, a golden eagle. Ogima had turned into an eagle also and off he flew toward the South. I spread my wings and flew after him in the same direction. After a while we arrived at a place where there were lots of tents and lots of people. It was the home of the Summer Birds.

Hallowell adds that "after returning North again the boy was left at their starting point after his guardian spirit had promised help whenever he wanted it. The boy's father came for him and took him home again."[5] We are not told about the course of the boy's life, except that for the Ojibwe the eagle suggests a leadership role.

Is this widespread practice simply an irrational superstition? I believe we can more legitimately understand it as an attempt by these cultures to make use of the connecting powers of dreaming to put together previously unconnected themes in the young person's life. The preparations for this dream, sometimes including days of fasting and contemplating one's future, and sometimes months of instruction by tribal elders as to the "career opportunities" open to a young person, make certain that the issue of career choice or future path becomes an emotionally meaningful concern for the dreamer. In this situation—not dissimilar from the situations after trauma and stress that we have discussed before—the dreaming mind will take the emotionally meaningful concern and make connections with any related material within the memory nets. And the dream may very well come up with an important connection in the form of a contextualizing image or metaphor—based on the youth's wishes, fears, experiences, and abilities.

I know that modern Westerners, too, sometimes make use of such a technique even though it is not legitimized by their culture. Here, where directed, conscious thought is most highly valued, a young person often will be encouraged to "think carefully about your career choice" and maybe "make lists of the pros and cons of the different possibilities." This works to a certain extent, but I knew of a number of cases where the career decision was really made, and felt right, only after it came together in a dream.

It is noteworthy that in these tribal societies the dream is not asked for in answer to any little problem like "what shall I wear to the tribal dance tomorrow?" Rather, the dreamer asks for help with a major life decision, which in our terms represents a powerful and presumably unresolved emotional concern. The importance of the problem is often further emphasized (made more of an emotional concern) by the techniques of incubation and preparation by the elders. The dream is in effect being asked to pull together available material from the young person's past experiences, personality characteristics, likes, dislikes, wishes, and fears, and come up with an image that may then help in making a decision. That is just what dreams are good at! In my view, the dream is being used appropriately as a place where broader connections can be made, where emotionally important themes can be integrated, and it may produce an image or series of images that will help in making the career choice. This appears to me to be very sensibly making use of the broad connective abilities of dreaming.

The final decision about his career is of course made by the initiate in the waking state, perhaps with help from other waking minds. But the "opinion" of the dream is taken into account. I think this same technique can be useful in our Western culture in trying to advise a young person making a difficult career choice—or other choice—now. I would certainly encourage her to consider everything carefully from the point of view of advantages and disadvantages in the normal waking mode, but I would also urge her to think more loosely, to daydream, and perhaps to spend a few days alone, away from other concerns, and try to incubate a dream on the topic. Why not make use of all our available resources including the broader, more connective possibilities of the dream, which sometimes afford us a new insight or new perspective on the problem?

The dream quest of the adolescent is one of many examples of an institutionalized use of dreams in various cultures. Dreams of this kind—big or important dreams of which society makes use—have been called "culture pattern" dreams.[6] Such dreams help the entire village make certain decisions, for instance, in the creation of dances or wedding and funeral ceremonies.

THE SOUL REMAINS ABOVE GROUND

The connecting power of dreams can be used in a variety of ways. The above example is a kind of practical behavioral use of dreams. I believe our connections in dreams also directly influence widespread cultural beliefs. As one prominent example, there is a belief in many cultures, and among some members of our culture as well, that when a person dies, his or her soul "remains above ground" in some manner for a time. This period of time varies from a few weeks or months to a number of years.[7] Often gifts or offerings of various kinds are given to the souls of the dead either to speed their journey to the other world or to make sure they feel friendly toward the survivors. These are cultures in which it is very important to placate the souls of the dead, especially in the period soon after death. Among the Shangaan people of South Africa, whenever a person dies away from his own village, it is necessary for a close relative or, lacking that, a good friend from the home village to journey by train to the place where the deceased met his death. The relative or friend then transports the body back to the native village. However, the most important part of the custom, which one must never neglect, is that while the body travels back in the baggage compartment of the train, the soul travels in the passenger car with the family member or friend, who must pay for an additional seat on the journey, to allow the soul to travel in comfort back to its native village.[8]

In some cultures, the soul is thought to have unfulfilled duties, or unfinished business with the living. Sometimes the soul of the deceased is thought to haunt the living, especially if the death has been a violent one. The period of time the soul is thought to remain above ground varies, but it is usually a few months or a few years. I suggest that a clear basis for this belief is that the dead person is indeed still with us in the sense that he or she is dreamt about by friends and loved ones for some months or years. As the years and decades pass, the departed appears less frequently and finally not at all in the dreams of the living. At about this time the soul is declared to have departed and moved on.

This view of the soul remaining with us does not strike me as a fanciful or outrageous belief; anyone we think about is, in some sense, with us. Someone close to us, emotionally important to us, whom we not only think of but dream about in the amazingly real picture language of dreams, is that much more real. And dreams about the dead can sometimes be especially powerful since, as we have noted, the dream has the ability to contextualize emotional concerns. Thus, the dream's connections bring back not only a simple memory image of the departed person but an image enhanced by the dreamer's concerns. My impression is that the recently dead are a particularly powerful focus for our emotional concerns, not only about the individual dead person but about relationships in general, and about our perception of our own life and death.

I have mentioned one patient, both of whose parents died in the course of two years. Both came back to him in dreams, but in remarkably different ways. In his only two dreams of his mother, he referred to her as smiling, and looking healthy; he was somehow saying goodbye to his mother and the feeling was of peace and contentment. This is quite common, in fact, in dreams of the departed.[9] The dreams about his father were quite different. His father came back in a number of dreams looking half-dead and half-alive, in some kind of pain. This alerted the dreamer to the fact that his relationship with his father had always been difficult and that there was a lot of "unfinished business" after his father's death. He realized there was still a good deal he had to think about and work on in terms of understanding his relationship to his father before they could be at peace. In terms of the beliefs of certain cultures, the father's soul was still above ground.

Dreams remind us that the dead are still with us, and call our attention to an important point for our own lives. A significant part of our existence is our existence in the minds of others, and this part does not die with our physical death.

THE DREAM AS A VOYAGE OF THE SOUL

Some cultures believe the soul of the sleeping person leaves the body, takes long voyages in dreams, and meets with other souls—

those of the living and the recently dead.[10] Although the word "soul" grates on the Western scientific ear, I believe its use here is not illegitimate. If we consider such meetings important and we wish to give a name to the part of ourselves that meets with our dead relatives and loved ones, it certainly cannot be our body, which is lying peacefully in bed; nor apparently is it our everyday mind: The experience of unexpectedly meeting (seeing, experiencing) someone in a dream is very different from and more resonant than simply thinking about her or remembering her. We can use a name such as "spirit" or "soul" and speak of our spirit or soul meeting the spirit or soul of a departed person. In some societies such meetings may be thought to occur in the "real world." In some it does not matter, or the distinction between "real world" and "imagined world" is not always clear. We can certainly recognize that something emotionally meaningful occurs, even if we believe that such a meeting occurs in the outer pathways of our dreaming memory nets rather than in the pathways of the physical world.

As a therapist, and also as a person who has dreamt about his own dead parents, I have no question that such encounters are psychologically meaningful and important. They are very real to me. Thin-boundary cultures may not make sharp distinctions between real in that sense and the real world of hard objects. In some cultures such encounters may be thought of as occurring in the "real world." My down-to-earth scientific (thick-boundary) colleagues, of course, say that these are totally different occurrences, as different as black and white. They tell me that those cultures think that souls are really out there meeting other souls, and I am just talking about a dream in your mind, nothing but a dream. Well, I agree that the meetings I am talking about presumably occur in the wider portions of the nets of our dreaming minds. We can call this "not real," but only in the sense that all our dreams, thoughts, virtues, and vices as well as love, hate, truth, and beauty are not real. I wonder whether those who talk of souls in other cultures are speaking of something so different. They may say that souls meet, but they may mean meet in a world that is important, that is just as real as waking reality rather than in exactly the same real world.[11] I'm not claiming that such encounters are "real" in exactly the same sense as my encounter at this moment with a pad of paper and a coffee cup, but there is no question that they are important, and that they can influence our lives.

THE IMAGES OF OUR RELIGIONS

We can also consider the actual images and icons that occur in all of our religions. In any number of religions, a god or a supernatural creature is portrayed as a bird or a lion with a man or woman's head, or a man with the head of an antelope or other animal. I would argue that these images probably derived at some point from dreams. They are the very stuff of dream connection or condensation—especially the powerful condensations that sometimes occur at the end of a long dream.

Some readers may feel that I am speaking only of distant or "primitive" religions that have little to do with modern man. Not so! What we have discussed relates to Western religions as well as to those we consider more exotic. For instance, I have suggested that the Christian hell is populated by creatures derived from nightmares.[12] Demons and devils of various kinds are typical dream condensations and they are the kinds of creatures frequently found in nightmares. I believe it is likely that they derived originally from the nightmares and dreams of those who formulated these beliefs. However, I do not in the least mean that our images of hell are arbitrary—that someone happened to have a dream one night and wrote it down and said, "Hey, this is a great image. Let's use it." Nor am I suggesting that hell is a cautionary tale dreamt up, literally or figuratively, to frighten people. Rather, I believe that hell, similarly to the dream quest or other culture pattern demons we have discussed, may have derived from dreams but was shaped culturally and clearly had some adaptive value in our culture. Hell can indeed be considered a gradually evolving, highly creative condensation contextualizing or picturing metaphorically our powerful guilts and concerns about sin and punishment.

Symmetry suggests that a few words about heaven are in order here. However, my impression is that for most of us heaven is not as clear-cut a picture as hell either in our dreams or in texts or imaginings. Heaven is more vague and ill-formed. Just as it was easier to discuss picturing negative or disturbing emotions in dreams, so do the pictures of hell and demons both in our dreams and elsewhere appear more clearly formed or easier to describe than pictures of bliss or heavenly creatures. Nonetheless, there is no question that we can dream of angels and of heaven. Although I am not religious in any conventional sense, I've had such dreams myself. Presumably such dreams are picturing our concepts of what is highest and/or our attempts to achieve it. One study has been completed in which persons capable of lucid dreaming (being aware in their dreams that they were dreaming and to some extent able to change their dreams) were asked to try to dream of "the highest." A number of beautiful images occurred, mostly involving glowing energy, sun, light, and flowers. This led to a number of paintings and other works of art, but not to any clear-cut, easily statable conclusions.[13]

BIG DREAMS, MYTHS, ARCHETYPES

It has been noted and can be seen by anyone who has kept track of dreams for a long time that at least certain rare dreams–the "big dreams"—sometimes have themes and imagery very much like those of myth and religion. We take part in heroic quests, we go down into dark caves and dungeons and at least some of the time come up triumphant. We slay dragons at times, though more commonly, in our nightmares, we run away from them.

In these instances our dreams appear to put us more in touch with our basic cultural idioms or themes. The incubation techniques of certain cultures appear to be adapted to promoting this process of getting in touch with our cultural roots, and it happens occasionally even without incubation. Kelly Bulkeley has written in detail on this aspect of dreaming and its ability to connect with the "root metaphors" of our culture.[14] Root metaphors imply basic underlying images and themes. For instance, the example of "hell" would represent one of the root metaphors of Christian culture.

There is also a commonality across cultures in these human creations. Jung has described common themes and "archetypes" in dreams, myths, and rituals among different cultures.[15] Joseph Campbell has elaborated this in great detail, tracing similarities in important stories and myths through various cultures of the world.[16] Our "big" dreams appear to allow us to access this material somehow, though for most of us this does not happen very often.

It might be an interesting study to determine under just what conditions and to whom these mythic dreams occur—or, in our terms, what sort of emotion or emotional concern is being contextualized by these large, often awesome, numinous, or mythic kinds of dreams? They are very far removed from nightmares and frightening dreams. The feeling tone can usually be described as positive, though not exactly as happiness. If there is any feeling either in the dream or perhaps in the background being pictured by the dream, it is something like awe or wonder. My dream series indicate that these dreams certainly do not occur when we are just recovering from trauma, when we are in a severely stressful situation, or when we are overcome by one disturbing emotion. Perhaps they occur when we are relatively at peace, when we have no immediate pressing concern. Or perhaps they occur when our most pressing concern is one that could be called spiritual or existential, an attempt to know ourselves better, to know our essence, or to find something higher.

The commonality of these dream stories, myths, and religions suggests a kind of commonality in human mental functioning in the way we are able to tell and organize stories. Certain themes, such as a heroic quest or an encounter with monsters, appear to recur repeatedly. This suggests a commonality in the structure of our minds. Jung spoke of archetypes, and in his view they lay at the depths of the unconscious; we are all somewhat similar in the archetypic depths of our unconscious.[17] In the model I have elaborated here I would talk rather of certain constraints in the looser, broader, more peripheral portions of our nets. The nets of our minds may be woven loosely, but my nets are not totally different from yours. There are biological constraints in the functioning of the cortex. There are certain common features in the weave and in the pathways taken by excitation when it travels along the nets.

The Immense and the Intense

Not only do we have big dreams and dreams in which we dream of great quests and important doings, but I believe that the whole idea of huge—incredibly big, incredibly powerful, etc.—is one that comes from our dreams, or at least is most accessible in our dreams and of course, to a lesser extent, in our daydreams.

In our ordinary waking thought, we indeed think of big people and little people, but the big people are only two or three times as large as the little ones. We think of big animals, such as horses and elephants, and little animals, such as mice and squirrels, but usually there's little more range than that. In our dreams, we are confronted with the huge, the vast, the unending. Leafing through a series of dreams in front of me, I frequently see references such as "a huge mountain has split"; "a huge tree has fallen down"; " a giant ladder going right up into the clouds"; "there's a tremendously high building that seems to go up to the sky"; "I am on an immense, vast, empty plain"; "I'm driving on and on through this endless tunnel." And many other images, for instance the tidal wave image we have discussed in previous chapters, certainly imply immensity.

Likewise, we sometimes dream about huge quantities: "millions of little ants coming out of the cellar." A quick comparison of 100 dreams with several other sorts of text has convinced me that words such as huge, vast, immense, occur far more often in the dreams than in comparison texts of equal length. It is no secret that our dreams are peopled with giants and strange, usually large, creatures; to some extent this may be related to our childhood, when everything and everyone around us seemed huge. But I think there is more to it than that. Our dreams contain not only giants and huge beings, but unusually powerful beings and forces and sometimes unusually intense experiences—glowing golden sculptures, or a powerful phallic pillar in one of Jung's early dreams, which he remembered his entire life. There is in fact a developing literature about intense mystical sorts of experiences in dreams. Some dreamers have experienced an intense golden light experience in lucid dreams, which is also reported in important religious and mystical experiences.[18] There are also groups of lucid dreamers who try to go beyond the usual lucid dream experience of being aware one is dreaming and continue toward the awareness of dreamless sleep as well and eventually a constant, free-floating awareness without any content.[19] Dreams can apparently lead us outward or inward in a number of interesting directions.

Thus the dream brings us closer to hugeness, huge power, intense emotion, and intense experience. It isn't far from there to the angels, demigods, and gods. Is the idea of an all-powerful and all-encompassing god an extension of these dream ideas? Or, on the other hand, is it possible that our capacity for experiencing the huge and the intense in dreams brings us closer to whatever powerful, intense forces there may be outside of us?

The relation of dreams to religion and religious thought is a huge (vast? endless? intense?) topic that we cannot discuss in detail here. Certainly religious texts are full of important dreams, and the founders of major religions attribute much of their wisdom to revelations in dreams and visions.

DREAMING AND PARANORMAL PHENOMENA

While we are thinking along the lines of the large and unusual, we can also ask, does dreaming, as many believe, perhaps give us a chance to experience "paranormal phenomena"? Is there such a thing as a telepathic dream or a precognitive dream, which many people claim to have experienced?

Although I personally have not experienced a convincing telepathic, clairvoyant, or precognitive dream, I am not willing to dismiss the possibility that such things can happen. Our knowledge is limited and I have no reason to believe that the forms of energy transmission or the forms of communication that have been discovered so far are necessarily the entire picture. There may be something more, and I will explain why I believe dreams might be an especially good place to look for that something more.

I have heard at least ten times from reliable people something like the following:

> Last year I had this very striking dream in which something awful happened to my mother. I think she was hurt or perhaps had died in my dream. I woke up very disturbed and after some time decided to call home (which is 200 miles away). I reached a member of the family who said, "It's strange that you called asking about your mother just now. She had a heart attack (or stroke or sudden illness) and was taken to the hospital just a few hours ago."

I have sometimes asked these people whether they have had such dreams at other times and then found that nothing had happened in reality, but they usually say that this is the only or almost the only time they can remember such a dream. These occurrences always seem to involve someone very close to the dreamer where there is a strong emotional bond. It is possible that these instances could all be coincidences, of course, but I am not convinced of it.

In fact, there have been attempts to study telepathy in dreams scientifically, and at least one study has provided statistically significant positive results. Krippner and Ullman set up a study in 1970 in which a person acting as a "receiver" slept in a sleep laboratory and was awakened during long REM sleep periods and asked to report dream content. A "sender" in another building had been informed when the receiver started a REM period; the sender at that point was to take one picture at random out of an envelope and concentrate on that picture, trying to "send" it. Judges who did not know which picture was looked at then tried to match the dream reports with the various pictures. In this study, some significant positive results were found. However, attempts to replicate this finding have met with mixed results.[20]

Interestingly, the other area in which some very positive results suggesting telepathy have been found involves not night dreaming itself but rather a daydreamlike condition referred to as the Ganzfeld phenomenon. Here subjects who are to "receive information" lie quietly in a room with no sound or with white noise and with only diffuse light (they usually have half Ping-Pong balls over their eyes to let only diffuse white light in). They are simply instructed to say whatever comes into their mind—describe any imagery, etc.—while they are in this relaxed, somewhat sensory-deprived state. Meanwhile, somewhere else, someone attempts to "send" images or material of one kind or another. Again, judges try to match the verbal productions of the receivers with the pictures or other material focused on by the senders. Although no single study of this kind is as well-known or has achieved such dramatic results as the Krippner-Ullman dream telepathy studies, there have now been enough separate Ganzfeld studies that the authors of a recent review in a prestigious psychological journal suggested that there is indeed something worth examining and that perhaps "Psi," the general name for these paranormal phenomena, does exist and is at least worth exploring further.[21]

Thus, although this whole field is full of controversy, it appears that there is at least a possibility that studies of telepathy will lead to a new field of scientific inquiry. And it is interesting that the most convincing studies among the hundreds or perhaps thousands that have been done, include a receiver who is either in REM sleep or lying relaxed in a sensory deprivation situation that encourages reverie or daydreaming. The best way I can summarize this for myself is to say that if it turns out that there is some form of energy or information transfer responsible for telepathy, I find it reasonable that we might be most susceptible to it when we are in the broadly connecting states of dreaming or daydreaming.

DREAMING, PLAY, AND ART

Dreaming is one of the broadening faculties of the human mind; other such faculties include play and art. In a sense, of course, dreaming *is* play. Dreaming involves the playful putting together of items in ways that they are not usually put together by waking thought. Dreaming concerns itself little with the immediate goals of waking. Play is generally described as allowing the child to get away from the requirements and goals of school or home, to try new possibilities and combinations—in other words, make new connections. In this sense play is much like dreaming.

Likewise, in a sense dreaming is art, as we have discussed. Dreaming has been called involuntary poetry and an incomplete

work of art. In fact for many people who do not consider themselves
to have any specific artistic talent or who have not developed a talent,
dreaming may be their closest approach to creating a work of art.

It is noteworthy that all three of these human faculties, which I
consider very essential parts of our makeup—dreaming, play, and
art—have been somewhat neglected or at least marginalized by
Western civilization in recent centuries. We have focused on the
scientific method, on deduction, on reaching a goal by the fastest
method possible. I am by no means trying to deride these goal-
directed activities; they are essential and useful parts of our lives, but
we are more than that! Dreaming, play, and art are different ways of
expressing parts of the "more" beyond straightforward science and
logic. In terms of our network model of the mind, all three of these
activities involve the looser, less direct, broader making of connections.

When Forster ended his novel *A Passage to India* with the injunction, "only connect," he was presumably thinking of relationships
between people, but it holds in other ways, too. If we can "only
connect" through our dreams, play, and art, in addition to our more
linear, focused waking connections, I believe we will have achieved
more of our human potential.

CULTURAL INFLUENCE AND BIAS

I have spoken briefly here of myths, root metaphors, archetypes,
and a number of religious and cultural beliefs without doing justice
to their complexity and richness. Although I am trying hard to accept
insights from other cultures insofar as I can, I am aware that I am a
product of my own culture and this influences the particular symbols
and metaphors I choose both in my waking and in my dreamlife and
may also influence my viewpoints and theories. This is an inescapa-
ble bias, and all I can do is point to a few places where I realize that
such cultural bias plays a role and at least accept in principle that
there are many other places where the role is less obvious and I may
not yet be aware of it.

For instance, I believe that what I have said about broad connectivity in dreams, connection making guided by emotion, and contex-

tualizing of emotional concerns is broad enough to be valid across cultures. However the specific images—the contextualizing images I have collected and chosen as illustrative examples—are heavily influenced by my culture. For instance the dream image of a journey by car representing the course of life or the course of a relationship is extremely common in modern American dreamers, but is unlikely to be so used in a culture where cars are unusual or associated with only certain groups, such as rich foreigners, and thus have totally different meanings. The common fear image of being chased by a gang of Nazis is of course an image of Western culture following the period of Nazi domination of Europe. Even our paradigmatic image of being overwhelmed by a tidal wave would be less likely in a hypothetical water-loving culture where periodic tidal waves are needed to flood parched land.

Dreaming Makes Us Human

In this chapter I have explored very briefly the ways in which dreaming connects us with larger cultural or human themes through root metaphors and archetypes. We have discussed how dreaming can be useful in a variety of ways, from career choice to understanding what many cultures mean by the soul. And I have suggested that dreams bring us in touch with a greater range in almost all dimensions from size (huge, vast) and quantity (millions and billions) to greater intensities of emotional experience and perhaps mystical experience. We have touched on the resemblances of dreaming, play, and art.

All of these enlargements or extensions in our lives can be related to a very simple mechanism I postulated at the beginning of our discussion: that we make connections more broadly in dreaming than in waking, and that the connections are by no means random but are guided by forces within us. I have called these forces emotional concerns but they can include larger existential, cultural, or religious concerns.

I believe all this greater connectedness and broadening is essential in our most human quest for increased knowledge, especially increased self-knowledge. Dreaming helps us fulfill the great task placed before us by the Delphic Oracle: "gnowthi seauton" (to know oneself).

If we think of ourselves only as complex calculating machines, at our best when solving arithmetic problems, then dreaming is useless. If we think of ourselves only as outfielders running to the right place to catch a fly ball, then dreaming is useless. If we think of ourselves only as need-fulfilling creatures—dashing about seeking food, shelter, mates, and when we obtain these that is the end of it—then perhaps we do not need dreaming. But insofar as we are more than this, our dreams are essential to us.

I am not trying to belittle waking; obviously we need our focused waking thought and activity. Waking is useful in achieving our goals as efficiently as possible. Waking is a hunt, dreaming is an exploration. Dreaming does not achieve an immediate goal, but connects us with other parts of ourselves, our pasts, our plans for the future, our stories and myths, our ancestors and descendants, our demons and gods. Dreaming makes us more human!

POSTSCRIPT: IN DREAMS BEGIN RESPONSIBILITIES

I have loved this phrase for many years. Its origins seem a bit uncertain. Poet Delmore Schwartz used "In dreams begin responsibilities" as the title of one of his first short stories and again as the title for his collected poetry.[22] He attributes the phrase to William Butler Yeats, who does not take credit for it, however, but attributes it in turn to "an old play."[23] Perhaps scholars have found a more exact origin, but it does not matter. I rather like the uncertainty. I like to consider it a phrase whose roots go back somewhere in the sands of time. I can imagine it as a phrase Adam might have mumbled to Eve or vice-versa after their first night together. But what does it mean? Are we meant to apply it to our literal dreams as opposed to our figurative dreams or imaginings? I cannot give you an answer, gentle reader, but there are some possible connections to what we have discussed about our dreams. If you have had a big dream, a powerful dream, an impactful dream, you can simply sit back and say to yourself or to others, "Wow, what a fascinating dream I had," or, as we have seen, you can stop smoking, you can create a new machine, a painting, a sonata, or a new religion.

You can change your life. You are free, I suppose, to do something or to do nothing at all. It is your dream. In dreams begin responsibilities.

APPENDIX

THE BOUNDARY QUESTIONNAIRE*

Please try to rate each of the statements from 0 to 4. 0 indicates no, not at all, or not at all true of me. 4 indicates yes, definitely, or very true of me.

Please try to answer all of the questions and statements as quickly as you can.

1. When I awake in the morning, I am not sure whether I am really awake for a few minutes.   0   1   2   3   4

2. I have had unusual reactions to alcohol.
   0   1   2   3   4

3. My feelings blend into one another.
   0   1   2   3   4

4. I am very close to my childhood feelings.
   0   1   2   3   4

5. I am very careful about what I say to people until I get to know them really well.   0   1   2   3   4

6. I am very sensitive to other people's feelings.
   0   1   2   3   4

---

*Reprinted with permission from Ernest Hartmann, *Boundaries in the Mind*. New York: Basic Books, 1991.

7. I like to pigeonhole things as much as possible.
   0   1   2   3   4

8. I like solid music with a definite beat.
   0   1   2   3   4

9. I think children have a special sense of joy and wonder that is
   later often lost.   0   1   2   3   4

10. In an organization, everyone should have a definite place and
    a specific role.   0   1   2   3   4

11. People of different nations are basically very much alike.
    0   1   2   3   4

12. There are a great many forces influencing us which science
    does not understand at all.   0   1   2   3   4

13. I have dreams, daydreams, nightmares in which my body or
    someone else's body is being stabbed, injured, or torn apart.
    0   1   2   3   4

14. I have had unusual reactions to marijuana.
    0   1   2   3   4

15. Sometimes I don't know whether I am thinking or feeling.
    0   1   2   3   4

16. I can remember things from when I was less than three years
    old.
    0   1   2   3   4

17. I expect other people to keep a certain distance.
    0   1   2   3   4

18. I think I would be a good psychotherapist.
    0   1   2   3   4

19. I keep my desk and worktable neat and well organized.
    0   1   2   3   4

20. I think it might be fun to wear medieval armor.
    0   1   2   3   4

21. A good teacher needs to help a child remain special.
    0   1   2   3   4

22. When making a decision, you shouldn't let your feelings get in
    the way.   0   1   2   3   4

23. Being dressed neatly and cleanly is very important.
    0   1   2   3   4

24. There is a time for thinking and there is a time for feeling; they
    should be kept separate.   0   1   2   3   4

25. My daydreams don't always stay in control.
    0   1   2   3   4

26. I have had unusual reactions to coffee or tea.
    0   1   2   3   4

27. For me, things are black or white; there are no shades of gray.
    0   1   2   3   4

28. I had a difficult and complicated childhood.
    0   1   2   3   4

29. When I get involved with someone, I know exactly who I am
    and who the other person is. We may cooperate, but we main-
    tain our separate selves.   0   1   2   3   4

30. I am easily hurt.   0   1   2   3   4

31. I get to appointments right on time.
    0   1   2   3   4

32. I like heavy solid clothing.   0   1   2   3   4

33. Children and adults have a lot in common. They should give
    themselves a chance to be together without any strict roles.
    0   1   2   3   4

34. In getting along with other people in an organization, it is very
    important to be flexible and adaptable.
    0   1   2   3   4

35. I believe many of the world's problems could be solved if only
    people trusted each other more.   0   1   2   3   4

36. Either you are telling the truth or you are lying; that's all there
    is to it.   0   1   2   3   4

37. I spend a lot of time daydreaming, fantasizing, or in reverie.
    0   1   2   3   4

38. I am afraid I may fall apart completely.
    0   1   2   3   4

39. I like to have beautiful experiences without analyzing them or
    trying to understand them in detail.
    0   1   2   3   4

40. I have definite plans for my future. I can lay out pretty well
    what I expect year by year at least for the next few years.
    0   1   2   3   4

41. I can usually tell what another person is thinking or feeling
    without anyone saying anything.   0   1   2   3   4

42. I am unusually sensitive to loud noises and to bright lights.
    0   1   2   3   4

43. I am good at keeping accounts and keeping track of my money.
    0   1   2   3   4

44. I like stories that have a definite beginning, middle, and end.
    0   1   2   3   4

45. I think an artist must in part remain a child.
    0   1   2   3   4

46. A good organization is one in which all the lines of responsibil-
    ity are precise and clearly established.
    0   1   2   3   4

47. Each nation should be clear about its interests and its own
    boundaries, as well as the interests and boundaries of other
    nations.   0   1   2   3   4

48. There is a place for everything, and everything should be in its
    place.   0   1   2   3   4

49. Every time something frightening happens to me, I have night-mares or fantasies or flashbacks involving the frightening event.   0   1   2   3   4

50. I feel unsure of who I am at times.   0   1   2   3   4

51. At times I feel happy and sad all at once.
0   1   2   3   4

52. I have a clear memory of my past. I could tell you pretty much what happened year by year.   0   1   2   3   4

53. When I get involved with someone, we sometimes get too close.   0   1   2   3   4

54. I am a very sensitive person.   0   1   2   3   4

55. I like things to be spelled out precisely and specifically.
0   1   2   3   4

56. I think a good teacher must remain in part a child.
0   1   2   3   4

57. I like paintings and drawings with clean outlines and no blurred edges.   0   1   2   3   4

58. A good relationship is one in which everything is clearly defined and spelled out.   0   1   2   3   4

59. People are totally different from each other.
0   1   2   3   4

60. When I wake up, I wake up quickly and I am absolutely sure I am awake.   0   1   2   3   4

61. At times I have felt as if I were coming apart.
0   1   2   3   4

62. My thoughts blend into one another.
0   1   2   3   4

63. I had a difficult and complicated adolescence.
0   1   2   3   4

64. Sometimes it's scary when one gets too involved with another
     person.   0   1   2   3   4

65. I enjoy soaking up atmosphere even if I don't understand
     exactly what's going on.   0   1   2   3   4

67.* I like paintings or drawings with soft and blurred edges.
     0   1   2   3   4

68. A good parent has to be a bit of a child too.
     0   1   2   3   4

69. I cannot imagine marrying or living with someone of another
     religion.   0   1   2   3   4

70. It is very hard to empathize truly with another person because
     people are so different.   0   1   2   3   4

71. All important thought involves feelings, too.
     0   1   2   3   4

72. I have dreams and daydreams or nightmares in which I see
     isolated body parts—arms, legs, heads, and so on.
     0   1   2   3   4

73. Things around me seem to change their size and shape.
     0   1   2   3   4

74. I can easily imagine myself to be an animal or what it might be
     like to be an animal.   0   1   2   3   4

75. I feel very separate and distinct from everyone else.
     0   1   2   3   4

76. When I am in a new situation, I try to find out precisely what is
     going on and what the rules are as soon as possible.
     0   1   2   3   4

77. I enjoy(ed) geometry: there are simple, straightforward rules,
     and everything fits.   0   1   2   3   4

There is no item 66 on the Boundary Questionnaire; there is a total of 145 items on the
questionnaire.

78. A good parent must be able to empathize with his or her children, to be their friend and playmate at the same time.
0   1   2   3   4

79. I cannot imagine living with or marrying a person of another race.   0   1   2   3   4

80. People are so different that I never know what someone else is thinking or feeling.   0   1   2   3   4

81. Beauty is a very subjective thing. I know what I like, but I wouldn't expect anyone else to agree.
0   1   2   3   4

82. In my daydreams, people kind of merge into one another or one person turns into another.   0   1   2   3   4

83. My body sometimes seems to change its size or shape.
0   1   2   3   4

84. I get overinvolved in things.   0   1   2   3   4

85. When something happens to a friend of mine or a lover, it is almost as if it happened to me.   0   1   2   3   4

86. When I work on a project, I don't like to tie myself down to a definite outline. I rather like to let my mind wander.
0   1   2   3   4

87. Good solid frames are very important for a picture or a painting.   0   1   2   3   4

88. I think children need strict discipline.
0   1   2   3   4

89. People are happier with their own kind than when they mix.
0   1   2   3   4

90. East is East, and West is West, and never the twain shall meet. (Kipling)   0   1   2   3   4

91. There are definite rules and standards, which one can learn, about what is and is not beautiful.   0   1   2   3   4

92. In my dreams, people sometimes merge into each other or become other people.   0   1   2   3   4

93. I believe I am influenced by forces which no one can understand.   0   1   2   3   4

94. When I read something, I get so involved that it can be difficult to get back to reality.   0   1   2   3   4

95. I trust people easily.   0   1   2   3   4

96. When I am working on a project, I make a careful detailed outline and then follow it closely.   0   1   2   3   4

97. The movies and TV shows I like best are the ones where there are good guys and bad guys and you always know who they are.   0   1   2   3   4

98. If we open ourselves to the world, we find that things go better than expected.   0   1   2   3   4

99. Most people are sane; some people are crazy; there is no in-between.   0   1   2   3   4

100. I have had déjà vu experiences.   0   1   2   3   4

101. I have a very definite sense of space around me.
0   1   2   3   4

102. When I really get involved in a game or in playing at something, it's sometimes hard to tell where the game stops and the rest of the world begins.   0   1   2   3   4

103. I am a very open person.   0   1   2   3   4

104. I think I would enjoy being an engineer.
0   1   2   3   4

105. There are no sharp dividing lines between normal people, people with problems, and people who are considered psychotic or crazy.   0   1   2   3   4

106. When I listen to music, I get so involved that it is sometimes difficult to get back to reality.   0   1   2   3   4

107. I am always at least a little bit on my guard.
      0   1   2   3   4

108. I am a down-to-earth, no-nonsense kind of person.
      0   1   2   3   4

109. I like houses with flexible spaces, where you can shift things
      around and make different uses of the same rooms.
      0   1   2   3   4

110. Success is largely a matter of good organization and keeping
      good records.   0   1   2   3   4

111. Everyone is a little crazy at times.   0   1   2   3   4

112. I have daymares.   0   1   2   3   4

113. I awake from one dream into another.
      0   1   2   3   4

114. Time slows down and speeds up for me. Time passes very
      differently on different occasions.   0   1   2   3   4

115. I feel at one with the world.   0   1   2   3   4

116. Sometimes I meet someone and trust him or her so completely
      that I can share just about everything about myself at the first
      meeting.   0   1   2   3   4

117. I think I would enjoy being the captain of a ship.
      0   1   2   3   4

118. Good fences make good neighbors.
      0   1   2   3   4

119. My dreams are so vivid that even later I can't tell them from
      waking reality.   0   1   2   3   4

120. I have often had the experience of different senses coming
      together. For example, I have felt that I could smell a color, or
      see a sound, or hear an odor.   0   1   2   3   4

121. I read things straight through from beginning to end. (I don't
      skip or go off on interesting tangents.)
      0   1   2   3   4

122. I have friends and I have enemies, and I know which are which.   0   1   2   3   4

123. I think I would enjoy being some kind of a creative artist.
0   1   2   3   4

124. A man is a man and a woman is a woman; it is very important to maintain that distinction.   0   1   2   3   4

125. I know exactly what parts of town are safe and what parts are unsafe.   0   1   2   3   4

126. I have had the experience of not knowing whether I was imagining something or it was actually happening.
0   1   2   3   4

127. When I recall a conversation or a piece of music, I hear it just as though it were happening there again right in front of me.
0   1   2   3   4

128. I think I would enjoy a really loose, flexible job where I could write my own job description.   0   1   2   3   4

129. All men have something feminine in them and all women have something masculine in them.   0   1   2   3   4

130. In my dreams, I have been a person of the opposite sex.
0   1   2   3   4

131. I have had the experience of someone calling me or speaking my name and not being sure whether it was really happening or I was imagining it.   0   1   2   3   4

132. I can visualize something so vividly that it is just as though it were happening right in front of me.   0   1   2   3   4

133. I think I could be a good fortune-teller or a medium.
0   1   2   3   4

134. In my dreams, I am always myself.
0   1   2   3   4

135. I see auras or fields of energy around people.
0   1   2   3   4

136. I can easily imagine myself to be someone of the opposite sex.   0   1   2   3   4

137. I like clear, precise borders.   0   1   2   3   4

138. I have had the feeling that someone who is close to me was in danger or was hurt, although I had no ordinary way of knowing it, and later found out that it was true.
0   1   2   3   4

139. I have a very clear and distinct sense of time.
0   1   2   3   4

140. I like houses where the rooms have definite walls and each room has a definite function.   0   1   2   3   4

141. I have had dreams that later came true.
0   1   2   3   4

142. I like fuzzy borders.   0   1   2   3   4

143. I have had "out of body" experiences during which my mind seems to leave, or actually has left, my body.
0   1   2   3   4

144. I like straight lines   0   1   2   3   4

145. I like wavy or curved lines better than I like straight lines.
0   1   2   3   4

146. I feel sure that I can empathize with the very old.
0   1   2   3   4

Scoring the Boundary Questionnaire

All the questions listed in the left-hand column (labeled "Thick to thin") are "thin" items; the questions in the right-hand column (labeled "Thin to thick") are "thick" items. The difference should be clear from reading the items.

Under each number in the left-hand column, enter the score the subject has circled for that item. Under each number in the right-hand column, enter the *inverse* of the subject's score, according to the following table:

$$4 = 0$$
$$3 = 1$$
$$2 = 2$$
$$1 = 3$$
$$0 = 4$$

Add the scores entered in both columns to obtain the scores on each of the twelve categories and the overall score (SumBound). On the average, the total for all questions is 250–300.

Boundary Questionnaire Score Sheet

Thick to thin						Thin to thick			Score
0				4		0		4	

Category 1: Sleep/wake/dream

1	13	25	37	49	72	60	134	
82	92	112	113	119	130			____

Category 2: Unusual experiences

2	14	26	38	50	61	(101, not included in the
73	83	93	100	114	120	score.)
126	131	135	138	141	143	____

Category 3: Thoughts, feelings, moods

3	15	39	51	62	74	27	139
84	94	102	106	115	127	
132	136					____

Category 4: Childhood, adolescence, adulthood

4	16	28	63	40	52	____

Category 5: Interpersonal

41	53	64	85	95	103	5	29	122	125
116	146					(17, 75, 107, not included in
						the score.)			____

Category 6: Sensitivity

6	18	30	42	54	____

Category 7: Neat, exact, precise

65	86	7	19	31	43	55
		76	96	108	121	____

Category 8: Edges, lines, clothing

67	109	123	133	142	145	44	57	77	87	97
128						104	117	137	140	144
						(8, 20, 32, not included in
						the score.)				____

Category 9: Opinions about children and others

9	21	33	45	56	68	88	
78							____

Boundary Questionnaire Score Sheet (*Continued*)

Thick to thin 0 4		Thin to thick 0 4					Score
Category 10: Opinions about organizations and relationships							
34 98		10	22	46	58	69	
		79	89	110			___
Category 11: Opinions about peoples, nations, groups							
11 35 105 111 129		23	47	59	70	80	
		90	99	118	124		___
Category 12: Opinions about beauty, truth							
12 71 81		24	36	48	91		___
		Total score (SumBound)					___

ENDNOTES

CHAPTER 1

1. Craig E (1992).
2. Campbell E (1987).
3. Siegel A (1996).
4. Summarized in a number of works by Lakoff and his associates, for instance, Lakoff and Johnson (1980), Lakoff (1987), Johnson (1987), and Lakoff (1993a).
5. Sacks O (1973).
6. States B (1995).
7. See Chapter 5 and notes to Chapter 5.
8. See Chapter 7 for a discussion and references.
9. Roffwarg H et al. (1966).
10. Hartmann E (1973).
11. See Chapter 11 for discussion and references.
12. Barrett D (1993).
13. See Chapter 9 for a detailed discussion.
14. See Chapter 5, especially Figure 3.
15. Discussed further in Chapter 9.

CHAPTER 2

1. Siegel A (1996).
2. Roussy et al. (1996). These authors found no incorporation of students' listed concerns. Saredi et al. (1997) did find some significant incorpora-

tion of concerns when these were specifically rehearsed ("incubated") before sleep. But these results were no longer significant when data were controlled for dream length. See also earlier studies such as Rados and Cartwright (1982).

3. Van der Kolk B *et al.* (1984).

4. Brenneis B (1994).

5. A similar case is described at length by K Muller (1996).

6. Greenberg R, personal communication.

7. Hartmann E *et al.* (1997).

8. The detailed scorings are presented here, from Hartmann E, Rosen R, and Grace, N (1998): A contextualizing image (CI) is a powerful central image in a dream that "contextualizes" (provides a picture context for) a dominant emotion. A paradigmatic CI is a dream we have frequently encountered, which goes something like, "I was overwhelmed by a tidal wave," or "I was swept away by a whirlwind," dreamt by someone who has recently escaped from a fire, been raped, or been through some other form of trauma. The dream does not picture the actual traumatic scene, but rather pictures the emotion, "I am terrified," "I feel overwhelmed." We are now examining whether contextualizing images in dreams can be scored reliably and whether they are more frequent and/or more intense after trauma.

Methods: The material analyzed here consists of 504 dreams reported by 10 subjects. The series ranged from five to 225 dreams per subject and were collected under very different circumstances after different traumas, making it difficult to combine results; thus the series will be presented individually. In several cases, dream series after trauma as well as at other times are available, so intrasubject comparisons are possible.

After establishing agreement between raters (see below), each dream was scored on a blind basis by two raters in the shorter dream series and one rater in the two longest series, on the following measures: (1) Presence or absence of a CI; (2) Intensity of the CI, on a scale of 0 to 3, where 0 means no CI; (3) Best guess as to what emotion is contextualized (out of a list of eighteen basic emotions we have found in dreams).

Interrater Reliability: Pearson product moment correlations were calculated on four sets of dream and daydream data. The mean r was .75 for measure (1) and .74 for measure (2).

Results: **Case 1**. A 28-year-old woman; eight dreams collected within three weeks after a violent rape. CIs present in 100%; mean intensity 2.53. Emotions contextualized: fear/terror; helplessness/vulnerability.

Case 2. A 30-year-old man from Central America; five dreams told to his therapist soon after a yearlong period of imprisonment and torture. CIs present in 100%; mean intensity 2.55. Emotions contextualized: helplessness/vulnerability; grief/loss; anger; power/mastery.

Case 3. A 25-year-old man whose twin brother died in an accident; 25 dreams in the year after the death, recorded in a dream log. CIs present in 72.6%; Intensity 1.30. Emotions contextualized: grief/loss; guilt; anger; helplessness.

Case 4. A 54-year-old woman with severe trauma from major surgery (poor surgical result); 21 dreams reported to her therapist. CIs in 85.7%; Intensity 1.50. Emotions contextualized: despair/helplessness; loss/sadness; helplessness/vulnerability.

Case 5. Thirteen dreams in a 35-year-old woman, just before and after a hysterectomy for a tumor that turned out to have metastasized. CIs in 53.8%; Intensity 1.12. Emotions contextualized: grief/loss; fear/terror; helplessness/vulnerability.

Case 6. A 40-year-old man who kept a dream log. Five dreams immediately after the death of his mother were compared with five dreams from a relatively peaceful period five years earlier, and five dreams ten years later. CIs in early period: 40.0%; Intensity 0.40. Emotions contextualized: frustration; fear. Period just after death: CIs in 70%; Intensity 1.15. Emotions: grief/loss; frustration. Period 10 years later: CIs in 50%; Intensity 0.50. Emotions: happiness/joy; shame/embarrassment.

Case 7. A 22-year-old woman who had two traumas. She heard of a good friend's suicide, and then seven weeks later another good friend fell off Case 7's roof and became paraplegic. Ten dreams before traumas: CIs in 20%; Intensity 0.21. Five dreams after first trauma: CIs in 60%; Intensity 0.62. Five dreams after second trauma: CIs in 60%; Intensity 0.90. Five dreams three years later: CIs in 0%; Intensity = 0. Emotions: various.

Case 8. A 50-year-old woman going through a very stressful time, as a good friend discovers she has metastatic cancer. Sixteen dreams are reported over two months. CIs in 62.5%; mean intensity 1.05. Emotions contextualized: helplessness/vulnerability; frustration.

Case 9. A 35-year-old man who kept a continuous dream log; one brother died unexpectedly of a heart attack and his other brother died of suicide four months later. We scored 255 dreams before, between, and after the traumas. Eighteen dreams before the first trauma: CIs in 77.7%; Intensity 1.22. Many emotions including awe, power, helplessness, shame. Count 179 dreams after the first brother's death and before the second: CIs in 75.4%; Intensity 1.53. Emotions: many. (Considering only the 10 dreams immediately after the first trauma: CIs in 70.0%; Intensity 1.60. Emotions: anger; frustration; power/mastery.) Total 58 dreams after the second trauma: CIs in 81.0%; Intensity 1.53. Emotions: many. (Considering the 10 dreams just after the second trauma: CIs in 80.0%; Intensity 1.82. Emotions: guilt, grief, anger, helplessness.)

Case 10. A 31-year-old man in Oklahoma City, one of whose best friends died in the federal building bombing. A complete dream log is available including 121 dreams—12 dreams in the weeks before the bombing, and

109 dreams after the bombing. Total 12 dreams before bombing: CIs in 58.3%; Intensity 1.17. Emotions: anger, frustration, guilt. Total 12 dreams immediately after the bombing: CIs in 100%; Intensity = 2.54. Emotions: disturbing, helplessness, anger. All 109 dreams in the year after the bombing: CIs in 69.7%; Intensity = 1.56. Emotions: many including helplessness/vulnerability; anger/frustration; power/mastery.

College Students: For purposes of comparison, a group of 40 recent dreams of college students were rated: CIs in 64 ± 44%; Intensity 1.19 ± 1.0.

Conclusions: CIs can be scored reliably. CIs appear to be more frequent and more intense after trauma, and at traumatic times within the same individual. The emotions after trauma usually include fear/terror and helplessness/vulnerability.

9.   Hartmann E *et al.* (1998).
10. Herman J (1992); Everstine D and Everstine L (1992).
11. Jouvet M (1962); Jacobson A *et al.* (1964).
12. See, for instance, Terr L (1991).
13. Hartmann E (1996b).
14. An excellent study of Palestinian children in the war-torn Gaza Strip has been done by Punamaki R (1997).

CHAPTER 3

1.   Breger L *et al.* (1971).
2.   Cartwright R (1991); Cartwright R (1992); Cartwright R and Lamberg L (1992).
3.   See for instance Garfield P (1988); Maybruck P (1989); Van de Castle R (1994).
4.   From Garfield P (1988) p. 179.
5.   Both examples from Maybruck P (1989) p. 30.
6.   Jung C (1935/1968).
7.   Cartwright R and Romanek I (1978); Robbins P and Houshi F (1983); Domhoff W (1996).
8.   From La Rue R (1970). This dream, and about 20 dreams in my files, disprove the old adage that you never die in your dreams.
9.   Hartmann E (1984).
10. Kasatkin V (1967, 1984).
11. Garfield P (1991).
12. These examples are from Garfield P (1991).
13. Garfield P (1991).
14. Both examples are from Sacks O (1996).
15. Freud (1953 [1900]).
16. These studies began quite soon after the discovery of REM sleep, with an excellent study by Dement W and Wolpert E (1958). For a review and

further references, see Ellman S and Antrobus J (1991) or Nielsen T (1993).

17. Nielsen T (1993).
18. Dement W and Wolpert E (1958).
19. Trenholme *et al.* (1984).
20. This is the view expressed by a number of biological researchers including J. A. Hobson (1988) and Michael Gazzaniga (1988). To be fair, Hobson insists he is not saying that dreams are totally meaningless but only that their production is random (activation of the forebrain by the brainstem) and that meaning is "added on later." However, the situation in REM sleep is very similar to that in waking—a great deal of quasi-random activations of the forebrain by the brainstem along with a varying amount of more structured activation from sensory pathways. Are waking thought and fantasy then also to be considered random with meaning "added on later"?
21. Freud S (1953 [1900]), pp. 96–121.
22. There are many approaches to the scripts of dreams. For instance, Fookson J and Antrobus J (1992), Baylor G and Deslauriers D (1986).
23. This too is not unique to dreaming, but rather occurs more as we move to the right on the continuum from focused waking to dreaming (see Chapter 5).

Chapter 4

1. Beradt C (1968 [1966]).
2. The distinction between night terrors and nightmares was first noted by Broughton (1968) and clarified by Fisher *et al.* (1968). It is discussed in detail by Hartmann E (1984).
3. Kramer M (1970); Nielsen T *et al.* (1991).
4. Harris I (1948); Engelhart R and Hale D (1990).
5. MacFarlane J *et al.* (1954); Ames L (1964); Beltramini A and Hertzig M (1983).
6. From Mack J (1989 [1970]).
7. The personality dimension "Thick vs. Thin Boundaries" is discussed in Chapter 13. See also Hartmann E (1991).
8. Hartmann E (1984, 1991).
9. Snyder F (1970); McCarley R and Hobson J (1979).
10. Based on a number of studies. See Nielsen T *et al.* (1991) and Strauch I and Meier B (1989) for recent studies and reviews.
11. This was a survey rather than a controlled study. Considered as a study, the methodology was flawed. When the judges first scored for a contextualizing image (CI) they read the whole dream, and might have been influenced in their judgement of a CI by an emotion actually mentioned

in the dream. Ideally, the mentioned emotion should have been removed when judges scored the CIs.

12. These are patients with damage to the medial portions of the frontal lobes, studied by Damasio A (1994).

13. This brings up complex issues concerning "access to consciousness." There may be competition between different emotional states for "access to consciousness," and there is certainly some sense of emotions building up to a point where they suddenly emerge into consciousness either in waking or in dreaming. Sometimes the emotions and concerns emerge very suddenly in a dream. A friend of mine, a successful therapist and author, had a great deal of conflict about getting things finished. A severe case of writer's block played a major role in his life. Every few months or so, he has what he calls a "punch dream," a dream that suddenly reminds him in a very powerful and emotional way of what he has been putting off or neglecting. These dreams could be extremely simple and direct. For instance, while he was putting off finishing a book and had missed several deadlines, he had a dream that he was back in school trying to take an exam, and someone kept yelling, "You haven't finished yet, you haven't finished yet." This has been going on for years. I asked him whether it occurred all the time. He said yes, that it occurred all the time except for a few occasions when he had just completed a dissertation or a book. At those points the dreams stopped for a few months.

   My friend has come to understand his emotional state, which frequently includes guilt and shame. He realizes that much of the time these emotions remain underground and he is not aware of them, but at certain times they break through to waking awareness and he becomes consciously guilty and often quite unhappy. At other times, for various reasons, he is less aware of these feelings during waking, but they suddenly break through and produce a punch dream. The dream seems to contextualize and focus his complex emotional state, and he reports that sometimes this is useful to him; sometimes he requires a "reminder" from his dreams to help him get back to work on a project and get it finished. For more on consciousness see Chapter 10, Note 10.

14. This is of course not a new idea. One can read Freud in this way: A day's residue activates a wish, generally a derivative of a childhood wish, that remains active—unfulfilled, or unresolved. Calvin Hall, in his quantitative "content analysis of dreams," speaks of our generally dreaming of unresolved problems (Hall C and Van de Castle R, 1966). His student G. Domhoff (1996) has recently published an excellent detailed summary of content analysis studies supporting the view that dreaming, like waking, cognition deals with ongoing personal concerns and interests. See also Klinger E (1990). A number of authors have suggested that dreams not only picture concerns or problems but attempt to solve them. (See Chapter 7.)

15. Interestingly, the facing of issues often need not be a long-term or detailed therapeutic endeavor: To a certain extent, the process works in a mechanical manner. A child who dreams frequently of a particular monster can be asked simply to relate that dream, talk about it, and if possible, write it down or draw it before going to bed. Often that particular nightmare will not recur, or at least not for a while. I have spoken to many parents and also several children who have discovered this for themselves. It's not a complete solution: Other nightmares with different creatures may continue to occur. Overall, it is certainly useful to help the child face whatever fears are being pictured by the night-mares, get them out in the open, and try to find some solution. Such a process is not necessarily simple and can often be done best with a therapist. This has been formalized to some extent by some therapists who work with dreams. Anne Wiseman, for instance, has a detailed program for treating children's nightmares along these lines (1989).

    Also, a whole technique has been developed for treating night-mares in adults that involves writing down the nightmare in detail, trying to give it a new and more optimistic ending, and writing down the new script (Krakow and Neidhardt, 1996), which definitely seems to help some nightmare sufferers. I have found this useful in a few cases, although I am not certain that writing a new ending for the nightmare is really essential. In some cases, simply writing the original nightmare, thinking about it, and facing the danger in some way was enough without inventing any new endings.

16. Compensation is referred to a number of times in Jung's work on dreams. It depends on the view that we all have portions of ourselves or our personalities that we express easily and openly. Jung calls this the Persona. But there are other parts hidden deep within ourselves, some-times referred to as the "inferior aspect of the psyche," including the Shadow and the Anima or Animus. These hidden aspects or portions emerge in dreams. For a detailed, fully referenced discussion of conti-nuity versus compensation and evidence for each view, see Shafton A (1995).

17. Hall C and Van de Castle R (1966); Nielsen T et al. (1991).

CHAPTER 5

1. Based mainly on the work of Rumelhart D, McClelland J, and their many collaborators in the PDP research group (Rumelhart and McClel-land, 1986; McClelland and Rumelhart, 1986). In such models a memory feature or an item of information is not a fixed text or series of letters at a fixed address (as it would be in a serial computer) but rather a pattern of activation among widely distributed units or subfeatures (microfea-

tures). Such a network can function at several levels: A higher-level memory feature could be stored as a distributed activation pattern of lower-level features (microfeatures), each of which is stored as an activation pattern of still lower-level units (perhaps neurons).

2. Rumelhart D and McClelland J (1986).

3. Cohen J et al. (1990).

4. Crick F and Mitchison G (1983, 1986) used a very early form of connectionist net (Hopkins net). More recent attempts to use a net model are by Cartwright R (1990); Fookson J and Antrobus J (1992); Palombo S (1992b); Globus G (1993).

5. Hartmann E (1973, 1976, 1991b,, 1995).

6. First, there are various mathematical treatments of activation functions for each unit in the net (McClelland and Rumelhart, 1986) and a somewhat different treatment of groups of units by Grossberg S (1987). Then, a higher-level description is attempted by a whole field of mathematics called Harmony Theory (Smolensky P, 1986) which may form part of a far-ranging branch of knowledge known as Complex Systems Theory (Bar Yam, 1997).

7. These common "generic" settings would be scored as either "unfamiliar" or "questionable" settings in the Hall–Van de Castle content analysis; the norms in students show that the sum of these two categories account for 57% of dream settings in males and 53% in females—similar to the findings in my dreams. Inge Strauch and her collaborators have recently confirmed these findings in children 11–13 years old, finding that settings in dreams were 62% "unfamiliar, distorted, or questionable" and only 38% familiar, while settings in waking fantasies were 80% familiar (Strauch I, 1996).

8. Freud S (1953 [1900]) pp. 279–304.

9. Boss M (1958); Craig E (1992).

10. Hartmann E (1973).

11. See Hobson J (1988) or Siegel J (1993) for summaries of these studies.

12. The terms "inhibitory sharpening" and "increased signal-to-noise ratio" have been used more or less interchangeably to describe the actions of norepinephrine (especially at beta-adrenergic receptors) (Foote S et al., 1975; Woodward D et al., 1979; Servan-Schreiber et al., 1990). Both terms refer to a strongly activated center or central path, in sharp contrast to an inhibited periphery or surrounding area.

13. Of course each of these simple sounding "abilities" is actually quite complex and most likely involves not one but several "tightly woven" regions. Recent brain-imaging studies and older neuropsychological studies show that language skills (perhaps the best-studied abilities) remove the participation of a number of widespread cortical regions. See, for instance, Petersen S et al. (1995).

14. Autoassociative nets have been given a number of names, especially

"attractor nets." For a recent mathematical, complex systems approach to feed-forward and autoassociative nets, see Bar Yam J (1997).

15. Singer J (1975); Klinger E (1990).

16. From Hartmann E (1996b). Details are as follows:

Methods: A questionnaire was mailed to 400 members of the Association for the Study of Dreams; these are persons known to be interested in their dreams, and most are frequent dream recallers. Questions included age, sex, and frequency of dream recall. Dream content was examined in two separate ways. In Part A, subjects were asked how often a given activity occurred in their dreams on a 5-point scale from "never" to "all the time; it's in most of my dreams." This question was asked concerning four activities—reading, writing (by hand), typing (word processing, etc.), and calculating. Later in the questionnaire, respondents were asked how much time they spent per day in each of these four activities. In Part B respondents were asked, "How prominent is each of the following activities in your dreams as opposed to your waking life?" They responded on a scale from 1 ("far more prominent in my waking life; it occurs little or not at all in my dreams") through 4 ("equally prominent") to 7 ("far more prominent in my dream life; it occurs little or not at all in my waking life"). The activities were walking, writing, talking with friends, reading, sexual activity, and typing.

Results: The 240 respondents were frequent dream recallers; they recalled 6.8 ± 5.8 dreams per week. (A) *Reading*: 48% of subjects responded "never" and an additional 36% said "hardly ever," although this group reported spending 150 ± 94 minutes per day reading. *Writing*: 56% of subjects said "never"; 36% "hardly ever." This group spent 106 + 87 minutes per day writing. *Typing*: 75% of subjects said "never"; 19% "hardly ever." This group spent 98 ± 97 minutes per day typing. *Calculating*: 73% of subjects said "never"; 22% "hardly ever." This group spent 23 ± 29 minutes per day calculating. In Part B, respondents were questioned about six different activities including three very disparate control activities:

(B) Relative Prominence of Six Activities in Waking and Dreaming (X ± SD) in 240 Respondents

Walking*	Talking w/friends*	Sexual activity*
2.9 ± 1.4	3.1 ± 1.3	3.4 ± 1.7
Writing**	Reading**	Typing**
1.4 ± 0.8	1.4 ± 0.8	1.4 ± 1.0

Each variable marked ** differed significantly from each variable marked * by pairwise t-tests ($P < .0001$). There were no significant differences between variables within the two groupings (* and **). There was no significant correlation between sex or age and any of these six variables. This table gives means ± standard deviations, whereas means ± SEM standard errors of the mean are plotted in Figure 4.

"Calculating" was not included among the activities here since preliminary studies showed that many people spend close to zero time (and energy) calculating, so that asking them to compare prominence of calculating in dreams vs. waking asked them to compare two quantities each close to zero, which they found very difficult.

17. For instance, the view that we dream about emotional stuff rather than dull stuff (and I agree with this in general) would explain the low values for the 3 R's. But it would not explain the fact that walking is rated about equal to sexual activity. Or one could explain the results on the basis that we dream about visually large things and not about small things (fine details). This would roughly explain the present results, but it is not very satisfying since most good dream recallers (including myself) can recall at least some dreams in which they examine an object carefully and are struck by the interesting and unusual small details. In any case, the results appear to establish that even those of us who engage in the 3-R activities a great deal in waking, dream about them little or not at all.

18. Hartmann E (1966).

19. The many conceptual and mathematical tools related to "complex systems analysis" (Bar Yam, 1997) might be applied to our focused waking-to-dreaming continuum, if we think of it as (relatively) within-subsystem functioning at one end, and across or between subsystems functioning at the other.

20. See Chapters 7 and 11.

CHAPTER 6

1. See for instance Lakoff G (1987); Lakoff G and Johnson M (1980); Johnson M (1987).

2. Lakoff G and Turner M (1989).

3. Simile is simply metaphor that includes terms such as "like." Thus, "man is a wolf" is considered a metaphor; "man is like a wolf" a simile, but there is no essential difference. When we speak of metaphor in pictures rather than words, the difference become entirely meaningless.

4. When I speak of visual or visual-spatial imagery, I am talking about the usual situation in sighted persons. People differ, but our imagery is certainly predominantly visual. In people blind from birth the visual

sense is lacking, but the dreams nonetheless have a very sensory quality made up especially of auditory-spatial and tactile-spatial elements. Helen Keller provides some striking examples of such dreams in her autobiography (Keller H 1990). See also Chapter 12.

5. Lifton R (1996).
6. Sacks O (1973).
7. Garfield P (1991) p. 320.
8. Barrett D (1994).
9. Nielsen T (1993).
10. Maybruck P (1989) p. 65.
11. See for instance Delaney G (1979), Faraday A (1974), Garfield P (1976 [1974]), Taylor J (1992).
12. Delaney G (1991) p. 21.
13. See the work of Lakoff, Johnson, Turner, and others (Note 1).
14. See for instance Winner E and Gardner H (1993).
15. Rumelhart D and Abrahamson A (1973); Sternberg R et al. (1993).
16. Sternberg R et al. (1993).
17. Aristotle (1941).
18. States B (1995, 1997).
19. Snyder F (1970).
20. Foulkes D (1982).
21. Rechtschaffen A and Buchignani C (1992).
22. Though I had not realized it when I wrote it, the title of this section—The Dream as Metaphor and Continuity—contains at least an echo of Schopenhauer's great work (1883 [1819]), *Die Welt als Wille und Vorstellung* (The World as Will and Idea). In fact, Schopenhauer's thesis (not on dreaming but on our entire mental world) involves one powerful central force—the will—surrounded by elaborations and continuities.

   The importance of metaphor in dreams has been mentioned or alluded to by many authors, perhaps even Aristotle, if we consider metaphor a noting of similarities. Montague Ullman (1969) has written an entire paper entitled "Dreaming as Metaphor in Motion."

CHAPTER 7

1. Hartmann E (1973, 1991b). Also see several discussions of dreaming functions vs. REM functions in Moffitt A et al. (1993).
2. Janet P (1904, 1973 [1889], 1983 [1911]), summarized in English with great clarity by van der Kolk B and van der Hart O (1989).
3. Freud's "The Aetiology of Hysteria" (1962 [1896]) presents his earlier view, while the later view occurs throughout his work. See for instance Freud S (1916–1917).

4. American Psychiatric Association Diagnostic and Statistical Manual IV (1994).
5. There is a large and growing literature on the effects of trauma. See for instance Herman J (1992); Van der Kolk B (1984).
6. Lessing D (1975).
7. For instance Herman J (1992); Everstine D and Everstine L (1992).
8. Mathematically, this rough or smooth spatial state can be represented, though imperfectly, by "phase space," in which the position of a rolling ball represents the "state" of the system. This is a representation in which the rolling ball settles into a dip or "valley," representing lower "computational energy." The lowest valley represents the least perturbation or the most relaxed state. The ball settling into the lowest valley here is equivalent to the flat, smooth sea in the spatial metaphor. See Smolensky P (1986).
9. "Harmony" theory is a field of applied mathematics, sometimes applied to neural and connectionist nets. See Smolensky P (1986).
10. Consolidation of memory has an established meaning in the extensive literature on learning and memory. Used chiefly in behavioral studies, it is usually defined as, and measured by, the degree to which an event (usually a food reward or a shock) that produced a behavior, can still be shown to produce that behavior at a later time. One can thus study how environmental changes, drugs, lesions, etc., affect memory consolidation. Consolidation in this sense is not at all what I mean in terms of a function of dreaming. For instance, a traumatic memory is well-recalled, and by behavioral tests would be considered "consolidated." Yet it is very poorly cross-connected or integrated.
11. French T and Fromm E (1964).
12. Greenberg R and Pearlman C (1975, 1993); Greenberg et al. (1992).
13. Breger L et al. (1971).
14. Cartwright R (1991); Cartwright R and Lamberg L (1992).
15. Reviewed in Fiss H (1993).
16. Fiss H (1986). Fosshage J (1983) as well as Fiss assigns dreams a role in integration or consolidation of the self.
17. Jones R (1970).
18. Goodenough D et al. (1975).
19. Koulack D (1991).
20. Palombo S (1978b). Palombo manages to fit his memory cycle model into a Freudian framework, retaining such features as dream censorship. Palombo has recently been reformulating some of his views in terms of a connectionist net view of the mind (1992b).
21. Hartmann E (1973).
22. Studies of REM deprivation (sometimes called "dream deprivation") do not, unfortunately, provide clear answers, for many reasons. This research will be discussed in Chapter 11. Another approach would be to

study people who appear to do less dreaming than most. If one can assume tentatively that "less dreaming" is related to less REM sleep and/or less dream recall, I have studied a relevant group that is very low on both measures. These are the "short sleepers"—people who get along well on less than six hours of sleep per night (Hartmann E *et al.*, 1971, 1972). I described them as psychologically normal in most ways. They were smooth, efficient "nonworriers" who tended to deal with problems by denial or by keeping busy. Many of them had very "thick boundaries" (see Chap. 13). I am now attempting to follow up these same people 25–30 years later to examine whether they have maintained their short-sleep/little-dreaming style and how they are functioning now. I expect some interesting results, but I doubt they will provide a clear-cut answer to the functions of sleep or dreaming.

23. Cartwright R (1991); Cartwright R and Lamberg L (1992).
24. Kramer M and Roth T (1980); Kramer M (1993). The correlation of mood change with number of characters in the dream was statistically significant after correcting for the number of tests done. It is unclear why "number of characters" should be especially important; possibly number of characters is one index of the complexity of the dream.
25. Roffwarg H *et al.* (1966).
26. Hartmann E (1973).

CHAPTER 8

1. Much of this section is from Hartmann E (1995), pp. 213–228. (Reprinted with permission, with some changes.)
2. Foulkes D (1962); Foulkes D and Vogel G (1965).
3. See the focused waking to dreaming continuum, Figure 5.
4. Freud S (1961 [1923]). (By "id" Freud referred to the inchoate mass of drives and impulses he sometimes referred to as a "boiling cauldron" containing the derivatives of our sexual and aggressive drives. This part of us is often not accepted as ourselves and thus is called "id," Latin for "it." The ego refers to the relatively calm, organized portions of ourselves, including conscious and unconscious elements, that we recognize as ourselves, hence the name "ego," Latin for "I.")
5. Herman J (1992); Everstine D and Everstine L (1992).
6. What I am speaking of here does not cover everything that is now called psychotherapy. I am referring to psychoanalysis and all the psychodynamic, "uncovering" therapies derived from it, including Jung's approach.
7. Jouvet M (1962); Jacobson *et al.* (1964).

8. A rare exception occurs in the pathological condition called REM Behavior Disorder that sometimes follows a stroke or other illness and produces damage to the pathways responsible for muscular inhibition in REM sleep. In these rare cases, the patient sits up or gets up, thrashes about, and appears to be acting out her dreams, which can be frightening for the bed partner or roommate and occasionally produces physical injury (Schenk C *et al.*, 1986).

9. A lucid dream refers to a dream in which one is aware that one is dreaming, without waking up. In such dreams (rare for most of us) the dreamer may indeed react in an "awakelike" manner to the dream content, and many even change it while still remaining asleep (LaBerge S, 1985; Gackenbach J and LaBerge S, 1988).

10. Though some idiosyncratic analysts, notably Jacques Lacan (1945), have tried.

11. Trosman H *et al.* (1960); Verdone P (1965).

12. Freud S (1957 [1912]).

13. Hartmann E *et al.* (1971, 1972).

14. Faraday A (1972, 1976 [1974]); Delaney G (1979, 1991); Garfield P (1976 [1974], 1991); Cartwright R and Lamberg L (1992), Taylor J (1992).

15. Jung C (1974); Hannah B (1981).

16. Perls F (1970, 1992 [1969]).

17. Gendlin E (1976).

18. Bosnak R (1988 [1986]).

19. Ullman M and Zimmerman N (1985); Ullman (1996).

20. Hillman D (1990). Information on dreamworking, dreamworking groups, and dream workshops can be obtained from the Association for the Study of Dreams (ASD), Box 1600, Vienna, VA 22183. There is also a newsletter devoted specifically to dreamworking—The Dream Network Journal, PO Box 1026, Moab, UT 84532-1026.

CHAPTER 9

1. Dement W (1974 [1972]), pp. 98–102.

2. Schatzman M (1983).

3. There has been one controlled research study on problem solving in sleep using similar puzzles. Rosalind Cartwright (1974) asked subjects to solve several kinds of crossword puzzles and word-associative problems. Subjects gave their best answers either after a period of sleep including at least one REM-period or an equivalent amount of waking time. No differences were found between the two conditions: Apparently a REM period did not help on these tasks. However, dream content was not examined.

4. Barrett D (1993).
5. Kaempffert W (1924).
6. Ramsay O and Rocky A (1984); also see Strunz F (1993).
7. Strunz F (1993).
8. Krippner S and Hughes W (1970b).
9. See for instance Fuster J (1989).
10. These were collected by Barrett D (1996a).
11. Hamburger P (1994).
12. Ellis H (1911), p. 286.
13. Billy Joel in a documentary: "The Power of Dreams." Linda Harrar, producer. Public Broadcasting System (1994).
14. Schonberg H (1992), pp. 171–172.
15. Hartmann E (1996c). Also see Chapter 5.
16. Stillinger J (1994).
17. Stevenson R (1925).
18. Koestler A (1964, 1978).
19. This quote is attributed to J. P. Richter, who wrote under the name of Jean Paul, by Charles Darwin (1871). I've been unable to find the original German reference.
20. Hunt H (1991a); Webb W (1992).
21. Eliot T (1920).
22. Kuiken D and Sikora S (1993); Busink R and Kuiken D (1996).
23. Busink R and Kuiken D (1996), p. 110.
24. Sullivan K (1998).
25. Rilke R (1907).

CHAPTER 10

1. Hobson J and McCarley R (1977); Hobson J (1988); Gazzaniga M (1988).
2. Newman E and Evans C (1965); Crick F and Mitchison G (1983).
3. For instance, Hartmann E (1967, 1973).
4. Starting with Boss M (1958). For an overview of existential therapy, see Craig E and Aanstoos C (1988).
5. Perls F (1970, 1992 [1969]).
6. Hartmann H (1958 [1939], 1964). See also Loewenstein R et al. (1966).
7. Freud S (1953 [1900]).
8. Freud S (1953 [1900]), p. 1.
9. Freud S (1953 [1900]), p. 608.
10. The astute reader may have noticed that I have hardly spoken of consciousness in this book. In fact, David Foulkes, whose work I greatly respect, was kind enough to send me a very positive note about an early version of the present theory in which he says I've caught exactly what

must be going on in dreaming except for one thing: I haven't dealt with the question of consciousness.

I plead guilty. I certainly have not dealt with the huge, vexed question of the nature of consciousness. (For those who feel deprived of discussions of huge, vexed questions, I refer to my early work on free will in Chapter 5, Note 19: Hartmann E, 1966). I do not think an understanding of the nature of consciousness is necessary to my discussion of dreaming. This is fortunate because neither I nor anyone else as far as I know currently has such an understanding. Nor do I believe a discussion of Freud's system, in which "Conscious" refers to one portion of the psychic apparatus (terminology which he later changed), is useful for our concerns here. However, let me mention very briefly some ways in which not so much consciousness, but rather what is conscious and unconscious, may be helpful to our discussion on dreaming.

First and most important, a great deal obviously goes on in the nets of our minds (in our brains and especially our cerebral cortices) without our being conscious of it. Included are many automatic behaviors—control of our breathing, control of our muscles when we are walking, etc.—of which we can become conscious if we focus on them). Also, material glimpsed or heard momentarily (subliminally) often does not become part of our conscious waking train of thought, but can affect our behavior. Likewise, there are emotions or emotional states of which we are not aware at a given time, but which are obviously affecting us, as we can often see when someone points it out to us: "You're right. I did sound angry. It must be such and such. . . . Yes, I'm still angry at John about that." Freud's discovery and exploration of repression is very relevant to the latter situations. And there is a great deal more. Using an old-fashioned phrase, a lot happens "below the level of awareness" and we only become conscious of some of it—probably only a small part of it. This situation holds 24 hours a day no matter what state we are in.

Out of all this activity in the nets of the mind (the cortex), what exactly becomes conscious? We cannot give a complete answer, but obviously levels of cortical activation are important. Overall, cortical activation levels are low in non-REM sleep, when we generally have little or no conscious experience, and high in both waking and REM sleep, when we are usually having conscious experiences. Furthermore, the location of cortical activation is clearly related to the content of conscious experience, as is most clear when we are awake and perceiving.

The intensity of a specific activation is also involved. A very quiet sound or a dim light may not enter our awareness, while a loud enough sound or a bright enough light does. And emotional connection makes a big difference: A mother will easily be aware of (hear) her own child's cry even when it is no louder than surrounding cries. John Antrobus and his collaborators have tried various ways of relating intensity of activation to presumed conscious experience in waking and dreaming (Antrobus J, 1991; Fookson and Antrobus, 1992).

In any case, I think we can be satisfied for now with a fairly simple quantitative model in which activation (excitation) is constantly playing across the cortex. When it reaches a certain level, we become conscious of it whether awake or asleep. I think this is sufficient for our purposes in this book. We have not tackled the question of the essence or basic nature of consciousness; rather, in a sense we have defined consciousness in practical terms as what occurs or what we experience under certain conditions or levels of cortical activation.

11. Freud S. Letter to Wilhelm Fliess, June 12, 1900. (Freud 1953 [1900], p. 121.)
12. Freud S (1953 [1900]), p. 121.
13. Freud S (1953 [1900]), p. 119.
14. Freud S (1953 [1900]), p. 151.
15. Freud at one point admitted that such PTSD dreams were exceptions to his "wish-fulfillment" thesis, since they followed an overriding principle of mental functioning—the compulsion to repeat, which took precedence over wish fulfillment.
16. On discussing my series of dreams after trauma—the dreams of tidal waves, for instance, from someone who has escaped from a fire—I have on two occasions had a very orthodox Freudian attempt a wish-fulfillment explanation along the lines of, "Well, water puts our fire, so maybe there is a wish in that dream after all." Unfortunately I do not find this very convincing. Perhaps tidal waves can put out fires, but surely gangs of Nazis, whirlwinds, or oncoming trains—metaphors frequently found at such times—can hardly play such a role.
17. Freud S (1953 [1900]), pp. 130–131.
18. Bokert E (1967).
19. See for instance an entire book summarizing research on Freud's various theories: Fisher S and Greenberg R (1985).
20. Freud S (1953 [1900]), pp. 229–305.
21. The overlapping zones of excitation in the nets of the mind (Chap. 5) can be considered a basis of Freud's mechanism of condensation, but may also underlie some of the other mechanisms of dreamwork—for instance, a representation by symbols. See our later discussion of sexual symbolism.
22. Well-trained therapists will be acutely aware of this issue and will do their best to understand their own wishes, needs, or agendas so that they can try to avoid imposing them on the patient.
23. Jung (1954), p. 549.
24. Hannah B (1981).
25. Freud S (1953 [1900]), pp. 350–404.
26. Stekel W (1911).
27. Freud S (1953 [1900]), pp. 359–360.
28. Zadra A and Nielsen T (1997).

29. Oberhelman S (1991). It is interesting that though Achmet provides simple symbolic and "prophetic" dream interpretation guidelines such as those cited, he warns that these should not be relied on by themselves. He states that they must be modified according to the dreamer's station, his health, and whatever else about him the interpreter knows. Achmet never makes quiet clear his views on the origins or sources of dreams. Though usually, as in the examples cited, he phrases the interpretations as prophecy, he nowhere calls dreams direct messages from the gods about the future. Rather he states that he learns as much as possible about the dreamer and uses this information in his interpretation. It appears likely that he used the dreams as well as other information about the dreamer to guess at the dreamer's psychological state, which leads him to a prediction as to how the dreamer's life will go in the future. Thus if a king appears strong and confident and dreams of a large, erect penis, Achmet guesses and predicts that this king's reputation will grow.

30. Dement W and Wolpert E (1958).

31. Studies by Dement and Wolpert and many others have failed to find initiation of REM periods by external stimuli. Dement and Wolpert (1958) also tried to introduce stimuli during non-REM sleep and did not find that these initiated non-REM dreams.

32. Reviewed in Arkin A and Antrobus J (1991) and Nielsen T (1993).

33. This formulation is from Fisher C (1965).

34. Hartmann H (1958 [1939]).

35. This has been discussed in Chapter 4.

36. Jung C (1954).

37. See for instance a detailed discussion of continuity versus compensation in Shafton A (1995).

38. Jung C (1968 [1935], 1974).

39. Reviewed in Shafton A (1995).

40. This table of course is oversimplified and thus not 100% accurate. For instance, Freud would not necessarily say no to point 7. Though forgotten dreams cannot be used in therapy and understanding, he would consider them perhaps serving their function in preserving sleep. Jung would probably agree with Freud on most points except point 2. Likewise, the biologist Crick and Mitchison (1983) do not claim that dreams are random activity, but rather that they include material that needs to be unlearned or thrown away (point 5).

CHAPTER II

1. Hartmann, E (1967). The work started with Aserinsky E and Kleitman N (1953).

2. Here's a little more detail on a night of sleep (Fig. 8). As an average adult human falls asleep, the body quiets down, there is a reduction of muscle activity, the eye movement muscles and other muscles become very quiescent, and pulse and respiratory rates slow down. Brain waves recorded in the electroencephalogram (EEG) start from a waking pattern of rapid activity mixed with 10 per second alpha activity and move through a series of changes: first, alpha activity drops out and the record is characterized by low-voltage fast activity (stage 1 sleep). Sleep spindles—spindle-shaped rapid activity at 12 to 15 per second emerge (stage 2), and then gradually slow waves (with a frequency of less than 4 per second) begin to dominate the record (stages 3 and 4). As sleep deepens in the first hour or two of the night, the record is dominated increasingly by the deep, slow waves (stage 4). However, the night does not continue in this way. The above patterns, which describe the stages of non-REM sleep, are interrupted three to five times a night by the appearance of a very different state. The first such interruption (REM sleep) usually appears 90 to 120 minutes after sleep onset. Sleep appears to lighten since the EEG again shows low-voltage fast activity, somewhat like sleep onset or even waking. But this sleep is not actually light; it is quite deep in terms of arousal threshold (the intensity of a stimulus needed to awakened the sleeper). The periods are characterized by rapid movements of the eyes (because of these the whole state is now called REM sleep) and by a number of other changes including an extremely low muscle potential in most muscles and an increased rate and increased variability of pulse and respiration. These periods of REM sleep together make up 20–25% of the night's sleep. The remainder of sleep is called non-REM sleep, with stages 1, 2, 3, and 4 to indicate the depth of sleep within it.

3. Jouvet M (1962); Snyder F (1963); Hartmann E (1967).

4. See Chapter 12 and notes to Chapter 12 for more details.

5. McCarley R and Hobson J (1975); Hobson J and Steriade M (1986).

6. Aserinsky E and Kleitman N (1953); Dement W and Kleitman N (1957).

7. Foulkes D (1962); Foulkes D and Vogel G (1965); Goodenough D (1967). There is still controversy as to whether non-REM dreams differ from REM dreams in important ways.

8. I am speaking of the states characterized by relatively high levels of cortical activation that appear to underlie conscious experience. Though it is easy to speak of "thinking vs. dreaming," we are probably dealing with a continuum (see Chapter 5).

9. Broughton R (1982); Solms M (1997).

10. Solms (1997) carefully delineates several different syndromes related to dreaming that can be produced by neurological lesions. One is the *syndrome of nonvisual dreaming*, which arises from damage to the medial occipitotemporal regions. A second, called *syndrome of global cessation of dreaming*, occurs first of all as an acute condition following various large

brain lesions; there is usually recovery within one year. More long-lasting and specific global cessation of dreaming occurs with parietal (especially inferior parietal) lesions of either hemisphere. It can also occur with deep bifrontal lesions. Third, he delineates a *symptom complex of dream-reality confusion*. This occurs with anterior limbic-frontal lesions. Finally, he finds a *syndrome of recurring nightmares*, with temporal-limbic seizure activity. Overall, Solms tends to use the terms "telencephalic lesions," which includes not only the cortex but subcortical white matter and in some cases cortical-limbic connections.

11. Nielsen *et al.* (1995).
12. Maquet P *et al.* (1996); Braun A *et al.* (1997); Sutton J *et al.* (1996).
13. Whitman R *et al.* (1969); Kramer M (1969); Hartmann E (1978, 1984, pp. 246–272). I have not been able to find any reviews published in recent years.
14. McCarley R *et al.* (1995).
15. See for instance Klawans *et al.* (1978).
16. Hartmann E *et al.* (1980).
17. There are also many case reports and small studies suggesting that noradrenergic blockers, especially beta blockers, produce an increase in vivid dreams and nightmares. I have reviewed this area briefly (Hartmann E, 1984). It appears that acetylcholine and norepinephrine have opposite effects on REM sleep and concomitantly on the intensity of dreaming. Dopamine may play a different role, intensifying dreams without altering REM sleep. In addition to the study of small doses of l-dopa vs. placebo, administered during the night (mentioned in text: Hartmann E *et al.*, 1980), we also studied the long-term effects of the dopamine blocker chlorpromazine (Hartmann E and Cravens J, 1974). We found that chlorpromazine produced a highly significant reduction in the measure of "appropriateness to each other of the setting, actions, and characters of the dream." In other words the dreams were disjointed and scattered. The two studies together suggest that dopamine plays a role in the intensity, connectedness, or flow of dreams, a role it may also play in waking mentation (Hartmann E, 1982).
18. Based on many studies. See Hobson J (1988) or Siegel A (1993) for reviews.
19. Hartmann E (1973).
20. Foote S *et al.* (1975); Woodward D *et al.* (1979); Servan-Schreiber *et al.* (1990).
21. McCarley R and Hobson J (1975).
22. Hartmann E (1967), pp. 148–149.
23. Parmeggiani and Sabbatini L (1972).
24. For recent reviews of the research on REM deprivation in humans and animals, see three comprehensive Chapters in *The Mind in Sleep* (Ellman S and Antrobus J, eds., 1991): Ellman S *et al.* (1991); Weinstein L *et al.* (1991); and Lewin I and Singer J (1991).

25. Reviewed in Smith C (1985, 1993).
26. De Koninck J *et al.* (1987).
27. Glaubman H and Hartmann E (1978). In this study, comparing the intense group situation with a central situation in the same subjects, the experimental situation showed significantly reduced REM latency, but only a trend toward increased REM-sleep time.
28. See reviews in Notes 24 and 25.
29. Zepelin H (1994).
30. Roffwarg H, Muzio J, Dement W (1966).
31. Hartmann E (1973).
32. Rechtschaffen, A *et al.* (1983); Rechtschaffen, A *et al.* (1989).
33. For animal studies, see Ellman S *et al.* (1991), pp. 329–368. Some of the human studies are reviewed in Greenberg R and Pearlman C (1993). The evidence is suggestive, but not very strong. I believe the most compelling descriptions of REM-deprived human behavior come from an old study by Agnew H *et al.* (1967) in which REM sleep deprivation was compared with stage 4 sleep deprivation in the same subjects. Performance tests did not show great differences, but the descriptions of social behavior did: Stage 4 deprivation produced plain physical tiredness or lethargy, whereas REM deprivation produced irritability and poor social behavior.

CHAPTER 12

1. Hartse K (1994); Amlaner C and Ball N (1994); Zepelin H (1994).
2. Hartse K (1994). See Chapter 11, Note 2 for details of the brain waves in humans.
3. Zepelin H (1994); Amlaner C and Ball N (1994).
4. Solodkin M *et al.* (1984).
5. Zepelin H (1994).
6. See Zepelin H (1994) for the overall picture. My collaborators and I contributed an early study on the elephant (Hartmann E *et al.*, 1967) in which we estimated the length of the REM/non-REM cycle to be 124 minutes in the adult. We also noticed that the elephant can obtain much of its non-REM sleep standing up but is always lying down when it has REM sleep. The last line of our report to the sleep society was, "If anyone asks why the elephant lies down, the elephant lies down to dream."
7. Zepelin H (1994).
8. Foulkes D (1990).
9. From Rainville R (1988).
10. Keller H (1990).
11. Kirtley D (1975).

12. Rainville R (1994).
13. Walsh W (1920); De Martino M (1954).
14. Vaughan C (1964). Physiological recordings were not made during this study, so one cannot be absolutely certain that the animals were fully asleep while pressing the bars, though they appeared to be. Because of muscle inhibition it is quite difficult though not impossible to perform such activities while remaining in REM sleep.
15. Henley K and Morrison A (1969); Jouvet M and Delorme J (1965).
16. Roffwarg H et al. (1966).
17. Foulkes D (1982).
18. Siegel A and Bulkeley K (1997).
19. Foulkes D (1982).
20. Stoddard F et al. (1996).
21. Terr L (1991).
22. Nader K (1996).

CHAPTER 13

1. There are numerous studies on dream recall—who recalls more or less dreams and what makes a difference in dream recall. For reviews, see Cohen D (1970); Goodenough D (1991); Tonay V (1993).
2. Hartmann E (1989, 1991a); Harrison R et al. (1989).
3. The Boundary Questionnaire is included as Appendix A.
4. McCrae (1994). "Openness to experience" is one of five basic dimensions of personality emerging from many lines of personality study (Costa and McCrae, 1992).
5. The overall correlation between SumBound (the total score where high scores are "thin") and frequency of dream recall in 757 persons tested was $r = .40$ ($p < .0001$) (Hartmann E et al., 1991). The correlation was $r = .56$ in a subgroup (n = 42) especially interested in dreaming, who were more aware of their dream recall frequency.
6. A comparison of frequent dreamers (seven or more dreams per week) and nondreamers (higher numbers always refer to thinner boundaries):

	Frequent dreamers (N = 64)	Nondreamers (N = 69)	t	p
SumBound total	314 ± 60	232 ± 40	9.2	<.0001
Personal total	208 ± 48	142 ± 32	9.2	<.0001
World total	106 ± 17	89 ± 17	5.6	<.0001
Sleep-dream-wake	23 ± 13	8 ± 7	8.6	<.0001
Unusual experiences	34 ± 13	15 ± 9	9.5	<.0001

Thoughts, feelings, moods	33 ± 11	24 ± 9	5.7	<.0001
Child, adolescent, adult	13 ± 4	10 ± 4	3.3	<.01
Interpersonal	27 ± 6	23 ± 6	3.7	<.001
Sensitivity	15 ± 3	12 ± 4	4.2	<.0001
Neat, exact, precise	21 ± 7	18 ± 6	3.4	<.001
Edges, lines, clothing	41 ± 8	33 ± 8	6.3	<.0001
Opinions about children	23 ± 5	20 ± 5	3.8	<.001
Opinions about organizations	26 ± 6	22 ± 6	4.4	<.0001
People, nations, groups	38 ± 7	32 ± 8	4.5	<.0001
Beauty, truth	19 ± 4	16 ± 4	4.1	<.0001

From Hartmann E (1991), with permission.

7. Hartmann E *et al.* (1991). Very similar results on dream recall are reported by Schredl M *et al.* (1996) and by Hartmann E, Rosen R, and Rand W (1998).

8. Hartmann E (1991a); Hartmann E *et al.* (unpublished data). We found similar relationships between boundaries and dream recall in groups of patients who could be given psychiatric diagnoses using DSM-IV. Although boundaries are not a measure of psychopathology, there were some groups that not unexpectedly scored very "thick" or very "thin." Patients diagnosed Obsessive-Compulsive Personality Disorder scored very thick on the boundary questionnaire, and reported few dreams. Patients diagnosed Schizotypal Personality Disorder or Borderline Personality Disorder scored very thin on the questionnaire, and recalled significantly more dreams than average.

There is an interesting condition (though not currently considered an official diagnostic category) called Alexithymia, referring literally to difficulty in putting feelings into words. People with this condition may be of normal intelligence, experience feelings, and are able to think and talk normally, but somehow the parts do not come together: They are unable to talk about their feelings. It has been found that alexithymics also have a poor fantasy life; they are unable to picture feelings very well (Sifneos P, 1967). This seems related to our concerns. In fact among our patient files available I have been able to find eight persons considered clinically alexithymic and who had scored high on a scale called the Toronto Alexithymia Scale, who had also taken the boundary questionnaire. As I expected, these persons obtained extremely thick scores on the boundary questionnaire. They appeared to have very solid boundaries in most senses; we also found that they remembered few dreams and that the dreams they did remember were relatively short, and not very vivid, emotional, or "dreamlike". This group of people, in other words, kept things very separate; did not make many connections among their thoughts, feelings, images, etc.; and thus had thick boundaries and indeed turned out to have little dreaming and not very dreamlike dreams.

9.   Hartmann E (1991a), pp. 245–246; Harrison R *et al.* (1989).
10. Kunzendorf R *et al.* (1997). These students took an abbreviated form of the boundary questionnaire: "BQ short form," which correlates well with the full questionnaire. Ratings of "dreamlikeness" produced results very similar to "bizarreness," though not quite as pronounced.
11. Hartmann E (1991a), pp. 238–241.
12. Griffith J *et al.* (1972); Ellinwood E (1968). These tentative results on the "chemistry of boundaries"—especially the intense thickening of boundaries produced by amphetamines (which increase norepinephrine and dopamine activity)—are consistent with studies reviewed earlier on the chemistry of dreaming. Roughly speaking, the left end of the continuum is related to more norepinephrine activity in the cortex, and the right end with less.

Chapter 14

1.   Crick F and Mitchison G (1983, 1986).
2.   Hobson J and McCarley R (1977); Hobson J (1988).
3.   Freud S (1953 [1900]), pp. 1–92.
4.   Lincoln J (1970 [1935]); Devereux G (1951, 1957); Eggan D (1955); D'Andrade R (1961); Hallowell I (1966); Dentan R (1986); Irwin L (1989). The "dream quest" is sometimes referred to as "vision quest" or "dream fast."
5.   Hallowell I (1966).
6.   For a discussion of culture pattern dreams, see Kracke W (1986, 1987).
7.   Krippner S and Thompson A (1996).
8.   Malan R (1994).
9.   Barrett D (1988–89); Garfield P (1997).
10. According to a review by Waud Kracke (1987), the thesis that "primitive peoples" believe dreams to be real experiences of their wandering souls was first put forward by Edward Tylor (1865). This generalization is broadly accepted today although it is considered an oversimplification, covering a variety of related beliefs in widely different cultures (Kracke W, 1986, 1987). See also Krippner S and Thompson A (1996). In 1871, E Tylor suggested that the entire concept of soul might derive from our dreams—the soul as an aspect of the self that leaves the body during sleep.
11. For instance, Waud Kracke (1987) discusses various cultural views on such meetings of souls. The meeting place may be a special and different reality where supernatural presences can be perceived; the place

may be a place of communication between minds other than the usual reality; dreams may be coded reports about a reality other than real experience; the dreamer's dream image may take part in actions with other dream images (rather than with real people). All these cases involve subtle nuances of meaning, but they suggest some caution in simply assuming that these cultures believe in a meeting of souls in the ordinary real world.

12. Hartmann E (1984).
13. Bogzaran F (1996).
14. Bulkeley K (1994).
15. Jung's thoughts on archetypes and basic human myths and beliefs are scattered throughout his writings. See especially Jung C (1954), Volumes 9, 10, 11.
16. Campbell J (1959–1967; 1983).
17. Jung C (1954, Vol 9, part I; 1974).
18. Gillespie G (1992).
19. Gillespie G (1988); Gackenbach J (1991); Gackenbach J and Sheikh A (1991); Shafton A (1995), pp. 472–485.
20. Krippner S and Ullman, M (1970), Ullman M and Krippner S (1970). Krippner S (1991).
21. Bem D and Honorton C (1994).
22. Schwartz D (1978 [1939]).

BIBLIOGRAPHY

Agnew, H. Jr., Webb, W., and Williams, R. (1967). Comparison of stage four and I-REM sleep deprivation. *Perceptual and Motor Skills* **24**:851–858.

American Psychiatric Association. (1994). *DSM-IV*. Washington, D.C.: American Psychiatric Association.

Amlaner, C., and Ball, N. (1994). Avian sleep. In *Principles and Practices of Sleep Medicine*. Kryger, M., Roth, T., Dement, W., eds. Philadelphia: W.B. Saunders Co.

Ames, L. (1964). Sleep and dreams in childhood. In *Problems of Sleep and Dreams in Children*. E. Harms, ed. New York: Pergamon Press.

Antrobus, J. (1991). Dreaming: Cognitive processes during cortical activation and high perceptual thresholds. *Psychological Review* **98**:96–121.

Antrobus, J., and Bertini, M.,eds. (1992). *The Neuropsychology of Sleep and Dreaming*. Hillsdale, NJ: Lawrence Erlbaum Associates.

Aristotle (1941). On Prophesying by Dreams. In *The Basic Works of Aristotle*. McKeon, R., ed. New York: Random House.

Arkin, A., and Antrobus, J. (1991). The effects of external stimuli applied prior to and during sleep on sleep experience. In *The Mind in Sleep: Psychology and Psychophysiology*, 2nd edition. Ellman, S., and Antrobus, J., eds. New York: John Wiley and Sons.

Aserinsky, E., and Kleitman, N. (1953). Regularly occurring periods of eye mobility and concomitant phenomena during sleep. *Science* **150**:763–766.

Bar Yam, Y. (1997). *Dynamics of Complex Systems*. Reading, MA: Addison-Wesley.

Barrett, D. (1988–89). Dreams of death. *Omega* **19**:95–101.

Barrett, D. (1993). The "committee of sleep": A study of dream incubation for problem solving. *Dreaming* **3**:115–122.

Barrett, D. (1994). Dreams in dissociative disorders. *Dreaming* **4**:165–175.

Barrett, D. (1996a). Dreams and creative problem solving. Presidential address to the Association for the Study of Dreams. Berkeley, CA.

Barrett, D. (1996b). *Trauma and Dreams*. Cambridge, MA: Harvard University Press.

Baylor, G., and Deslauriers, D. (1986). Dreams as problem solving: A method of study. Part 1: Background and theory. *Imagination, Cognition and Personality* **6**(2):105–118.

Bem, D., and Honorton, C. (1994). Does Psi exist? Replicable evidence for an anomalous process of information transfer. *Psychological Bulletin* 115:4–27.

Beradt, C. (1968 [1966]). *The Third Reich of Dreams*. Chicago: Quadrangle.

Bogzaran, F. (1996). Images of the lucid mind: A phenomenological study of lucid dreaming and modern painting. Dissertation abstract. Ann Arbor, MI: University of Michigan.

Bokert, E. (1967). The effects of thirst and a related verbal stimulus on dream reports. Doctoral dissertation, New York University (University Microfilm 68–6041, 1968).

Bosnak, R. (1988 [1986]). *A Little Course in Dreams*. Boston: Shambhala.

Boss, M. (1958). *The Analysis of Dreams*. New York: Philosophical Library.

Braun, A., Balkin, T., Wesenten, N., Carson, R., Varga, M., Baldwin, P., Selbie, S., Belenky, G., and Herscovitch, P. (1997). Regional cerebral blood flow throughout the sleep-wake cycle. *Brain* 120:7.

Breger, L., Hunter, I., and Lane, R.W. (1971). *The Effect of Stress on Dreams*. New York: International Universities Press.

Brenneis, B. (1994). On the relationship of dream content, trauma, and mind: A view from inside out or outside in? In *The Inner World in the Outer World*. New Haven: Yale University Press.

Broughton, R. (1968). Sleep disorders: Disorders of arousal? *Science* 159:1070–1078.

Broughton, R. (1982). Neurology and dreaming. *Psychiatric Journal of the University of Ottawa* 7:101–110.

Bulkeley, K. (1994). *The Wilderness of Dreams*. Albany: State University of New York.

Businck, R., and Kuiken, D. (1996). Identifying types of impactful dreams: A replication. *Dreaming* 6:97–119.

Campbell, E. (1987). On dreams. In *Dreams Are Wiser Than Men*. Russo, R., ed. Berkeley, CA: North Atlantic Books.

Campbell, J. (1959–1967). *The Masks of God*. 4 Vols. New York: Viking/Penguin.

Campbell, J. (1983). *The Way of the Animal Powers*. Vol. 1. San Francisco: Harper and Row.

Cartwright, R. (1974). Problem solving; waking and dreaming. *Journal of Abnormal Psychology* 83:451–455.

Cartwright, R. (1990). A network model of dreams. In *Sleep and Cognition*. Bootzin, R., Kihlstrom, J., and Schacter, D., eds. Arlington, VA: American Psychological Association.

Cartwright, R. (1991). Dreams that work: The relation of dream incorporation to adaptation to stressful events. *Dreaming* 1:3–10.

Cartwright, R. (1992). "Masochism" in dreaming and its relation to depression. *Dreaming* 2:79–84.

Cartwright, R., and Lamberg, L. (1992). *Crisis Dreaming: Using Dreams to Solve Your Problems*. New York: Harper Collins Publications.

Cartwright, R., and Romanek, I. (1978). Repetitive dreams of normal subjects. *Sleep Research* 7:174.

Cohen, D. (1970). Current research on the frequency of dream recall. *Psychological Bulletin* 73:433–440.

Cohen, J.D., Dunbar, K., and McClelland, J.L. (1990). On the control of automatic processes: A parallel distributed processing account of the stroop effect. *Psychological Review* 97:332–361.

Costa, P. Jr., and McCrae, R. (1992). Four ways five factors are basic. *Personality and Individual Differences* **13**:653–665.

Craig, E. (1992). Paper presented to the Association for the Study of Dreams. Charlottesville, VA.

Craig, E., and Aanstoos, C., eds. (1988). Psychotherapy for freedom. *Humanistic Psychologist* **16**:1.

Crick, F., and Mitchison, G. (1983). The function of dream sleep. *Nature* **304**:111–114.

Crick, F., and Mitchison, G. (1986). REM sleep and neural nets. *Journal of Mind and Behavior* **7**:229–249.

D'Andrade, R. (1961). Anthropological studies of dreams. In *Psychological Anthropology*. Hsu F., ed. Homewood, IL: Dorsey Press.

Damasio, A. R. (1994). *Descartes' Error*. New York: G.P. Putnam's Sons.

Darwin, C. (1871). *The Descent of Man*. London: Murray, p. 74.

De Koninck, J., Christ, G., and Lorrain, D. (1987). Intensive language learning and REM sleep: More evidence of a performance factor. *Sleep Research* **16**:201.

De Martino, M. (1954). Some characteristics of the manifest dream content of mental defectives. *Journal of Clinical Psychology* **10**:175–178.

Delaney, G. (1979). *Living Your Dreams*. San Francisco: Harper and Row.

Delaney, G. (1991). *Breakthrough Dreaming*. New York: Bantam.

Dement, W. (1974 [1972]). *Some Must Watch While Some Must Sleep*. San Francisco: W.H. Freeman.

Dement, W., and Kleitman, N. (1957). Cyclic variations in EEG during sleep and their relation to eye movements, body motility, and dreaming. *Electroencephalography Clinical Neurophysiology* **9**:673–690.

Dement, W., and Wolpert, E.A. (1958). The relation of eye movements, body motility, and external stimuli to dream content. *Journal of Experimental Psychology* **55**:543–553.

Dentan, R. (1986). Ethnographic considerations of the cross cultural study of dreams. In *Sleep & Dreams: A Source Book*. Gackenbach, J., ed. New York: Garland.

Devereux, G. (1951). *Dream and Reality: The Psychotherapy of a Plains Indian*. Albany: New York University Press.

Devereux, G. (1957). Dream learning and individual ritual differences in Mohave shamanism. *American Anthropologist* **59**:1036–1045.

Domhoff, G. (1996). *Finding Meaning in Dreams: A Quantitative Approach*. New York: Plenum Press.

Dufresne, A., and Baylor, G. (1992). Partially automated dream analysis: An application and extension of Foulkes' scoring system for latent structures. *Dreaming* **2**: 149–160.

Eggan, D. (1955). The personal use of myth in dreams. *Journal of American Folklore* **68**:445–463.

Eliot, T.S. (1920). *The Sacred Wood: Essays on Poetry and Criticism*. Minella, NY: Dover Publications.

Ellinwood, E. (1968). Amphetamine psychosis. II. Theoretical implications, *Journal of Neuropsychiatry* **4**:45–54.

Ellis, H. (1911). *The World of Dreams*. Boston: Houghton-Mifflin.

Ellman, S., and Antrobus, J., eds. (1991). *The Mind in Sleep: Psychology and Psychophysiology*, 2nd edition. New York: John Wiley and Sons.

Ellman, S., Spielman, D., and Lipschutz-Brach, L. (1991). REM deprivation update. In

The Mind in Sleep: Psychology and Psychophysiology, 2nd edition. Ellman, S., and Antrobus, J., eds. New York: John Wiley and Sons.

Ellman, S., Spielman, A., Luck, D., Steiner, S., and Halperin, R. (1991). REM deprivation: a review. In *The Mind in Sleep: Psychology and Psychophysiology*, 2nd edition. Ellman, S., and Antrobus, J., eds. New York: John Wiley and Sons.

Englehart, R., and Hale, D., Punishment, nail-biting and nightmares: A cross-cultural study. *Journal of Multicultural Counseling and Development* 18:126–132.

Everstine D., and Everstine L. (1992). *The Trauma Response: Treatment for Emotional Injury*. New York: W.W. Norton and Company.

Faraday, A. (1972). *Dream Power*. London: Hodder and Stoughton.

Faraday, A. (1974). *The Dream Game*. New York: Harper and Row.

Faraday, A. (1976 [1974]). *The Dream Game*. New York: Perennial Library.

Fisher, C. (1965). Psychoanalytic implications of recent research on sleep and dreaming. *Journal of the American Psychoanalytic Association* 4:5–48.

Fisher, C., Byrne, J.V., and Edwards, A. (1968). NREM and REM nightmares. *Psychophysiology* 5:221–222.

Fisher, S., and Greenberg, R. (1985). *The Scientific Credibility of Freud's Theories and Therapy*. New York: Columbia University Press.

Fiss, H. (1986). An empirical for a self-psychology of dreaming. *Journal of Mind and Behavior* 7:161–191.

Fiss, H. (1993). The "royal road" to the unconsciousness revisited: A signal detection model of dream function. In *The Functions of Dreaming*. Moffitt, A., Kramer, M., and Hoffman, R., eds. Albany, NY: State University of New York Press.

Fookson, J., and Antrobus, J. (1992). A connectionist model of bizarre thought and imagery. In *The Neuropsychology of Sleep and Dreaming*. Antrobus, J., and Bertini, M., eds. Hillsdale, NJ: Lawrence Erlbaum Associates.

Foote, S.L., Freedman, R., and Oliver, A.P. (1975). Effects of putative neurotransmitters on neuronal activity in monkey auditory cortex. *Brain Research* 86:229–242.

Fosshage, J. (1983). The psychological function of dreams: a revised psychoanalytical perspective. *Psychoanalysis and Contemporary Thought* 6:641–667.

Foulkes, D. (1962). Dream reports from different stages of sleep. *Journal of Abnormal and Social Psychology* 65:14–25.

Foulkes, D. (1982). *Children's Dreams: Longitudinal Studies*. New York: Wiley.

Foulkes, D. (1990). Dreaming and consciousness. *European Journal of Cognitive Psychology* 2:39–55.

Foulkes D., and Vogel, G. (1965). Mental activity of sleep onset. *Journal of Abnormal Psychology* 70:231–243.

French, T., and Fromm, E. (1964). *Dream Interpretation*. New York: Basic Books.

Freud, S. (1953 [1900]). *The Interpretation of Dreams*, standard edition, Vols. 4 and 5. London: Hogarth.

Freud, S. (1957 [1912]). Recommendation to physicians practicing psychoanalysis. In *Complete Psychological Works of Sigmund Freud*, standard ed., Vol. 12. London: Hogarth Press.

Freud, S. (1961 [1923]). *The Ego and the Id*. London: Hogarth Press.

Freud, S. (1962 [1896]). The aetiology of hysteria. In *Complete Psychological Works*, standard ed., Vol. 3. London: Hogarth Press.

Fuster, J. (1989). *The Prefrontal Cortex*. New York: Raven Press.

Gackenbach, J. (1986). *Sleep and Dreams: A Sourcebook.* New York: Garland Publishing Libraries.

Gackenbach, J. (1991). Frameworks for understanding lucid dreams: A review. *Dreaming* 1:109–128.

Gackenbach, J., and LaBerge, S., eds. (1988). *Conscious Mind, Sleeping Brain: Perspectives on Lucid Dreaming.* New York: Plenum.

Gackenbach, J., and Sheikh, A. (eds.) *Dream Images: A Call to Mental Arms.* Amityville, NY, Baywood.

Garfield, P. (1976 [1974]). *Creative Dreaming.* New York: Ballantine.

Garfield, P. (1988). *Women's Bodies, Women's Dreams.* New York: Ballantine Books.

Garfield, P. (1991). *The Healing Power of Dreams.* New York: Simon and Schuster.

Garfield, P. (1997). *The Dream Messenger.* New York: Simon and Schuster.

Gazzaniga, M. (1988) *Mind Matters.* Boston: Houghton-Mifflin.

Gendlin, E.T. (1986). *Let Your Body Interpret Your Dreams.* Wilmette, IL: Chiron.

Gillespie, G. (1988). When does lucid dreaming become transpersonal experience. *Psychiatric Journal of the University of Ottawa* 13:107–110.

Gillespie, G. (1992). Light in lucid dreams: A review. *Dreaming* 2:167–179.

Glaubman, H., and Hartmann, E. (1978). Daytime state and nighttime sleep: A sleep study after a marathon group experience. *Perceptual and Motor Skills* 46:711–715.

Globus, G. (1993). Connectionism and sleep. In *The Functions of Dreaming.* Moffitt, A., Kramer, M., and Hoffman, R., eds. Albany, NY: State University of New York Press.

Goodenough, D. (1967). Some recent studies of dream recall. In *Experimental Studies of Dreaming.* Witkin, H., and Lewis, H., eds. New York: Random House.

Goodenough, D. (1991). Dream recall: History and current status of the field. In *The Mind in Sleep.* Ellman, S., and Antrobus, J., eds. New York: John Wiley and Sons.

Goodenough, D., Witkin, H., Koulack, D., and Cohen, H. (1975). The effects of stress films on dream affect and on respiration and eye-movement during rapid-eye movement sleep. *Psychophysiology* 15:313–320.

Greenberg, R. Personal communication.

Greenberg, R., and Pearlman, C. (1975). A psychoanalytic dream continuum: The source and function of dreams. *International Review of Psychoanalysis* 2:441–448.

Greenberg, R., and Pearlman, C. (1993). An integrated approach to dream theory: Contributions from sleep research and clinical practice. In *The Functions of Dreaming.* Moffitt, A., Kramer, M., and Hoffman, R., eds. Albany, NY: State University of New York Press.

Greenberg, R., Katz, H., Schwartz, W., and Pearlman, C. (1992). A research based reconsideration of psychoanalytic dream theory. *Journal of the American Psychoanalytic Association* 40:531–550.

Griffith, J., Cavanaugh, J., Held, J., and Oates, J. (1972). Dextroamphetamine: Evaluation of psychomimetic properties in man. *Archives of General Psychiatry* 26:97–100.

Grossberg, S. (1987). Competitive learning: From interactive activation to adaptive resonance. *Cognitive Science* 11:23–63.

Hall, C.S., and Van de Castle, R.L. (1966). *The Content Analysis of Dreams.* New York: Meredith.

Hallowell, A. (1966). The role of dreams in the Ojibwa culture. In *The Dream and Human Societies.* Von Grunebaum, G., and Caillois, R., eds. Berkeley: University of California Press.

Hamburger, P. (1994). Mrs. Roosevelt, eight feet tall. *The New Yorker.* Oct. 24, pp. 54–60.

Hannah B. (1981). *Encounters with the Soul: Active Imagination as Developed by C.G. Jung.* Boston: Sigo Press.

Harrar, L. (Producer) (1994). *The Power of Dreams.* Discovery Channel.

Harris, I. (1948). Observations concerning typical anxiety dreams. *Psychiatry* **11**:301–309.

Harrison, R., Hartmann, E., and Bevis, J. (1989). *The Hartmann Boundary Questionnaire: A Measure of Thin and Thick Boundaries.* Unpublished. Presented in part to The Eastern Psychological Association. Boston, April 1989.

Hartmann, E. (1966). The psychophysiology of free will. In *Psychoanalysis, A General Psychology.* Lowenstein, R., Newman, L., Schur, M., and Solnit, A., eds. New York: International Universities Press, pp. 521–536.

Hartmann, E. (1967). *The Biology of Dreaming.* Springfield, IL: Charles C. Thomas.

Hartmann, E. (1970). A note on the nightmare. In *Sleep and Dreaming.* Hartmann, E., ed. Boston: Little, Brown and Co., pp. 192–197.

Hartmann, E. (1973). *The Functions of Sleep.* New Haven: Yale University Press.

Hartmann, E. (1976). Discussion of "The Changing Use of Dreams in Psychoanalytic Practice." *International Journal of Psychoanalysis* **57**:331–334.

Hartmann, E. (1978). *The Sleeping Pill.* New Haven: Yale University Press.

Hartmann, E. (1982). From the biology of dreaming to the biology of the mind. *Psychoanalytic Study of the Child* **37**:303–335.

Hartmann, E. (1984). *The Nightmare: The Psychology and Biology of Terrifying Dreams.* New York: Basic Books.

Hartmann, E. (1989). Boundaries of dreams, boundaries of dreamers: Thin and thick boundaries as a new personality dimension. *Psychiatric Journal of the University of Ottawa* **14**:557–560.

Hartmann, E. (1991a). *Boundaries in the Mind: A New Psychology of Personality.* New York: Basic Books.

Hartmann, E. (1991b). Dreams that work or dreams that poison: What does dreaming do? *Dreaming* **1**:23–25.

Hartmann, E. (1995). Making connections in a safe place: Is dreaming psychotherapy? *Dreaming* **5**:213–228.

Hartmann, E. (1996a). Outline for a theory on the nature and functions of dreaming. *Dreaming* **6**:147–169.

Hartmann, E. (1996b). Post-traumatic nightmares versus ordinary nightmares: Who develops what kind of nightmares? In *Trauma and Dreams.* Barrett, D., ed. Cambridge, MA: Harvard University Press, pp. 100–113.

Hartmann, E. (1996c). We do not dream of the three R's: A study and implications. *Sleep Research* **25**:136.

Hartmann, E., Baekeland, F., Zwilling, G., and Hoy, P. (1971). Sleep need: How much sleep and what kind? *American Journal of Psychiatry* **127**:1001–1008.

Hartmann, E., Baekeland, F., and Zwilling, G. (1972). Psychological differences between long and short sleepers. *Archives of General Psychiatry* **26**:463–468.

Hartmann, E., and Cravens, J. (1974). Long-term psychotropic drug administration: Effects on dream content and on REM density. *Sleep Research* **3**:119.

Hartmann, E., Russ, D., Oldfield, M., Falke, R., and Skoff, B. (1980). Dream content: Effects of L-DOPA. *Sleep Research* **9**:153.

Hartmann, E., Elkin, R., and Garg, M. (1991). Personality and dreaming: The dreams of people with very thick or very thin boundaries. *Dreaming* **1**:311–324.

Hartmann, E., Rosen, R., Gazells, N., and Moulton H. (1997). Contextualizing images in dreams—images that picture or provide a context for an emotion. *Sleep Research* **26**:274.

Hartmann, E., Rosen, R., and Grace, N. (1998). Contextualizing images in dreams: More frequent and more intense after trauma. *Sleep* **21**(suppl.):284.

Hartmann, E., Rosen, R., and Rand, W. (1998). Personality structure and dream content. *Dreaming* **8**:31–39.

Hartmann, H. (1958 [1939]). *Essays on Ego Psychology*. New York: International Universities Press.

Hartse, K. (1994). Sleep in insects and nonmammalian vertebrates. In *Principles and Practices of Sleep Medicine*. Kryger, M., Roth, T., and Dement, W., eds. Philadelphia: W.B. Saunders Co.

Henley, K., and Morrison, A. (1969). Release of organized behavior during desynchronized sleep in cats with pontine lesions. *Psychophysiology* **6**:245.

Henley, K., and Morrison, A. (1974). A re-evaluation of the effects of lesions of the pontine tegmentum and locus coeruleus on phenomena of paradoxical sleep in the cat. *Acta Neurobiologiae Experimentalis* **34**:215–232.

Herman, J. (1992). *Trauma and Recovery*. New York: Basic Books.

Hillman, D. (1990). The emergence of the grassroots dream movement. In *Dreamtime & Dreamwork*. Krippner, S., ed. Los Angeles: Jeremy Tarcher, Inc.

Hobson, J. (1988). *The Dreaming Brain*. New York: Basic Books.

Hobson, J., and McCarley, R. (1977). The brain as a dream state generator: An activation-synthesis hypothesis of the dream process. *American Journal of Psychiatry* **134**:1335–1348.

Hobson, J., and Steriade, M. (1986). Neuronal basis of behavioral state control. In *Handbook of Physiology*, Vol. 4: *The Nervous System*. Mountcastle, V., ed. Bethesda, MD: American Physiological Society, pp. 701–823.

Hunt, H. (1991a). Dreams as literature/science of dreams: An essay. *Dreaming* **1**:235–242.

Hunt, H. (1991b). Lucid dreaming as a meditative state: Some evidence from long-term meditators in relation to the cognitive-psychological bases of transpersonal phenomena. In *Dream Images: A Call to Mental Arms*. Gackenbach and Sheikh, eds. Amityville, NY: Baywood.

Irwin, L. (1989). The bridge of dreams: Myth dreams and visions in native North America. Unpublished doctoral dissertation. Indiana University.

Jacobson, A., Kales, A., Lehman, D., and Hoedemacher, F. (1964). Muscle tonus in human subjects during sleep and dreaming. *Experimental Neurology* **10**:418–424.

Janet, P. (1904). L'amnésie et la dissociation des souvenirs par l'émotion. *Journal de Psychologie* **4**:417–453.

Janet, P. (1973 [1889]). L'automatisme psychologique: Essai de psychologie expérimentale sur les formes inférieures de l'activité humaine. Paris: Société Pierre Janet.

Janet, P. (1983 [1911]). L'état mental des hystériques, 2nd ed. Paris: Félix Alcan.

Johnson, M. (1987). *The Body in the Mind: The Bodily Basis of Meaning, Reason and Imagination*. Chicago: University of Chicago Press.

Jones, R. (1970). *The New Psychology of Dreaming*. New York: Grune and Stratton.

Jouvet, M. (1962). Récherches sur les structures nerveuses et les mécanismes responsables des differentes phases du sommeil physiologique. *Archives Italiennes de Biologie* **100**:125–206.

Jouvet, M., and Delorme, J. (1965). Locus coeruleus et sommeil paradoxal. *Comptes Rendues de la Société de Biologie* **159**:895–899.

Jung, C. (1954). *The Development of Personality.* The Collected Works of C.G. Jung. Bollingen series XX. 18 Vols. CW 9-I. The Archetypes and the Collective Unconscious (1959; 2nd edition, 1968). CW 9-II. Aion (1959; 2nd edition, 1968). CW 10. Civilization in Transition (1964; 2nd edition 1970). CW 11. Psychology and Religion: West and East (1958; 2nd edition, 1969). Princeton, NJ: Princeton University Press.

Jung, C. (1968 [1935])*Analytical Psychology: Its Theory and Practice.* New York: Vintage Books.

Jung, C. (1974). *Dreams.* Princeton, NJ: Princeton University Press.

Kaempffert, W. (1924). *A Popular History of American Invention,* Vol. II. New York: Scribner's.

Kasatkin, V. (1967). *Theory of Dreams.* St. Petersburg, Russia: Meditsina.

Kasatkin, V. (1984). Diagnosis by dreams. *International Journal of Paraphysics* **18**:104–106.

Keller, H. (1990). *The Story of My Life.* New York: Bantam Doubleday.

Kirtley, D. (1975). *The Psychology of Blindness.* Chicago: Nelson-Hall.

Klawans, H., Moskovitz, C., Lupton, M., and Sharf, B. (1978). Induction of dreams by levodopa. *Harefuah,* **45**:57–59.

Klinger, E. (1990). *Daydreaming.* Los Angeles: Jeremy P. Tarcher.

Koestler, A. (1964). *The Act of Creation.* New York: Vintage Books.

Koestler, A. (1978). *Janus.* New York: Vintage Books.

Koulack, D. (1991). *To Catch a Dream.* Albany, NY: State University of New York Press.

Kracke, W. (1979). Dreaming in Kagwahiv: Dream beliefs and their psychic uses in an Amazonian culture. *Psychoanalytical Study of Society* **8**:119–171.

Kracke, W. (1986). Myth in dreams, thought in images: An Amazonian contribution to the psychoanalytic theory of the primary process. In *Dreaming, the Anthropology and Psychology of the Imaginal.* Tedlock, B., ed. London: Cambridge University Press.

Kracke, W. (1987). "Everyone who dreams has a bit of shaman": Cultural and personal meanings of dreams—evidence from the Amazon. *Psychiatric Journal of the University of Ottawa* **12**:65–71.

Krakow, B., and Neidhardt, J. (1996). *Conquering Bad Dreams and Nightmares.* New York: Berkeley.

Kramer, M. (1969). *Dream Psychology and the New Biology of Dreaming.* Springfield, IL: Charles C. Thomas.

Kramer, M. (1970). Manifest dream content in normal and psychopathologic states. *Archives of General Psychiatry* **22**:149–159.

Kramer, M. (1993). The selective mood regulatory function of dreaming: an update and revision. In *The Functions of Dreaming.* Moffit, A., Kramer, M., Hoffman, R., eds. Albany: State University of New York Press.

Kramer, M., and Roth, T. (1980). The relationship of dream content to night-morning mood change. In *Proceedings of the 4th European Congress on Sleep Research,* Tirgo-Mures, 1978. Basel: Karger, pp. 621–624.

Krippner, S. (1991). An experimental approach to the anomalous dream. In *Dream Images: A Cell to Mental Arms.* Gackenbach, J., and Sheikh, A., eds. Amityville, NY, Baywood.

Krippner, S., and Hughes, W. (1970a). Dreams and human potential. *Journal of Humanistic Psychology* **10**:1–20.

Krippner, S., and Hughes, W. (1970b). Genius at work. *Psychology Today* **June**:40–43.

Krippner, S., and Thompson, A. (1996). A 10-facet model of dreaming applied to dream practices of sixteen Native American cultural groups. *Dreaming* 6:71–96.

Krippner, S., and Ullman, M. (1970). Telepathy and dreams: A controlled experiment with electro-encephalogram–electro-oculogram monitoring. *Journal of Nervous and Mental Disease* 15:394–403.

Kuiken, D., and Sikora, S. (1993). The impact of dreams on waking thoughts and feelings. In *The Functions of Dreaming*. Moffitt, A., et al., eds. Albany: State University of New York Press.

Kunzendorf, R., Hartmann, E., Cohen, R., and Cutler, J., (1997). Bizarreness of the dreams and daydreams reported by individuals with thin and thick boundaries. *Dreaming* 7:265–271.

LaBerge, S. (1985). *Lucid Dreaming*. Los Angeles: Jeremy P. Tarcher.

Lacan, J. (1945). *Écrits: A Selection*. London: Routledge, pp. 30–113.

Lakoff, G. (1987). *Women, Fire, and Dangerous Things*. Chicago: University of Chicago Press.

Lakoff, G. (1993a). The contemporary theory of metaphor. In *Metaphor and Thought*. Ortony, A., ed. Cambridge: Cambridge University Press.

Lakoff, G. (1993b). How metaphor structures dreams: The theory of conceptual metaphor applied to dream analysis. *Dreaming* 3:77–98.

Lakoff, G., and Johnson, M. (1980). *Metaphors We Live By*. Chicago: University of Chicago Press.

Lakoff, G., and Turner, M. (1989). *More Than Cool Reason: A Field Guide to Poetic Metaphor*. Chicago: University of Chicago Press.

LaRue, R. (1996). Unpublished work (1970). In Domhoff, G.W. (1996).

Lessing, D. (1975). *My Father. Small Personal Voice*. New York: Random House, p. 87.

Levin, R. (1990). Psychoanalytic theory on the function of dreaming: A review of the empiral dream research. *Empirical Studies of Psychoanalytic Theories* 3.

Lewin, I., and Singer, J. (1991). Psychological effects of REM ("dream") deprivation upon waking mentation. In *The Mind in Sleep: Psychology and Psychophysiology*, 2nd edition. Ellman, S., and Antrobus, J., eds. New York: John Wiley and Sons.

Lifton, R. (1996). Dreaming well: On death and history. In *Trauma and Dreams*. Barrett, D., ed. Cambridge, MA: Harvard University Press.

Lincoln, J. (1970 [1935]). *The Dream in Primitive Cultures*. New York: Johnson Reprint.

Loewenstein, R., Newman, L., Schur, M., and Solnit, A. (1966). *Psychoanalysis: A General Psychology*. New York: International Universities Press.

MacFarlane, J., Allen, L., and Honzik, M. (1954). *A Developmental Study of the Behavior Problems of Normal Children Between Twenty-one Months and Fourteen Years*. Berkeley: University of California Press.

Mack, J. (1989 [1970]). *Nightmares and Human Conflict*. New York: Columbia University Press.

MacKenzie, N. (1965). *Dreams and Dreaming*. New York: Vanguard.

Malan, R. (1991). *My Traitor's Heart*. New York: Vintage (International).

Maquet, P., Peters, J., Aerts, J., Delfiore, G., Degueldre, C., Luxen, A., and Franck , G. (1996). Functional neuroanatomy of human rapid-eye-movement sleep and dreaming. *Nature* 383:163–166.

Maybruck, P. (1989). *Pregnancy and Dreams*. Los Angeles: Jeremy P. Tarcher.

McCarley, R., Greene, R., Rainnie, D., and Portas, C. (1995). Brain stem neuromodulation and REM sleep. *Seminars in Neurosciences* 7:341–354.

McCarley, R., and Hobson, J. (1975). Neuronal excitability modulation over the sleep cycle: a structural and mathematical model. *Science* **189**:58–60.

McCarley, R., and Hobson, J. (1979). The form of dreams and the biology of sleep. In *Handbook of Dreams: Research, Theories and Applications.* Wolman, B., ed. New York: Van Nostrand Reinhold.

McClelland, J., and Rumelhart, D., eds. (1996). *Parallel Distributed Processing; Explorations in the Microstructure of Cognition.* 2 Vols. Cambridge, MA: MIT Press.

McCrae, R. (1994). Openness to experience: expanding the boundaries of factor V. *European Journal of Personality* **8**:251–272.

Moffitt, A., Kramer, M., and Hoffmann, R., eds. (1993). *The Functions of Dreaming.* Albany: State University of New York.

Muller, K. (1996). Jasmine: Dreams in the psychotherapy of a rape survivor. In *Trauma and Dreams.* Barrett, D., ed. Cambridge, MA: Harvard University Press.

Nader, K. (1996). Children's traumatic dreams. In *Trauma and Dreams.* Barrett, D., ed. Cambridge, MA: Harvard University Press.

Newman, E., and Evans, C. (1965). Human dream processes as analogous to computer programme clearance. *Nature* **206**:534.

Nielsen, T. (1993). Changes in the kinesthetic content of dreams following somatosensory stimulation of leg muscles during REM sleep. *Dreaming* **3**:99–113.

Nielsen, T., Deslauriers, D., and Baylor, G. (1991). Emotions in dream and waking event reports. *Dreaming* **1**:287–300.

Nielsen, T., Germain, A., and Ovellet, L. (1995). Atonia-signalled hypnagogic imagery: Comparative EEG mapping of sleep onset transitions, REM sleep, and wakefulness. *Sleep Research* **24**:133.

Oberhelman, S., ed. (1991). *The Oneirocriticon of Achmet.* Lubbock, Texas: Texas Tech University Press.

Palombo, S. (1978a). *Dreaming and Memory: A New Information-Processing Model.* New York: Basic Books.

Palombo, S. (1978b). The adaptive function of dreams. *Psychoanalysis and Contemporary Thought* **1**:443–476.

Palombo, S. (1992a). The eros of dreaming. *International Journal of Psychoanalysis* **73**:637–646.

Palombo, S. (1992b). Connectivity and condensation in dreaming. *Journal of the American Psychoanalytic Association* **40**:1139–1159.

Parmeggiani, P., and Sabattini, L. (1972). Electromyographic aspects of postural, respiratory and thermoregulatory mechanisms in sleeping cats. *Electroencephalography and Clinical Neurophysiology* **33**:1–13.

Perls F. (1970). *Four Lectures in Gestalt Therapy.* Fagan, J., and Shepherd, I., eds. Palo Alto, CA: Science and Behavior Books.

Perls, F. (1992 [1969]). *Gestalt Therapy Verbatim.* Highland, NY: Gestalt Journal.

Petersen, S., Fox, P., Posner, M., Mintun, M., and Raiche, M. (1988). Positron emission tomographic studies of the cortical anatomy of single-word processing. *Nature* **331**:585–589.

Punamaki, R. (1997). Determinants and mental health effects of dream recall among children living in traumatic conditions. *Dreaming* **7**:235–264.

Rados, R., and Cartwright, R. (1982). Where do dreams come from? A comparison of presleep and REM sleep thematic content. *Journal of Abnormal Psychology* **91**:433–436.

Rainville, R. (1988). *Dreams Across the Life Span.* Boston: American Press.

Rainville, R. (1994). The role of dreams in the rehabilitation of the adventitiously blind. *Dreaming* 4:155–163.

Ramsay, O., and Rocke, A. (1984). Kekule's dreams: Separating the fiction from the fact. *Chemistry in Britain* 20:1093–1094.

Rechtschaffen, A., and Buchignani, C. (1992). The visual appearance of dreams. In *The Neuropsychology of Sleep and Dreams*. Antrobus, J., and Bertini, M., eds. Hillside, NJ: Lawrence Erlbaum, pp. 143–155.

Rechtschaffen, A., Gilliland, M, Bergmann, B., and Winter, J. (1983). Physiological correlates of prolonged sleep deprivation in rats. *Science* 221:182–184.

Rechtschaffen, A., Bergmann, B., Everson, C., Kushida, C., and Gilliland, M. (1989). Sleep deprivation in the rat. X. Integration and discussion of the findings. *Sleep* 12:68–87.

Rilke, R. (1907). *Selected Poems*. Berkeley, CA: University of California Press.

Robbins, P., and Houshi, F. (1983). Some observations on recurrent dreams. *Bulletin of the Menninger Clinic* 47:262–265.

Roffwarg, H.P., Muzio, J., and Dement, W.C. (1966). Ontogenetic development of the human sleep-dream cycle. *Science* 152:604–619.

Roussy, F., Camirand, C., Foulkes, D., De Koninck, J., Loftis, M., and Kerr, N. (1996). Does early-night REM dream content reliably reflect presleep state of mind? *Dreaming* 6:121–130.

Rumelhart, D., and Abrahamson, A. (1973). A model for analogical reasoning. In *Metaphor and Thought*. Ortony, A., ed. New York: Cambridge University Press.

Rumelhart, D.E., and McClelland, J.L. (1986). On learning the past tenses of verbs. In *Parallel Distributed Processing*, Vol. 2. *Psychological and Biological Models*. McClelland, J.L., Rumelhart, D.E., and PDP Research Group, eds. Cambridge, MA: MIT Press.

Sacks, O. (1973). *Awakenings*. Garden City, NY: Doubleday and Company.

Sacks, O. (1996). Neurological Dreams. In *Trauma and Dreams*. Barrett, D., ed. Cambridge, MA: Harvard University Press.

Salley, R. (1988). Subpersonalities with dreaming functions in a patient with multiple personalities. *Journal of Nervous and Mental Disease* 176:112–115.

Saredi, R., Baylor, G., Meier, B., and Strauch, I. (1997). Current concerns and REM-dreams: A laboratory study of dream incubation. *Dreaming* 7:3.

Schatzman, M. (1983). Sleeping on problems really can solve them. *New Scientist* 11:416–417.

Schenck C., Bundlie, S., Ettinger, M., and Mahowald, M. (1986). Chronic behavioral disorders of human REM sleep: A new category of parasomnia. *Sleep* 9:293–308.

Schneider, E. (1953). *Coleridge, Opium, and Kubla Kahn*. Chicago: University of Chicago Press.

Schonberg, H. (1992). *Horowitz: His Life and Music*. New York: Simon and Schuster.

Schopenhauer, A. (1883 [1819]). *The World as Will and Idea*, 4 Vols. New York: Charles Scribner.

Schredl, M., Kleinferchner, P., and Gell, T. (1996). Dreaming and personality: Thick vs. thin boundaries. *Dreaming* 6:219–223.

Schredl, M., Pallmer, R., and Montasser, A. (1996). Anxiety dreams in school-aged children. *Dreaming* 6:265–270.

Schwartz, D. (1978 [1939]). *In Dreams Begin Responsibilities*. New York: New Directions.

Servan-Schreiber, D., Printz, H.W., and Cohen, J.D. (1990). A network model of catecholamine effects: Gain, signal-to-noise ratio and behavior. *Science* **249**:892–895.

Shafton, A. (1995). *Dream Reader: Contemporary Approaches to the Understanding of Dreams*. Albany: State University of New York.

Siegel, A. (1993). Brainstem mechanisms generating REM sleep. In *Principles and Practice of Sleep Medicine*. Kryger, M.H., Roth, T., and Dement, W.C., eds. Philadelphia: W.B. Saunders Company, pp. 125–144.

Siegel, A. (1996). Dreams of firestorm survivors. In *Trauma and Dreams*. Barrett, D., ed. Cambridge, MA: Harvard University Press.

Siegel, A., and Bulkeley, K. (1997). *Dreamcatching*. New York: Three Rivers Press.

Sifneos, P. (1967). Clinical observations on some patients suffering from a variety of psychosomatic diseases. *Acta Medica Psychosomatica* **13**:339.

Singer, J. (1975). *The Inner World of Daydreaming*. New York: Harper and Row.

Smith C. (1985). Sleep states and learning: A review of the animal literature. *Neuroscience and Biobehavioral Revisions* **9**:157–168.

Smith, C. (1993). REM sleep and learning: Some recent findings. In Moffitt *et al.* (1993).

Smolensky, P. (1986). Information processing in dynamical systems: foundations of harmony theory. In *Parallel Distributed Processing*, Vol. 1. Rumelhart, D.E., McClelland, J.L., and PDP Research Group, eds. Cambridge, MA: MIT Press.

Snyder, F. (1963). The new biology of dreaming. *Archives of General Psychiatry* **8**:381–391.

Snyder, F. (1970). The phenomenology of dreaming. In *The Psychodynamic Implications of the Physiological Studies on Dreams*. Madow, H., and Snow, L.H., eds. Springfield, IL: Charles C. Thomas, pp. 124–151.

Solms, M. (1997). *The Neuropsychology of Dreams*. Mahwah, New Jersey: Lawrence Erlbaum Associates.

Solodkin, M., Cardona, A., and Corsi-Cabrera, M. (1984). Paradoxical sleep augmentation after imprinting in the domestic chick. *Physiology and Behavior* **35**:343–348.

States, B. (1995). Dreaming "accidentally" of Harold Pinter: The interplay of metaphor and metonymy in dreams. *Dreaming* **5**:229–245.

States, B. (1997). *Seeing in the Dark*. New Haven: Yale University Press.

Stekel, W. (1911). *Die Sprache des Träumes*. Wiesbaden: J.F. Bergmann.

Sternberg, R., Tourangeau, R., and Nigro, G. (1993). Metaphor, induction, and social policy: The convergence of macroscopic and microscopic views. In *Metaphor and Thought*. Ortony, A., ed. Cambridge: Cambridge University Press.

Stevenson, R. (1925). A chapter on dreams. In *Memories and Portraits, Random Memories, Memories of Himself*. New York: Scribner's.

Stillinger, J. (1994). *Coleridge and Textual Instability: The Multiple Versions of the Major Poems*. New York: Oxford, pp. 73–79.

Stoddard, F., Chedekel, D., and Shakun, L. (1996). Dreams and nightmares of burned children. In *Trauma and Dreams*. Barrett, D., ed. Cambridge, MA: Harvard University Press.

Strauch, I. (1996). Personal communication.

Strauch, I., and Meier, B. (1989). Das emotionale Erleben im REM-Traum. *Schweizerische Zeitschrift fur Psychologie* **48**(4):233–240.

Strauch, I., and Meier, B. (1992). *Den Traumen auf der Spur*. Bern: Verlag Hans Huber.

Strunz, F. (1993). Preconscious mental activity and scientific problem-solving. *Dreaming* **3**:281–294.

Sullivan, K. (1998). *Recurring Dreams: A Journey to Wholeness*. Freedom, CA: Crossing Press.

Sutton, J., Breiter, H., Caplan, J., Huang-Hellinger, K., Kwong, J., Hobson, A., and Rosen, B. (1996). Human brain activation during REM sleep detected by fMRI. *Society of Neuroscience Abstracts* **22**:690.

Taylor, J. (1992). *Where People Fly and Water Runs Uphill: Using Dreams to Tap the Wisdom of the Unconscious*. New York: Warner.

Terr, L. (1991). Childhood traumas: An outline and overview. *American Journal of Psychiatry* **148**:10–20.

Tonay, V. (1993). Personality correlates of dream recall: Who remembers? *Dreaming* 3:1–8.

Trosman, H., Rechtschaffen, A., Offenkrantz, W., and Wolpert, E. (1960). Studies in the psychophysiology of dreams. IV. Relations among dreams in sequence. *Archives of General Psychiatry* 3:602–607.

Trenholme, I., Cartwright, R., and Greenberg, G. (1984). Dream dimension during a life change. *Psychiatry Research* 12:35–45.

Turner, M. (1987). *Death Is the Mother of Beauty: Mind, Metaphor, Criticism*. Chicago: University of Chicago Press.

Tylor, E. (1865). *Researches into the Early History of Mankind and the Development of Civilization*, 3rd ed. New York: Henry Holt and Company.

Tylor, E. (1871). *Primitive Culture*. New York: Brentano.

Ullman, M. (1969). Dreaming as metaphor in motion. *Archives of General Psychiatry* 21:696–703.

Ullman, M. (1996). *Appreciating Dreams*. Thousand Oaks, CA: Sage Publications.

Ullman, M., and Krippner, S. (1970). *Dream Studies and Telepathy: An Experimental Approach*. New York: Parapsychology Foundation.

Ullman, M., and Zimmerman, N. (1985). *Working with Dreams*. Los Angeles: Tarcher.

Van de Castle, R.L. (1994). *Our Dreaming Mind*. New York: Ballantine Books.

Van der Kolk, B., ed. (1984). *Post-traumatic Stress Disorder: Psychological and Biological Sequelae*. Washington, DC: American Psychiatric Press.

Van der Kolk, B., Blitz, R., Burr, W., Sherry, S., and Hartmann, E. (1984). Nightmares and trauma: A comparison of nightmares after combat with lifelong nightmares in veterans. *American Journal of Psychiatry* 141:187–190.

Van der Kolk, B., Pelcovitz, D., Roth, S., Mandel, F., McFarlane, A., and Herman, J. (1996). Dissociation, somatization, and affect dysregulation: The complexity of adaptation to trauma. *American Journal of Psychiatry* 153:83–93.

Van der Kolk, B., and Van der Hart, O. (1989). Pierre Janet and the breakdown of adaptation in psychological trauma. *American Journal of Psychiatry* 146:1530–1540.

Van der Kolk, B., and Van der Hart, O. (1991). The intrusive past: The flexibility of memory and the engraving of trauma. *Am Imago* 48:425–454.

Vaughan, C. (1964). Behavioral evidence for dreaming in rhesus monkeys. *Physiologist* 7:275.

Verdone, P. (1965). Temporal reference of manifest dream content. *Perceptual & Motor Skills* 20:1253–1268.

Walsh, W. (1920). *Dreams of the feebleminded*. *Medical Record* 97:395–398.

Webb, W. (1992). A dream is a poem: A metaphorical analysis. *Dreaming* 2:191–201.

Weinstein, L., Schwartz, D., and Ellman, S. (1991). Sleep mentation as affected by REM deprivation: A new look. In *The Mind in Sleep: Psychology and Psychophysiology*, 2nd edition. Ellman, J., and Antrobus, J. New York: John Wiley and Sons.

Whitman, R., Kramer, M., Ornstein, P., and Balride, B. (1969). Drugs and dream content. *Experimental Medicine and Surgery* 27:210–223.

Winner, E., and Gardner, H. (1993). Metaphor and irony: Two levels of understanding. In *Metaphor and Thought*. Ortony, A., ed. New York: Cambridge University Press.

Wiseman, A. (1989). *Nightmare Help: A Guide for Parents and Children*. Cambridge: Ten Speed Press.

Woodward, D., Moises, H., Waterhouse, B., Hoffer, B., and Freedman, R. (1979). Modulatory action of norepinephrine in the central nervous system. *Federation Proceedings* **38**:2109–2116.

Zadra, A., and Nielsen., T. (1997). Typical dreams: A comparison of 1958 versus 1996 student samples. *Sleep Research* **7**:280–281.

Zepelin, H. (1994). Mammalian sleep. *Principles and Practices of Sleep Medicine* **2**:69–80.

INDEX